D1297425

There shall come forth a rod out of the
root of Jesse
And a flower shall rise up out of this root

J.G. Mears, S.J.

Other Works by the Editor

A modernized version of John Norris' translation of "*Amoris Effigies*"

A translation into English of Saint Bernard, *On the Love of God*

The Complete Poems of Francis Thompson, edited with textual notes

An Introduction to Chaucer and Langland

The English Renaissance and the Age of Elizabeth

If any be
That shall with rites of reverent piety
Approach this strong
Sad soul of sovereign Song,
Nor fail and falter with the intimidate throng;
If such there be,
These, these are only they
Have trod the self-same way.

—Francis Thompson, *A Captain of Song*

Coventry Patmore

C O V E N T R Y   P A T M O R E

MYSTICAL POEMS OF NUPTIAL LOVE

The Wedding Sermon, The Unknown Eros
and Other Odes

Edited with Notes by
TERENCE L. CONNOLLY, S.J., PH.D.
Professor of English Literature at
Boston College Graduate School

BOSTON
BRUCE HUMPHRIES, INC.
PUBLISHERS

PRINTED IN THE UNITED STATES OF AMERICA

TO MARY

"My Lady, yea the Lady of my Lord,
Who didst the first descry
The burning secret of virginity
We know with what reward!"

FOREWORD

"Theology and philosophy are the soul of truth; but they must be clothed with flesh, to create an organism which can come down and live among men. Therefore Christ became incarnate, to create Christianity. Be it spoken with reverence, a great poet, who is likewise a great thinker, does for truth what Christ did for God, the Supreme Truth." (*Form and Formalism,* Francis Thompson.) But when a poet has fulfilled so high a destiny, it is not always easy to discover the full meaning of his words. This is particularly true of Coventry Patmore. And because it is true, many of his willing readers have been discouraged. As Mrs. Meynell has expressed it: "The beauty was there, but it was an uncertain magnificence, a glow from a doubtful fire, a pealing call of an uncertain word, remote as thunder, the heart-piercing utterance of an obscure grief—obscure as waters are obscure because they are profound, not because they are turbid." (*Second Person Singular,* p. 102.)

Only those who have studied Patmore's poetry can appreciate how true are the words of the man and the woman who knew Patmore most intimately and best appreciated his work. In their words the present writer found the chief inspiration of this effort to elucidate Patmore's meaning and to help others attain to the apocalypse of hidden delight and spiritual exaltation in his poetry. Here the truths of conjugal love and genuine mysticism are blent as intimately and as reverently as they are in the inspired words of Holy Scripture and in the sublimest utterances of the Savior of the World. Those truths, in the perfection of the lyrical form which Patmore has given them, cannot but delight and expand the hearts of those who believe. They may, even, attract those who are repelled by the unadorned and austere truths of Christian dogma.

In Patmore's essay, *Real Apprehension,* we read: "To see rightly is the first of human qualities; right feeling and right acting are usually its consequences." Because so few today see rightly on the subject of mysticism and human love, there is little right feeling and less right acting where these subjects are concerned. But as Patmore reminds us: "There are two ways of seeing: one is to comprehend, which is to see all round a thing, or to embrace it; one is to apprehend, which is to see it in part, or to take hold of it. A thing may be taken hold of which is much too big for embracing. Real apprehension implies reality in that which is apprehended. You cannot 'take hold' of that which is nothing."

Today souls, like drowning men, are everywhere grasping at nothing because they have relinquished their hold on a God Whom they have found too big for embracing. The surest way to save them is Patmore's way because it is God's way—"For the invisible things of Him, from the creation of the world, are clearly seen, being understood by the things that are made."

In one of the most significant letters in the Collection of Thompsoniana at Boston College, Patmore, writing to Francis Thompson, characterizes Thompson's poetry as "song that is also prophecy." And such is Patmore's poetry. It sings of the visible things of time as so many prophecies of the invisible things of eternity. His central theme, as he sums it up in the letter just referred to, is *"Dieu et ma Dame"*—the title of one of his greatest essays. The order is deliberate and scrupulously observed. *Dieu,* first. Then, *ma dame.*

T. L. C.

CONTENTS

INTRODUCTION

Marriage today is not looked upon as possessing any special sacredness. Indeed, these are the days of marriage bonds sundered and happy homes broken "not secretly nor under cover," says Pius X., "but openly, with all sense of shame put aside, now by word again by writings, by theatrical productions of every kind, by romantic fiction, by amorous and frivolous novels, by cinematographs portraying in vivid scene, in addresses broadcast by radio telephony, in short by all the inventions of modern science, the sanctity of marriage is trampled upon and derided; divorce, adultery, all the basest vices either are extolled or at least are depicted in such colours as to appear to be free of all reproach and infamy."

What then can be said except words of gratitude for any book that would surround married life with a philosophy of love that transcends all earthly bounds and finds its consummation beyond the boundaries of Heaven? The more truly transcendental the philosophy the deeper must its roots lie in the familiar ground of human capacity and experience. And every heart that beats knows, or should know from experience, that its capacity for love has never been completely filled. We learn of the unknown from what we know, of the unseen from what we see. And our knowledge of the love of God for his creatures may well be glimpsed from the human love of a man for a woman.

Coventry Patmore with a bold stroke of genius took woman in the person of the wife, and made his startling statement, "The proper study of mankind is woman." Meaning, that in every wife there is a potential man, and in her, then, is the proper study of life. To him woman is the reflector of "those transmitters of divinity, the angels!" She "will consent to be small only when the man is great. Therefore, if a man confesses that he loves Heaven more than his wife it is not because he loves her less, but because he and she are parts of one whole, which derives its own centre from God." And any woman who has "no higher interest than herself only half loves a man."

Ennobled by the grace of the Sacrament nuptial love should grow with the years, for husband and wife "in applying themselves to careful observance, however laborious, of their duties, will find the power of that grace becoming more effectual as time goes on. Love for their children far more than their love for each other, will strengthen their union and intensify their yearning for the perfect love of eternity." Patmore took all the common places of his married life seriously comparing always the human love with the divine, scanning in all his love "the love which is between Himself."

The relation of the love of God to the soul is prototypic of the relation of lovers after, as well as before, marriage. Indeed there are some very striking analogies between this human love, or married life, and the Divine love that exists between God and the soul—or we may add between God and His Church. For as Pius XI continues in his encyclical on *Christian Marriage,* Christ our Lord and Redeemer, "desired marriage to be and made it the mystical image of his own ineffable union with the Church." Osbert Burdett among many other writers noted these analogies. We set them down here in our own words.

First, we should remember that "the soul, with regard to God, who is her life, is feminine." So, in this sense, just as man is the lover of woman, so God is the Lover of the soul. Now a lover is one who greatly exaggerates the difference between one young woman and another. He chooses one especially from all others. In the Divine order God has chosen us all. Each soul serves Him in a different manner and is able to offer to Him different gifts. No two are the same in their relations to Him, yet He is the life of all.

In both there is courtship, setbacks, and finally a bethrothal. In the Divine order God leads the soul carefully, slowly to the very summit of love which is Himself. In each love there is a great desire for sacrifice. But the measure of sacrifice is the measure of love. His love, indeed, was a love without measure.

In human love, the lover must desire his beloved and prove it. In the Divine order God desires us so much that he sent His Only Son into the world to save all souls.

The only unforgiveable sin in either the human or divine love is persistent infidelity. This being so, past weaknesses and lapses, if they are really past, increase rather than diminish the human and the divine lover's affection. Such is the glory of Mary Magdalen.

In either case, the lover desires the person of his love in contemplation rather than service from her. Services cannot replace, but they can prove. Mary's is the better part.

In either case the human or the divine lover has command which he rarely uses. Rather he delights in persuasion. "Come to me all you that labour and are burdened and I will refresh you."

There is a mutual desire to be captive. And is not God the adorable Prisoner in our tabernacles—guarded by two flickering tapers?

In both loves inattention is the most mortal offense. We may accept Christ or reject Him, love or repudiate—but to be supinely indifferent is impossible.

And in both loves there is an utter indissolubility of the union of the two lovers when it shall have reached its formal stage.

Coventry Patmore's philosophy, then, *is* the philosophy of nuptial love. He is one of the foremost of its philosophical inquirers. He is the chief poet, if not the only one, who thought nuptial love worthy of *serious* song. Even in his best years he has never been accorded more than a position of a minor, which fact may possibly indicate then, and now, how great is the gulf between public sincerity and public morals. He wrote for those who have ears to hear. "The higher and purer the strain, the smaller will be the number of those who have ears for it." He really and truly loved God. From this love he built his ladder, rung by rung, from the Deanery in Salisbury close to the summit of Christian mysticism. From this love an eleven-year-old agnostic grew into a seventy-three-year-old lover, completely enveloped by that Love Who was "his Life and his Light."

This book really needs no introduction except by way of commendation. It is a comprehensive and exhaustive study of Patmore's philosophy, supported with quotations from Scripture, from the Saints, Augustine, Bernard, Ignatius, Thomas Aquinas, and a long list of mystical writers. Patmore had himself said, "I make it my only claim to be heard, that these are the sources from which I have derived my matter."

Patmore uses symbols and parables of rich mysticism to express realities clear to the perception though dark to the understanding. Father Connolly interprets them with deep sympathy and casts upon them the glowing light of theology. Fresh from his excursions into the works of Saint Bernard—and his recent translation of *Saint Bernard on the Love of God,* he comes well prepared to reveal the splendor of Patmore's philosophy. He has not failed to notice that Patmore at times in applying his message, "follows instinct rather than the positive teaching of the Church." But these instances are very rare and are due sometimes to prevailing opinions, especially the political, when Patmore wrote.

Love, pure love, is surely the most gratifying of all gifts. Nuptial love can be raised to lofty heights of perfection or dragged in the mire and destroyed. This is a book on nuptial love. If it is going to be read carelessly instead of studied carefully, it should not, in our opinion, be read at all—and we might add what Saint Bernard said concerning the *Canticle of Canticles,* it should not be touched "except by ears and hearts which are chastened and wise." Eyes that are closed or blind never receive the pure light.

Indeed, Patmore and his writings become doubly important these days when we consider the widespread movement within the Church to teach and preach love of God. For, as he tells us, human love with all its delights and joys, all its sorrows and tragedies, all its yearnings and hopes is *madness* if there be no satisfaction for it hereafter in the final contemplation of the Beatific Vision.

And if you could ask Patmore who or what *is* love, he would climax all his words with the three words of Saint John, *"God is Love."*

JOACHIM V. BENSON, M.S.SS.T.

COVENTRY PATMORE: SOME BIOGRAPHICAL NOTES

The personal experiences of Coventry Patmore, the man, are so intimately connected with his work as a poet that a commentator upon his poetry must become his biographer. And so it has proved. For those unaquainted with Patmore and his work, therefore, it will be necessary to set down here the sequence of events that most strongly influenced him. First among these was his marriage to Emily Augusta Andrews, his wife for fifteen years, and the mother of six of his children. Her deep spirituality gradually drew her husband to a deeper religious faith and more profound appreciation of Christian truths. After her death it was her influence that led him to the Church which, through invincible ignorance, she had feared and hated. The spiritual struggle entailed in this step, the inspiration of "A Farewell," is expressed with a poignancy unsurpassed even by "Azalea" and "Departure" which reveal the awfulness of the poet's grief after his first wife's death in 1862.

Less than two years later Patmore visited Rome and was there received into the Catholic Church. This was the most important of Patmore's experiences—literally, the Great Divide of his life and of his art. As a consequence, a comparative study of his poetry written before and after his conversion affords one of the most interesting examples in modern literature, of the effect of the Catholic faith as the inspiration of poetry. There is, as Champneys remarks, "an essential coherence in idea" between the poet's earlier and later work, but, "comparison of the two gives abundant evidence of development: the ideal and transcendental are consistently assuming more and more predominance over the actual, and human love is ever increasingly allocated to its function to serve as the mere symbol of the Divine Love which had come to take complete possession of his intellect and imagination." (*Poems,* Introduction, p. xxxii.) To facilitate a comparison of the Odes with the poet's earlier work, the "Wedding Sermon," the best expression of his non-Catholic inspiration, has been included in the present volume.

Within a few months after his conversion Patmore married his second wife, Marianne Caroline Byles, a devout Catholic. The fearful soul-struggle between his love for his dead wife and his love for the woman who was to take her place is the theme of "Tired Memory."

In 1873 Patmore's favorite child, Emily Honoria, entered the novitiate of the Society of the Holy Child Jesus. Until her death in 1882 she led a life of rare sanctity and detachment which deeply influenced her father. Two years before her death, Patmore's second wife died and he took as his third wife, Harriet Robson, his daughter's closest friend.

Almost as great as the spiritual influence of his wives and daughter was the influence of Mrs. Meynell to whom he paid such noble tributes as we read in his essay, "Distinction." But this friendship, like most of Patmore's friendships, ended unhappily and greatly saddened his last days, the days of a rejected prophet such as he describes himself in "Dead Language."

But greater than the merely human love of the noble women who played so important a part in Patmore's life, was his love of the one entirely sinless woman who was the Mother of Christ. This is abundantly clear from his life, his prose-writings, and especially from one of his greatest odes, "The Child's Purchase." For Patmore the beauty and loveliness of all other women was but a reflection of the beauty and loveliness of Mary. And the beauty and loveliness of Mary were but a reflection of the beauty and loveliness of Jesus Christ, Who was God-made-Man. The Incarnation, not merely a dogma to which a cold intellectual assent is given, but a truth which pervades and possesses one, in its essence and in all its corollaries, was the centre of Patmore's life and art. It was all summed up in the last words and action of this great soul as described in a single sentence by his daughter Bertha who was the only witness: "Papa asked Mamma to kiss him. He put his arms around her neck, and said: 'I love you, dear, but the Lord is my Life and my Light.'" Only the reader who fully grasps the signficance of that incident with all its inferences and implications is prepared to understand and to enjoy the poetry of Coventry Patmore.

CHRONOLOGY OF BIOGRAPHICAL DATA

1823, July 23, born at Woodford Green, Epping Forest, Essex.

1839–1840, a student at Collège de France, during which time he fell in love with Miss Gore.

1844, Poems published.

1845, his father and mother went to the Continent leaving Patmore and his younger brother to their own resources.

1846–1862, wrote his early prose.

1846, met Tennyson about this time.
November 18, appointed to a position in the British Museum through the influence of Monckton Milnes.

1847, May 17, engaged to Emily Augusta Andrews.
September 11, married.

1853, Tamerton Church Tower, published.

1854, The Betrothal (Pt. I of *The Angel in the House*) published.

1856, The Espousals (Pt. II of *The Angel in the House*) published.
Estranged from Tennyson.

1860, Faithful Forever (Pt. III of *The Angel in the House*) published.

1862, July 5, his first wife, Emily Augusta Patmore died.
Children's Garland (An Anthology for Children) published.

1863, Victories of Love (Pt. IV of *The Angel in the House*) published.

1864, February, visited Rome with Aubrey de Vere.
May, was received into the Catholic Church.
Engaged to Marianne Caroline Byles.
July 18, married his second wife.

1865, retired from British Museum because of ill health.

1866, went to live at Heron's Ghyll, Sussex.

1867, embittered by the passage of the second Reform Bill aimed at the landed gentry.

1868, Nine Odes privately printed.

1873, his daughter, Emily Honoria, entered the Society of the Holy Child Jesus, at the Convent of St. Leonard.

1874, left Heron's Ghyll.

1875, went to live at the Mansion, Hastings.

1877, Bryan Waller Proctor: An Autobiographical Fragment (edited with notes by Patmore) published.
The Unknown Eros (Odes I–XXXI) published anonymously.
Visited Lourdes.

1878, Amelia and Tamerton Church Tower published.
The Unknown Eros (Odes I–XLVI) published bearing the author's name for the first time.

1879, Poems, undated, published. The fourth volume *The Unknown Eros,* contained 42 odes in the order subsequently retained.

1880, April 8, his daughter Emily, Sister Mary Christina, S.H.C.J., took her final vows.
April 12, Marianne Caroline Patmore, his second wife, died.
Saint Bernard on the Love of God, translated by Patmore and his second wife, published.

1881, September 13, married Harriet Robson, who survived her husband.

1882, his daughter Emily, Sister Mary Christina, died.

1883, February 24, his son, Henry, died.
Sponsa Dei, a prose expression of his love-theme destroyed by Patmore.

1884, Henry's poems published.

1889, Principle in Art published.

1891, went to live at Lymington.
Beginning of friendship with Mrs. Meynell.

1893, Religio Poetae published.

1894, beginning of friendship with Francis Thompson.

1895, Rod, Root and Flower, published.

1896, November 26, died, at Lymington, Hampshire.

THE WEDDING SERMON

THE WEDDING SERMON

1

The truths of Love are like the sea
For clearness and for mystery.
Of that sweet love which, startling, wakes
Maiden and Youth, and mostly breaks
The word of promise to the ear,
But keeps it, after many a year,
To the full spirit, how shall I speak?
My memory with age is weak,
And I for hopes do oft suspect
The things I seem to recollect.
Yet who but must remember well
'Twas this made heaven intelligible
As motive, though 'twas small the power
The heart might have, for even an hour,
To hold possession of the height
Of nameless pathos and delight!

2

In Godhead rise, thither flow back
All loves, which, as they keep or lack,
In their return, the course assign'd,
Are virtue or sin. Love's every kind,
Lofty or low, of spirit or sense,
Desire is, or benevolence.
He who is fairer, better, higher
Than all His works, claims all desire,
And in His Poor, His Proxies, asks
Our whole benevolence: He tasks,

Howbeit, His People by their powers;
And if, my Children, you, for hours,
Daily, untortur'd in the heart,
Can worship, and time's other part
Give, without rough recoils of sense,
To the claims ingrate of indigence,
Happy are you, and fit to be
Wrought to rare heights of sanctity,
For the humble to grow humbler at.
But if the flying spirit falls flat,
After the modest spell of prayer
That saves the day from sin and care,
And the upward eye a void descries,
And praises are hypocrisies,
And, in the soul, o'erstrain'd for grace,
A godless anguish grows apace;
Or, if impartial charity
Seems, in the act, a sordid lie,
Do not infer you cannot please
God, or that He His promises
Postpones, but be content to love
No more than He accounts enough.
Account them poor enough who want
Any good thing which you can grant;
And fathom well the depths of life
In loves of Husband and of Wife,
Child, Mother, Father; simple keys
To what cold faith calls mysteries.

3

The love of marriage claims, above
All other kinds, the name of love,
As perfectest, though not so high
As love which Heaven with single eye
Considers. Equal and entire,
Therein benevolence, desire,
Elsewhere ill-join'd or found apart,
Become the pulses of one heart,

Which now contracts, and now dilates,
And, both to the height exalting, mates
Self-seeking to self-sacrifice.
Nay, in its subtle paradise
(When purest) this one love unites
All modes of these two opposites,
All balanced in accord so rich
Who may determine which is which?
Chiefly God's Love does in it live,
And nowhere else so sensitive;
For each is all that the other's eye,
In the vague vast of Deity,
Can comprehend and so contain
As still to touch and ne'er to strain
The fragile nerves of joy. And then
'Tis such a wise goodwill to men
And politic economy
As in a prosperous State we see,
Where every plot of common land
Is yielded to some private hand
To fence about and cultivate.
Does narrowness its praise abate?
Nay, the infinite of man is found
But in the beating of its bound,
And, if a brook its banks o'erpass,
'Tis not a sea. but a morass.

4

No giddiest hope, no wildest guess
Of Love's most innocent loftiness
Had dared to dream of its own worth,
Till Heaven's bold sun-gleam lit the earth.
Christ's marriage with the Church is more,
My Children, than a metaphor.
The heaven of heavens is symbol'd where
The torch of Psyche flash'd despair.
But here I speak of heights, and heights

Are hardly scaled. The best delights
Of even this homeliest passion, are
In the most perfect souls so rare,
That they who feel them are as men
Sailing the Southern ocean, when,
At midnight, they look up, and eye
The starry Cross, and a strange sky
Of brighter stars; and sad thoughts come
To each how far he is from home.

5

Love's inmost nuptial sweetness see
In the doctrine of virginity!
Could lovers, at their dear wish, blend,
'Twould kill the bliss which they intend;
For joy is love's obedience
Against the law of natural sense;
And those perpetual yearnings sweet
Of lives which dream that they can meet
Are given that lovers never may
Be without sacrifice to lay
On the high altar of true love,
With tears of vestal joy. To move
Frantic, like comets to our bliss,
Forgetting that we always miss,
And so to seek and fly the sun,
By turns, around which love should run,
Perverts the ineffable delight
Of service guerdon'd with full sight
And pathos of a hopeless want,
To an unreal victory's vaunt,
And plaint of an unreal defeat.
Yet no less dangerous misconceit
May also be of the virgin will,
Whose goal is nuptial blessing still,
And whose true being doth subsist,
There where the outward forms are miss'd,

In those who learn and keep the sense
Divine of 'due benevolence,'
Seeking for aye, without alloy
Of selfish thought, another's joy,
And finding in degrees unknown
That which in act they shunn'd, their own.
For all delights of earthly love
Are shadows of the heavens, and move
As other shadows do; they flee
From him that follows them; and he
Who flies, for ever finds his feet
Embraced by their pursuings sweet.

6

Then, even in love humane, do I
Not counsel aspirations high,
So much as sweet and regular
Use of the good in which we are.
As when a man along the ways
Walks, and a sudden music plays,
His step unchanged, he steps in time,
So let your Grace with Nature chime.
Her primal forces burst, like straws,
The bonds of uncongenial laws.
Right life is glad as well as just,
And, rooted strong in 'This I must,'
It bears aloft the blossom gay
And zephyr-toss'd, of 'This I may;'
Whereby the complex heavens rejoice
In fruits of uncommanded choice.
Be this your rule: seeking delight,
Esteem success the test of right;
For 'gainst God's will much may be done,
But nought enjoy'd, and pleasures none
Exist, but, like to springs of steel,
Active no longer than they feel
The checks that make them serve the soul,

They take their vigour from control.
A man need only keep but well
The Church's indispensable
First precepts, and she then allows,
Nay, more, she bids him, for his spouse,
Leave even his heavenly Father's awe,
At times, and His immaculate law,
Construed in its extremer sense.
Jehovah's mild magnipotence
Smiles to behold His children play
In their own free and childish way,
And can His fullest praise descry
In the exuberant liberty
Of those who, having understood
The glory of the Central Good,
And how souls ne'er may match or merge,
But as they thitherward converge,
Take in love's innocent gladness part
With infantine, untroubled heart,
And faith that, straight t'wards heaven's far Spring,
Sleeps, like the swallow, on the wing.

7

Lovers, once married, deem their bond
Then perfect, scanning nought beyond
For love to do but to sustain
The spousal hour's delighted gain.
But time and a right life alone
Fulfil the promise then foreshown.
The Bridegroom and the Bride withal
Are but unwrought material
Of marriage; nay, so far is love,
Thus crown'd, from being thereto enough,
Without the long, compulsive awe
Of duty, that the bond of law
Does oftener marriage-love evoke,

Than love, which does not wear the yoke
Of legal vows, submits to be
Self-rein'd from ruinous liberty.
Lovely is love; but age well knows
'Twas law which kept the lover's vows
Inviolate through the year or years
Of worship pieced with panic fears,
When she who lay within his breast
Seem'd of all women perhaps the best.
But not the whole, of womankind,
Or love, in his yet wayward mind,
Had ghastly doubts its precious life
Was pledged for aye to the wrong wife.
Could it be else? A youth pursues
A maid, whom chance, not he, did choose,
Till to his strange arms hurries she
In a despair of modesty.
Then, simply and without pretence
Of insight or experience,
They plight their vows. The parents say
'We cannot speak them yea or nay;
'The thing proceedeth from the Lord!'
And wisdom still approves their word;
For God created so these two
They match as well as others do
That take more pains, and trust Him less
Who never fails, if ask'd, to bless
His children's helpless ignorance
And blind election of life's chance.
Verily, choice not matters much,
If but the woman's truly such,
And the young man has led the life
Without which how shall e'er the wife
Be the one woman in the world?
Love's sensitive tendrils sicken, curl'd
Round folly's former stay; for 'tis
The doom of all unsanction'd bliss
To mock some good that, gain'd, keeps still
The taint of the rejected ill.

8

Howbeit, though both were perfect, she
Of whom the maid was prophecy
As yet lives not, and Love rebels
Against the law of any else;
And, as a steed takes blind alarm,
Disowns the rein, and hunts his harm,
So, misdespairing word and act
May now perturb the happiest pact.
The more, indeed, is love, the more
Peril to love is now in store.
Against it nothing can be done
But only this: leave ill alone!
Who tries to mend his wife succeeds
As he who knows not what he needs.
He much affronts a worth as high
As his, and that equality
Of spirits in which abide the grace
And joy of her subjected place;
And does the still growth check and blurr
Of contraries, confusing her
Who better knows what he desires
Than he, and to that mark aspires
With perfect zeal, and a deep wit
Which nothing helps but trusting it.
So, loyally o'erlooking all
In which love's promise short may fall
Of full performance, honour that
As won, which aye love worketh at!
It is but as the pedigree
Of perfectness which is to be
That our best good can honour claim;
Yet honour to deny were shame
And robbery; for it is the mould
Wherein to beauty runs the gold
Of good intention, and the prop
That lifts to the sun the earth-drawn crop
Of human sensibilities.

Such honour, with a conduct wise
In common things, as, not to steep
The lofty mind of love in sleep
Of over much familiarness;
Not to degrade its kind caress,
As those do that can feel no more,
So give themselves to pleasures o'er;
Not to let morning-sloth destroy
The evening-flower, domestic joy;
Not by uxoriousness to chill
The warm devotion of her will
Who can but half her love confer
On him that cares for nought but her;—
These, and like obvious prudences
Observed, he's safest that relies,
For the hope she will not always seem,
Caught, but a laurel or a stream,
On time; on her unsearchable
Love-wisdom; on their work done well,
Discreet with mutual aid; on might
Of shared affliction and delight;
On pleasures that so childish be
They're 'shamed to let the children see,
By which life keeps the valleys low
Where love does naturally grow;
On much whereof hearts have account,
Though heads forget; on babes, chief fount
Of union, and for which babes are
No less than this for them, nay far
More, for the bond of man and wife
To the very verge of future life
Strengthens, and yearns for brighter day,
While others, with their use, decay;
And, though true marriage purpose keeps
Of offspring, as the centre sleeps
Within the wheel, transmitting thence
Fury to the circumference,
Love's self the noblest offspring is,
And sanction of the nuptial kiss;

Lastly, on either's primal curse,
Which help and sympathy reverse
To blessings.

9

God, who may be well
Jealous of His chief miracle,
Bids sleep the meddling soul of man,
Through the long process of this plan,
Whereby, from his unweeting side,
The Wife's created, and the Bride,
That chance one of her strange, sweet sex
He to his glad life did annex,
Grows more and more, by day and night,
The one in the whole world opposite
Of him, and in her nature all
So suited and reciprocal
To his especial form of sense,
Affection, and intelligence,
That, whereas love at first had strange
Relapses into lust of change,
It now finds (wondrous this, but true!)
The long-accustom'd only new,
And the untried common; and, whereas
An equal seeming danger was
Of likeness lacking joy and force,
Or difference reaching to divorce,
Now can the finish'd lover see
Marvel of me most far from me,
Whom without pride he may admire,
Without Narcissus' doom desire,
Serve without selfishness, and love
'Even as himself,' in sense above
Niggard 'as much,' yea, as she is
The only part of him that's his.

10

I do not say love's youth returns;
That joy which so divinely yearns!

But just esteem of present good
Shows all regret such gratitude
As if the sparrow in her nest,
Her woolly young beneath her breast,
Should these despise, and sorrow for
Her five blue eggs that are no more.
Nor say I the fruit has quite the scope
Of the flower's spiritual hope.
Love's best is service, and of this,
Howe'er devout, use dulls the bliss.
Though love is all of earth that's dear,
Its home, my Children, is not here:
The pathos of eternity
Does in its fullest pleasure sigh.
  Be grateful and most glad thereof.
Parting, as 'tis, is pain enough.
If love, by joy, has learn'd to give
Praise with the nature sensitive,
At last, to God, we then possess
The end of mortal happiness,
And henceforth very well may wait
The unbarring of the golden gate,
Wherethrough, already, faith can see
That apter to each wish than we
Is God, and curious to bless
Better than we devise or guess;
Not without condescending craft
To disappoint with bliss, and waft
Our vessels frail, when worst He mocks
The heart with breakers and with rocks,
To happiest havens. You have heard
Your bond death-sentenced by His Word.
What, if, in heaven, the name be o'er,
Because the thing is so much more?
All are, 'tis writ, as angels there,
Nor male nor female. Each a stair
In the hierarchical ascent
Of active and recipient
Affections, what if all are both

By turn, as they themselves betroth
To adoring what is next above,
Or serving what's below their love?
  Of this we are certified, that we
Are shaped here for eternity,
So that a careless word will make
Its dint upon the form we take
For ever. If, then, years have wrought
Two strangers to become, in thought,
Will, and affection, but one man
For likeness, as none others can,
Without like process, shall this tree
The king of all the forest, be,
Alas, the only one of all
That shall not lie where it doth fall?
Shall this unflagging flame, here nurs'd
By everything, yea, when reversed,
Blazing, in fury, brighter, wink,
Flicker, and into darkness shrink,
When all else glows, baleful or brave,
In the keen air beyond the grave?
  Beware; for fiends in triumph laugh
O'er him who learns the truth by half!
Beware; for God will not endure
For men to make their hope more pure
Than His good promise, or require
Another than the five-string'd lyre
Which He has vow'd again to the hands
Devout of him who understands
To tune it justly here! Beware
The Powers of Darkness and the Air,
Which lure to empty heights man's hope,
Bepraising heaven's ethereal cope,
But covering with their cloudy cant
Its ground of solid adamant,
That strengthens ether for the flight
Of angels, makes and measures height,
And in materiality
Exceeds our Earth's in such degree

As all else Earth exceeds! Do I
Here utter aught too dark or high?
Have you not seen a bird's beak slay
Proud Psyche, on a summer's day?
Down fluttering drop the frail wings four,
Missing the weight which made them soar.
Spirit is heavy nature's wing,
And is not rightly anything
Without its burden, whereas this,
Wingless, at least a maggot is,
And, wing'd, is honour and delight
Increasing endlessly with height.

11

If unto any here that chance
Fell not, which makes a month's romance,
Remember, few wed whom they would.
And this, like all God's laws, is good;
For nought's so sad, the whole world o'er,
As much love which has once been more.
Glorious for light is the earliest love;
But worldly things, in the rays thereof,
Extend their shadows, every one
False as the image which the sun
At noon or eve dwarfs or protracts.
A perilous lamp to light men's acts!
By Heaven's kind, impartial plan,
Well-wived is he that's truly man
If but the woman's womanly,
As such a man's is sure to be.
Joy of all eyes and pride of life
Perhaps she is not; the likelier wife!
If it be thus; if you have known,
(As who has not?) some heavenly one,
Whom the dull background of despair
Help'd to show forth supremely fair;
If memory, still remorseful, shapes
Young Passion bringing Eshcol grapes

To travellers in the Wilderness,
This truth will make regret the less:
Mighty in love as graces are,
God's ordinance is mightier far;
And he who is but just and kind
And patient, shall for guerdon find,
Before long, that the body's bond
Is all else utterly beyond
In power of love to actualise
The soul's bond which it signifies,
And even to deck a wife with grace
External in the form and face.
A five years' wife, and not yet fair?
Blame let the man, not Nature, bear!
For, as the sun, warming a bank
Where last year's grass droops gray and dank,
Evokes the violet, bids disclose
In yellow crowds the fresh primrose,
And foxglove hang her flushing head,
So vernal love, where all seems dead,
Makes beauty abound.
Then was that nought,
That trance of joy beyond all thought,
The vision, in one, of womanhood?
Nay, for all women holding good,
Should marriage such a prologue want,
'Twere sordid and most ignorant
Profanity; but, having this,
'Tis honour now, and future bliss;
For where is he that, knowing the height
And depth of ascertain'd delight,
Inhumanly henceforward lies
Content with mediocrities!

THE UNKNOWN EROS

"Deliciæ meæ esse cum filiis hominum."

PROVERBS VIII. 31.

PROEM

'MANY speak wisely, some inerrably:
Witness the beast who talk'd that should have bray'd,
And Caiaphas that said
Expedient 'twas for all that One should die;
But what avails
When Love's right accent from their wisdom fails,
And the Truth-criers know not what they cry!
Say, wherefore thou,
As under bondage of some bitter vow,
Warblest no word,
When all the rest are shouting to be heard?
Why leave the fervid running just when Fame
'Gan whispering of thy name
Amongst the hard-pleased Judges of the Course?
Parch'd is thy crystal-flowing source?
Pierce, then, with thought's steel probe, the trodden ground,
Till passion's buried floods be found;
Intend thine eye
Into the dim and undiscover'd sky
Whose lustres are the pulsings of the heart,
And promptly, as thy trade is, watch to chart
The lonely suns, the mystic hazes and throng'd sparkles bright
That, named and number'd right
In sweet, transpicuous words, shall glow alway
With Love's three-stranded ray,
Red wrath, compassion golden, lazuline delight.'
  Thus in reproof of my despondency,
My Mentor; and thus I:
  O, season strange for song!
And yet some timely power persuades my lips.
Is't England's parting soul that nerves my tongue,
As other Kingdoms, nearing their eclipse,

Have, in their latest bards, uplifted strong
The voice that was their voice in earlier days?
Is it her sudden, loud and piercing cry,
The note which those that seem too weak to sigh
Will sometimes utter just before they die?
  Lo, weary of the greatness of her ways,
There lies my Land, with hasty pulse and hard,
Her ancient beauty marr'd,
And, in her cold and aimless roving sight,
Horror of light;
Sole vigour left in her last lethargy,
Save when, at bidding of some dreadful breath,
The rising death
Rolls up with force;
And then the furiously gibbering corse
Shakes, panglessly convuls'd, and sightless stares,
Whilst one Physician pours in rousing wines,
One anodynes,
And one declares
That nothing ails it but the pains of growth.
  My last look loth
Is taken; and I turn, with the relief
Of knowing that my life-long hope and grief
Are surely vain,
To that unshapen time to come, when She,
A dim, heroic Nation long since dead,
The foulness of her agony forgot,
Shall all benignly shed
Through ages vast
The ghostly grace of her transfigured past
Over the present, harass'd and forlorn,
Of nations yet unborn;
And this shall be the lot
Of those who, in the bird-voice and the blast
Of her omniloquent tongue,
Have truly sung
Or greatly said,
To shew as one

With those who have best done,
And be as rays,
Thro' the still altering world, around her changeless head.
  Therefore no 'plaint be mine
Of listeners none,
No hope of render'd use or proud reward,
In hasty times and hard;
But chants as of a lonely thrush's throat
At latest eve,
That does in each calm note
Both joy and grieve;
Notes few and strong and fine,
Gilt with sweet day's decline,
And sad with promise of a different sun.
  'Mid the loud concert harsh
Of this fog-folded marsh,
To me, else dumb,
Uranian Clearness, come!
Give me to breathe in peace and in surprise
The light-thrill'd ether of your rarest skies,
Till inmost absolution start
The welling in the grateful eyes,
The heaving in the heart.
Winnow with sighs
And wash away
With tears the dust and stain of clay,
Till all the Song be Thine, as beautiful as Morn,
Bedeck'd with shining clouds of scorn;
And Thou, Inspirer, deign to brood
O'er the delighted words, and call them Very Good.
This grant, Clear Spirit; and grant that I remain
Content to ask unlikely gifts in vain.

BOOK I

I

SAINT VALENTINE'S DAY

Well dost thou, Love, thy solemn Feast to hold
In vestal February;
Not rather choosing out some rosy day
From the rich coronet of the coming May,
When all things meet to marry!
  O, quick, prævernal Power
That signall'st punctual through the sleepy mould
The Snowdrop's time to flower,
Fair as the rash oath of virginity
Which is first-love's first cry;
O, Baby Spring,
That flutter'st sudden 'neath the breast of Earth
A month before the birth;
Whence is the peaceful poignancy,
The joy contrite,
Sadder than sorrow, sweeter than delight,
That burthens now the breath of everything,
Though each one sighs as if to each alone
The cherish'd pang were known?
At dusk of dawn, on his dark spray apart,
With it the Blackbird breaks the young Day's heart;
In evening's hush
About it talks the heavenly-minded Thrush;
The hill with like remorse
Smiles to the Sun's smile in his westering course;
The fisher's drooping skiff
In yonder sheltering bay;

The choughs that call about the shining cliff;
The children, noisy in the setting ray;
Own the sweet season, each thing as it may;
Thoughts of strange kindness and forgotten peace
In me increase;
And tears arise
Within my happy, happy Mistress' eyes,
And, lo, her lips, averted from my kiss,
Ask from Love's bounty, ah, much more than bliss!
  Is't the sequester'd and exceeding sweet
Of dear Desire electing his defeat?
Is't the waked Earth now to yon purpling cope
Uttering first-love's first cry,
Vainly renouncing, with a Seraph's sigh,
Love's natural hope?
Fair-meaning Earth, foredoom'd to perjury!
Behold, all amorous May,
With roses heap'd upon her laughing brows,
Avoids thee of thy vows!
Were it for thee, with her warm bosom near,
To abide the sharpness of the Seraph's sphere?
Forget thy foolish words;
Go to her summons gay,
Thy heart with dead, wing'd Innocencies fill'd,
Ev'n as a nest with birds
After the old ones by the hawk are kill'd.
  Well dost thou, Love, to celebrate
The noon of thy soft ecstasy,
Or e'er it be too late,
Or e'er the Snowdrop die!

II

WIND AND WAVE

The wedded light and heat,
Winnowing the witless space,
Without a let,
What are they till they beat
Against the sleepy sod, and there beget
Perchance the violet!
Is the One found,
Amongst a wilderness of as happy grace,
To make Heaven's bound;
So that in Her
All which it hath of sensitively good
Is sought and understood
After the narrow mode the mighty Heavens prefer?
She, as a little breeze
Following still Night,
Ripples the spirit's cold, deep seas
Into delight;
But, in a while,
The immeasurable smile
Is broke by fresher airs to flashes blent
With darkling discontent;
And all the subtle zephyr hurries gay,
And all the heaving ocean heaves one way,
T'ward the void sky-line and an unguess'd weal;
Until the vanward billows feel
The agitating shallows, and divine the goal,
And to foam roll,
And spread and stray
And traverse wildly, like delighted hands,
The fair and fleckless sands;

And so the whole
Unfathomable and immense
Triumphing tide comes at the last to reach
And burst in wind-kiss'd splendours on the deaf'ning beach,
Where forms of children in first innocence
Laugh and fling pebbles on the rainbow'd crest
Of its untired unrest.

III

WINTER

I, singularly moved
To love the lovely that are not beloved,
Of all the Seasons, most
Love Winter, and to trace
The sense of the Trophonian pallor on her face.
It is not death, but plenitude of peace;
And the dim cloud that does the world enfold
Hath less the characters of dark and cold
Than warmth and light asleep,
And correspondent breathing seems to keep
With the infant harvest, breathing soft below
Its eider coverlet of snow.
Nor is in field or garden anything
But, duly look'd into, contains serene
The substance of things hoped for, in the Spring,
And evidence of Summer not yet seen.
On every chance-mild day
That visits the moist shaw,
The honeysuckle, 'sdaining to be crost
In urgence of sweet life by sleet or frost,
'Voids the time's law
With still increase
Of leaflet new, and little, wandering spray;
Often, in sheltering brakes,
As one from rest disturb'd in the first hour,
Primrose or violet bewilder'd wakes,
And deems 'tis time to flower;
Though not a whisper of her voice he hear,
The buried bulb does know
The signals of the year,

And hails far Summer with his lifted spear.
The gorse-field dark, by sudden, gold caprice,
Turns, here and there, into a Jason's fleece;
Lilies, that soon in Autumn slipp'd their gowns of green,
And vanish'd into earth,
And came again, ere Autumn died, to birth,
Stand full-array'd, amidst the wavering shower,
And perfect for the Summer, less the flower;
In nook of pale or crevice of crude bark,
Thou canst not miss,
If close thou spy, to mark
The ghostly chrysalis,
That, if thou touch it, stirs in its dream dark;
And the flush'd Robin, in the evenings hoar,
Does of Love's Day, as if he saw it, sing;
But sweeter yet than dream or song of Summer or Spring
Are Winter's sometime smiles, that seem to well
From infancy ineffable;
Her wandering, languorous gaze,
So unfamiliar, so without amaze,
On the elemental, chill adversity,
The uncomprehended rudeness; and her sigh
And solemn, gathering tear,
And look of exile from some great repose, the sphere
Of ether, moved by ether only, or
By something still more tranquil.

IV

BEATA

Of infinite Heaven the rays,
Piercing some eyelet in our cavern black,
Ended their viewless track
On thee to smite
Solely, as on a diamond stalactite,
And in mid-darkness lit a rainbow's blaze,
Wherein the absolute Reason, Power, and Love,
That erst could move
Mainly in me but toil and weariness,
Renounced their deadening might,
Renounced their undistinguishable stress
Of withering white,
And did with gladdest hues my spirit caress,
Nothing of Heaven in thee showing infinite,
Save the delight.

V

THE DAY AFTER TO-MORROW

Perchance she droops within the hollow gulf
Which the great wave of coming pleasure draws,
Not guessing the glad cause!
Ye Clouds that on your endless journey go,
Ye Winds that westward flow,
Thou heaving Sea
That heav'st 'twixt her and me,
Tell her I come;
Then only sigh your pleasure, and be dumb;
For the sweet secret of our either self
We know.
Tell her I come,
And let her heart be still'd.
One day's controlled hope, and then one more,
And on the third our lives shall be fulfill'd!
Yet all has been before:
Palm placed in palm, twin smiles, and words astray.
What other should we say?
But shall I not, with ne'er a sign, perceive,
Whilst her sweet hands I hold,
The myriad threads and meshes manifold
Which Love shall round her weave:
The pulse in that vein making alien pause
And varying beats from this;
Down each long finger felt, a differing strand
Of silvery welcome bland;
And in her breezy palm
And silken wrist,
Beneath the touch of my like numerous bliss
Complexly kiss'd,
A diverse and distinguishable calm?

What should we say!
It all has been before;
And yet our lives shall now be first fulfill'd,
And into their summ'd sweetness fall distill'd
One sweet drop more;
One sweet drop more, in absolute increase
Of unrelapsing peace.
O, heaving Sea,
That heav'st as if for bliss of her and me,
And separatest not dear heart from heart,
Though each 'gainst other beats too far apart,
For yet awhile
Let it not seem that I behold her smile.
O, weary Love, O, folded to her breast,
Love in each moment years and years of rest,
Be calm, as being not.
Ye oceans of intolerable delight,
The blazing photosphere of central Night,
Be ye forgot.
Terror, thou swarthy Groom of Bride-bliss coy,
Let me not see thee toy.
O, Death, too tardy with thy hope intense
Of kisses close beyond conceit of sense;
O, Life, too liberal, while to take her hand
Is more of hope than heart can understand;
Perturb my golden patience not with joy,
Nor, through a wish, profane
The peace that should pertain
To him who does by her attraction move.
Has all not been before?
One day's controlled hope, and one again,
And then the third, and ye shall have the rein,
O Life, Death, Terror, Love!
But soon let your unrestful rapture cease,
Ye flaming Ethers thin,
Condensing till the abiding sweetness win
One sweet drop more;
One sweet drop more in the measureless increase
Of honied peace.

VI

TRISTITIA

Darling, with hearts conjoin'd in such a peace
That Hope, so not to cease,
Must still gaze back,
And count, along our love's most happy track,
The landmarks of like inconceiv'd increase,
Promise me this:
If thou alone should'st win
God's perfect bliss,
And I, beguiled by gracious-seeming sin,
Say, loving too much thee,
Love's last goal miss,
And any vows may then have memory,
Never, by grief for what I bear or lack,
To mar thy joyance of heav'n's jubilee.
Promise me this;
For else I should be hurl'd,
Beyond just doom
And by thy deed, to Death's interior gloom,
From the mild borders of the banish'd world
Wherein they dwell
Who builded not unalterable fate
On pride, fraud, envy, cruel lust, or hate;
Yet loved too laxly sweetness and heart's ease,
And strove the creature more than God to please.
For such as these
Loss without measure, sadness without end!
Yet not for this do thou disheaven'd be
With thinking upon me.
Though black, when scann'd from heaven's surpassing bright,
This might mean light,

Foil'd with the dim days of mortality.
For God is everywhere.
Go down to deepest Hell, and He is there,
And, as a true but quite estranged Friend,
He works, 'gainst gnashing teeth of devilish ire,
With love deep hidden lest it be blasphemed,
If possible, to blend
Ease with the pangs of its inveterate fire;
Yea, in the worst
And from His Face most wilfully accurst
Of souls in vain redeem'd,
He does with potions of oblivion kill
Remorse of the lost Love that helps them still.
Apart from these,
Near the sky-borders of that banish'd world,
Wander pale spirits among willow'd leas,
Lost beyond measure, sadden'd without end,
But since, while erring most, retaining yet
Some ineffectual fervour of regret,
Retaining still such weal
As spurned Lovers feel,
Preferring far to all the world's delight
Their loss so infinite,
Or Poets, when they mark
In the clouds dun
A loitering flush of the long sunken sun,
And turn away with tears into the dark.
Know, Dear, these are not mine
But Wisdom's words, confirmed by divine
Doctors and Saints, though fitly seldom heard
Save in their own prepense-occulted word,
Lest fools be fool'd the further by false hope,
And wrest sweet knowledge to their own decline;
And (to approve I speak within my scope)
The Mistress of that dateless exile gray
Is named in surpliced Schools *Tristitia.*
But, O, my Darling, look in thy heart and see
How unto me,
Secured of my prime care, thy happy state,

In the most unclean cell
Of sordid Hell,
And worried by the most ingenious hate,
It never could be anything but well,
Nor from my soul, full of thy sanctity,
Such pleasure die
As the poor harlot's, in whose body stirs
The innocent life that is and is not hers:
Unless, alas, this fount of my relief
By thy unheavenly grief
Were closed.
So, with a consecrating kiss
And hearts made one in past all previous peace,
And on one hope reposed,
Promise me this!

VII

THE AZALEA

There, where the sun shines first
Against our room,
She train'd the gold Azalea, whose perfume
She, Spring-like, from her breathing grace dispersed.
Last night the delicate crests of saffron bloom,
For this their dainty likeness watch'd and nurst,
Were just at point to burst.
At dawn I dream'd, O God, that she was dead,
And groan'd aloud upon my wretched bed,
And waked, ah, God, and did not waken her,
But lay, with eyes still closed,
Perfectly bless'd in the delicious sphere
By which I knew so well that she was near,
My heart to speechless thankfulness composed.
Till 'gan to stir
A dizzy somewhat in my troubled head—
It *was* the azalea's breath, and she *was* dead!
The warm night had the lingering buds disclosed,
And I had fall'n asleep with to my breast
A chance-found letter press'd
In which she said,
'So, till to-morrow eve, my Own, adieu!
Parting's well-paid with soon again to meet,
Soon in your arms to feel so small and sweet,
Sweet to myself that am so sweet to you!'

VIII

DEPARTURE

It was not like your great and gracious ways!
Do you, that have nought other to lament,
Never, my Love, repent
Of how, that July afternoon,
You went,
With sudden, unintelligible phrase,
And frighten'd eye,
Upon your journey of so many days,
Without a single kiss, or a good-bye?
I knew, indeed, that you were parting soon;
And so we sate, within the low sun's rays,
You whispering to me, for your voice was weak,
Your harrowing praise.
Well, it was well,
To hear you such things speak,
And I could tell
What made your eyes a growing gloom of love,
As a warm South-wind sombres a March grove.
And it was like your great and gracious ways
To turn your talk on daily things, my Dear,
Lifting the luminous, pathetic lash
To let the laughter flash,
Whilst I drew near,
Because you spoke so low that I could scarcely hear.
But all at once to leave me at the last,
More at the wonder than the loss aghast,
With huddled, unintelligible phrase,
And frighten'd eye,
And go your journey of all days
With not one kiss, or a good-bye,
And the only loveless look the look with which you pass'd:
'Twas all unlike your great and gracious ways.

IX

EURYDICE

Is this the portent of the day nigh past,
And of a restless grave
O'er which the eternal sadness gathers fast;
Or but the heaped wave
Of some chance, wandering tide,
Such as that world of awe
Whose circuit, listening to a foreign law,
Conjunctures ours at unguess'd dates and wide,
Does in the Spirit's tremulous ocean draw,
To pass unfateful on, and so subside?
Thee, whom ev'n more than Heaven loved I have,
And yet have not been true
Even to thee,
I, dreaming, night by night, seek now to see,
And, in a mortal sorrow, still pursue
Thro' sordid streets and lanes
And houses brown and bare
And many a haggard stair
Ochrous with ancient stains,
And infamous doors, opening on hapless rooms,
In whose unhaunted glooms
Dead pauper generations, witless of the sun,
Their course have run;
And ofttimes my pursuit
Is check'd of its dear fruit
By things brimful of hate, my kith and kin,
Furious that I should keep
Their forfeit power to weep,
And mock, with living fear, their mournful malice thin.
But ever, at the last, my way I win

To where, with perfectly sad patience, nurst
By sorry comfort of assured worst,
Ingrain'd in fretted cheek and lips that pine,
On pallet poor
Thou lyest, stricken sick,
Beyond love's cure,
By all the world's neglect, but chiefly mine.
Then sweetness, sweeter than my tongue can tell,
Does in my bosom well,
And tears come free and quick
And more and more abound
For piteous passion keen at having found,
After exceeding ill, a little good;
A little good
Which, for the while,
Fleets with the current sorrow of the blood,
Though no good here has heart enough to smile.

X

THE TOYS

My little Son, who look'd from thoughtful eyes
And moved and spoke in quiet grown-up wise,
Having my law the seventh time disobey'd,
I struck him, and dismiss'd
With hard words and unkiss'd,
His Mother, who was patient, being dead.
Then, fearing lest his grief should hinder sleep,
I visited his bed,
But found him slumbering deep,
With darken'd eyelids, and their lashes yet
From his late sobbing wet.
And I, with moan,
Kissing away his tears, left others of my own;
For, on a table drawn beside his head,
He had put, within his reach,
A box of counters and a red-vein'd stone,
A piece of glass abraded by the beach
And six or seven shells,
A bottle with bluebells
And two French copper coins, ranged there with careful art,
To comfort his sad heart.
So when that night I pray'd
To God, I wept, and said:
Ah, when at last we lie with tranced breath,
Not vexing Thee in death,
And Thou rememberest of what toys
We made our joys,
How weakly understood,
Thy great commanded good,
Then, fatherly not less
Than I whom Thou hast moulded from the clay
Thou'lt leave Thy wrath, and say,
'I will be sorry for their childishness.'

XI

TIRED MEMORY

The stony rock of death's insensibility
Well'd yet awhile with honey of thy love
And then was dry;
Nor could thy picture, nor thine empty glove,
Nor all thy kind, long letters, nor the band
Which really spann'd
Thy body chaste and warm,
Thenceforward move
Upon the stony rock their wearied charm.
At last, then, thou wast dead.
Yet would I not despair,
But wrought my daily task, and daily said
Many and many a fond, unfeeling prayer,
To keep my vows of faith to thee from harm.
In vain.
'For 'tis,' I said, 'all one,
The wilful faith, which has no joy or pain,
As if 'twere none.'
Then look'd I miserably round
If aught of duteous love were left undone,
And nothing found.
But, kneeling in a Church, one Easter-Day,
It came to me to say:
'Though there is no intelligible rest,
In Earth or Heaven,
For me, but on her breast,
I yield her up, again to have her given,
Or not, as, Lord, Thou wilt, and that for aye.'
And the same night, in slumber lying,
I, who had dream'd of thee as sad and sick and dying,

And only so, nightly for all one year,
Did thee, my own most Dear,
Possess,
In gay, celestial beauty nothing coy,
And felt thy soft caress
With heretofore unknown reality of joy.
But, in our mortal air,
None thrives for long upon the happiest dream,
And fresh despair
Bade me seek round afresh for some extreme
Of unconceiv'd, interior sacrifice
Whereof the smoke might rise
To God, and 'mind Him that one pray'd below.
And so,
In agony, I cried:
'My Lord, if Thy strange will be this,
That I should crucify my heart,
Because my love has also been my pride,
I do submit, if I saw how, to bliss
Wherein She has no part.'
And I was heard,
And taken at my own remorseless word.
O, my most Dear,
Was't treason, as I fear?
'Twere that, and worse, to plead thy veiled mind,
Kissing thy babes, and murmuring in mine ear,
'Thou canst not be
Faithful to God, and faithless unto me!'
Ah, prophet kind!
I heard, all dumb and blind
With tears of protest; and I cannot see
But faith was broken. Yet, as I have said,
My heart was dead,
Dead of devotion and tired memory,
When a strange grace of thee
In a fair stranger, as I take it, bred
To her some tender heed,
Most innocent
Of purpose therewith blent,

And pure of faith, I think, to thee; yet such
That the pale reflex of an alien love,
So vaguely, sadly shown,
Did her heart touch
Above
All that, till then, had woo'd her for its own.
And so the fear, which is love's chilly dawn,
Flush'd faintly upon lids that droop'd like thine,
And made me weak,
By thy delusive likeness doubly drawn,
And Nature's long suspended breath of flame
Persuading soft, and whispering Duty's name,
Awhile to smile and speak
With this thy Sister sweet, and therefore mine;
Thy Sister sweet,
Who bade the wheels to stir
Of sensitive delight in the poor brain,
Dead of devotion and tired memory,
So that I lived again,
And, strange to aver,
With no relapse into the void inane,
For thee;
But (treason was't?) for thee and also her.

XII

MAGNA EST VERITAS

Here, in this little Bay,
Full of tumultuous life and great repose,
Where, twice a day,
The purposeless, glad ocean comes and goes,
Under high cliffs, and far from the huge town,
I sit me down.
For want of me the world's course will not fail:
When all its work is done, the lie shall rot;
The truth is great, and shall prevail
When none cares whether it prevail or not.

XIII

1867

In the year of the great crime,
When the false English Nobles and their Jew,
By God demented, slew
The Trust they stood twice pledged to keep from wrong,
One said, Take up thy Song,
That breathes the mild and almost mythic time
Of England's prime!
But I, Ah, me,
The freedom of the few
That, in our free Land, were indeed the free,
Can song renew?
Ill singing 'tis with blotting prison-bars,
How high soe'er, betwixt us and the stars;
Ill singing 'tis when there are none to hear;
And days are near
When England shall forget
The fading glow which, for a little while,
Illumes her yet,
The lovely smile
That grows so faint and wan,
Her people shouting in her dying ear,
Are not two daws worth two of any swan!
Ye outlaw'd Best, who yet are bright
With the sunken light,
Whose common style
Is Virtue at her gracious ease,
The flower of olden sanctities,
Ye haply trust, by love's benignant guile,
To lure the dark and selfish brood
To their own hated good;

Ye haply dream
Your lives shall still their charmful sway sustain,
Unstifled by the fever'd steam
That rises from the plain.
Know, 'twas the force of function high,
In corporate exercise, and public awe
Of Nature's, Heaven's, and England's Law
That Best, though mix'd with Bad, should reign,
Which kept you in your sky!
But, when the sordid Trader caught
The loose-held sceptre from your hands distraught,
And soon, to the Mechanic vain,
Sold the proud toy for nought,
Your charm was broke, your task was sped,
Your beauty, with your honour, dead,
And though you still are dreaming sweet
Of being even now not less
Than Gods and Goddesses, ye shall not long so cheat
Your hearts of their due heaviness.
Go, get you for your evil watching shriven!
Leave to your lawful Master's itching hands
Your unking'd lands,
But keep, at least, the dignity
Of deigning not, for his smooth use, to be,
Voteless, the voted delegates
Of his strange interests, loves and hates.
In sackcloth, or in private strife
With private ill, ye may please Heaven,
And soothe the coming pangs of sinking life;
And prayer perchance may win
A term to God's indignant mood
And the orgies of the multitude,
Which now begin;
But do not hope to wave the silken rag
Of your unsanction'd flag,
And so to guide
The great ship, helmless on the swelling tide
Of that presumptuous Sea,
Unlit by sun or moon, yet inly bright

With lights innumerable that give no light,
Flames of corrupted will and scorn of right,
Rejoicing to be free.
  And, now, because the dark comes on apace
When none can work for fear,
And Liberty in every Land lies slain,
And the two Tyrannies unchallenged reign,
And heavy prophecies, suspended long
At supplication of the righteous few,
And so discredited, to fulfilment throng,
Restrain'd no more by faithful prayer or tear,
And the dread baptism of blood seems near
That brings to the humbled Earth the Time of Grace,
Breathless be song,
And let Christ's own look through
The darkness, suddenly increased,
To the gray secret lingering in the East.

XIV

'IF I WERE DEAD'

'If I were dead, you'd sometimes say, Poor Child!'
The dear lips quiver'd as they spake,
And the tears brake
From eyes which, not to grieve me, brightly smiled.
Poor Child, poor Child!
I seem to hear your laugh, your talk, your song.
It is not true that Love will do no wrong.
Poor Child!
And did you think, when you so cried and smiled,
How I, in lonely nights, should lie awake,
And of those words your full avengers make?
Poor Child, poor Child!
And now, unless it be
That sweet amends thrice told are come to thee,
O God, have Thou *no* mercy upon me!
Poor Child!

XV

PEACE

O England, how hast thou forgot,
In dullard care for undisturb'd increase
Of gold, which profits not,
The gain which once thou knew'st was for thy peace!
Honour is peace, the peace which does accord
Alone with God's glad word:
'My peace I send you, and I send a sword.'
O England, how hast thou forgot,
How fear'st the things which make for joy, not fear,
Confronted near.
Hard days? 'Tis what the pamper'd seek to buy
With their most willing gold in weary lands.
Loss and pain risk'd? What sport but understands
These for incitements! Suddenly to die,
With conscience a blurr'd scroll?
The sunshine dreaming upon Salmon's height
Is not so sweet and white
As the most heretofore sin-spotted soul
That darts to its delight
Straight from the absolution of a faithful fight.
Myriads of homes unloosen'd of home's bond,
And fill'd with helpless babes and harmless women fond?
Let those whose pleasant chance
Took them, like me, among the German towns,
After the war that pluck'd the fangs from France,
With me pronounce
Whether the frequent black, which then array'd
Child, wife, and maid,
Did most to magnify the sombreness of grief,
Or add the beauty of a staid relief

And freshening foil
To cheerful-hearted Honour's ready smile!
  Beneath the heroic sun
Is there then none
Whose sinewy wings by choice do fly
In the fine mountain-air of public obloquy,
To tell the sleepy mongers of false ease
That war's the ordained way of all alive,
And therein with goodwill to dare and thrive
Is profit and heart's peace?
  But in his heart the fool now saith:
'The thoughts of Heaven were past all finding out,
Indeed, if it should rain
Intolerable woes upon our Land again,
After so long a drought!'
  'Will a kind Providence our vessel whelm,
With such a pious Pilot at the helm?'
  'Or let the throats be cut of pretty sheep
That care for nought but pasture rich and deep?'
  'Were 't Evangelical of God to deal so foul a blow
At people who hate Turks and Papists so?'
  'What, make or keep
A tax for ship and gun,
When 'tis full three to one
Yon bully but intends
To beat our friends?'
  'Let's put aside
Our costly pride.
Our appetite's not gone
Because we've learn'd to doff
Our caps, where we were used to keep them on.'
  'If times get worse,
We've money in our purse,
And Patriots that know how, let who will scoff,
To buy our perils off.
Yea, blessed in our midst
Art thou who lately didst,
So cheap,
The old bargain of the Saxon with the Dane.'

Thus in his heart the fool now saith;
And, lo, our trusted leaders trust fool's luck,
Which, like the whale's 'mazed chine,
When they thereon were mulling of their wine,
Will some day duck.
Remnant of Honour, brooding in the dark
Over your bitter cark,
Staring, as Rispah stared, astonied seven days,
Upon the corpses of so many sons,
Who loved her once,
Dead in the dim and lion-haunted ways,
Who could have dreamt
That times should come like these!
Prophets, indeed, taught lies when we were young,
And people loved to have it so;
For they teach well who teach their scholars' tongue!
But that the foolish both should gaze,
With feeble, fascinated face,
Upon the wan crest of the coming woe,
The billow of earthquake underneath the seas,
And sit at ease,
Or stand agape,
Without so much as stepping back to 'scape,
Mumbling, 'Perchance we perish if we stay:
'Tis certain wear of shoes to stir away!'
Who could have dreamt
That times should come like these!
Remnant of Honour, tongue-tied with contempt,
Consider; you are strong yet, if you please.
A hundred just men up, and arm'd but with a frown,
May hoot a hundred thousand false loons down,
Or drive them any way like geese.
But to sit silent now is to suborn
The common villany you scorn.
In the dark hour
When phrases are in power,
And nought's to choose between
The thing which is not and which is not seen,
One fool, with lusty lungs,

Does what a hundred wise, who hate and hold their tongues,
Shall ne'er undo.
In such an hour,
When eager hands are fetter'd and too few,
And hearts alone have leave to bleed,
Speak ; for a good word then is a good deed.

XVI

A FAREWELL

With all my will, but much against my heart,
We two now part.
My Very Dear,
Our solace is, the sad road lies so clear.
It needs no art,
With faint, averted feet
And many a tear,
In our opposed paths to persevere.
Go thou to East, I West.
We will not say
There's any hope, it is so far away.
But, O, my Best,
When the one darling of our widowhead,
The nursling Grief,
Is dead,
And no dews blur our eyes
To see the peach-bloom come in evening skies,
Perchance we may,
Where now this night is day,
And even through faith of still averted feet,
Making full circle of our banishment,
Amazed meet;
The bitter journey to the bourne so sweet
Seasoning the termless feast of our content
With tears of recognition never dry.

XVII

1880-85

Stand by,
Ye Wise, by whom Heav'n rules!
Your kingly hands suit not the hangman's tools.
When God has doom'd a glorious Past to die,
Are there no knaves and fools?
For ages yet to come your kind shall count for nought.
Smoke of the strife of other Powers
Than ours,
And tongues inscrutable with fury fraught
'Wilder the sky,
Till the far good which none can guess be wrought.
Stand by!
Since tears are vain, here let us rest and laugh,
But not too loudly; for the brave time's come,
When Best may not blaspheme the Bigger Half,
And freedom for our sort means freedom to be dumb.
Lo, how the dross and draff
Jeer up at us, and shout,
'The Day is ours, the Night is theirs!'
And urge their rout
Where the wild dawn of rising Tartarus flares.
Yon strives their Leader, lusting to be seen.
His leprosy's so perfect that men call him clean!
Listen the long, sincere, and liberal bray
Of the earnest Puller at another's hay
'Gainst aught that dares to tug the other way,
Quite void of fears
With all that noise of ruin round his ears!
Yonder the people cast their caps o'erhead,
And swear the threaten'd doom is ne'er to dread

That's come, though not yet past.
All front the horror and are none aghast;
Brag of their full-blown rights and liberties,
Nor once surmise
When each man gets his due the Nation dies;
Nay, still shout 'Progress!' as if seven plagues
Should take the laggard who would stretch his legs.
Forward! glad rush of Gergesenian swine;
You've gain'd the hill-top, but there's yet the brine.
Forward! to meet the welcome of the waves
That mount to 'whelm the freedom which enslaves.
Forward! bad corpses turn into good dung,
To feed strange futures beautiful and young.
Forward! God speed ye down the damn'd decline,
And grant ye the Fool's true good, in abject ruin's gulf
As the Wise see him so to see himself!
  Ah, Land once mine,
That seem'd to me too sweetly wise,
Too sternly fair for aught that dies,
Past is thy proud and pleasant state,
That recent date
When, strong and single, in thy sovereign heart,
The thrones of thinking, hearing, sight,
The cunning hand, the knotted thew
Of lesser powers that heave and hew,
And each the smallest beneficial part,
And merest pore of breathing, beat,
Full and complete,
The great pulse of thy generous might,
Equal in inequality,
That soul of joy in low and high;
When not a churl but felt the Giant's heat,
Albeit he simply call'd it his,
Flush in his common labour with delight,
And not a village-Maiden's kiss
But was for this
More sweet,
And not a sorrow but did lightlier sigh,
And for its private self less greet,

The whilst that other so majestic self stood by!
Integrity so vast could well afford
To wear in working many a stain,
To pillory the cobbler vain
And license madness in a lord.
On that were all men well agreed;
And, if they did a thing,
Their strength was with them in their deed,
And from amongst them came the shout of a king!
  But, once let traitor coward meet,
Not Heaven itself can keep its feet.
Come knave who said to dastard, 'Lo,
'The Deluge!' which but needed 'No!'
For all the Atlantic's threatening roar,
If men would bravely understand,
Is softly check'd for evermore
By a firm bar of sand.
But, dastard listening knave, who said,
' 'Twere juster were the Giant dead,
That so yon bawlers may not miss
To vote their own pot-belly'd bliss.'
All that is past!
We saw the slaying, and were not aghast.
But ne'er a sun, on village Groom and Bride,
Albeit they guess not how it is,
At Easter or at Whitsuntide,
But shines less gay for this!

XVIII

THE TWO DESERTS

Not greatly moved with awe am I
To learn that we may spy
Five thousand firmaments beyond our own.
The best that's known
Of the heavenly bodies does them credit small.
View'd close, the Moon's fair ball
Is of ill objects worst,
A corpse in Night's highway, naked, fire-scarr'd, accurst;
And now they tell
That the Sun is plainly seen to boil and burst
Too horribly for hell.
So, judging from these two,
As we must do,
The Universe, outside our living Earth,
Was all conceiv'd in the Creator's mirth,
Forecasting at the time Man's spirit deep,
To make dirt cheap.
Put by the Telescope!
Better without it man may see,
Stretch'd awful in the hush'd midnight,
The ghost of his eternity.
Give me the nobler glass that swells to the eye
The things which near us lie,
Till Science rapturously hails,
In the minutest water-drop,
A torment of innumerable tails.
These at the least do live.
But rather give
A mind not much to pry
Beyond our royal-fair estate

Betwixt these deserts blank of small and great.
Wonder and beauty our own courtiers are,
Pressing to catch our gaze,
And out of obvious ways
Ne'er wandering far.

XIX

CREST AND GULF

Much woe that man befalls
Who does not run when sent, nor come when Heaven calls;
But whether he serve God, or his own whim,
Not matters, in the end, to any one but him;
And he as soon
Shall map the other side of the Moon,
As trace what his own deed,
In the next chop of the chance gale, shall breed.
This he may know:
His good or evil seed
Is like to grow,
For its first harvest, quite to contraries:
The father wise
Has still the hare-brain'd brood;
'Gainst evil, ill example better works than good;
The poet, fanning his mild flight
At a most keen and arduous height,
Unveils the tender heavens to horny human eyes
Amidst ingenious blasphemies.
Wouldst raise the poor, in Capuan luxury sunk?
The Nation lives but whilst its Lords are drunk!
Or spread Heav'n's partial gifts o'er all, like dew?
The Many's weedy growth withers the gracious Few!
Strange opposites, from those, again, shall rise.
Join, then, if thee it please, the bitter jest
Of mankind's progress; all its spectral race
Mere impotence of rest,
The heaving vain of life which cannot cease from self,
Crest altering still to gulf
And gulf to crest

In endless chace,
That leaves the tossing water anchor'd in its place!
Ah, well does he who does but stand aside,
Sans hope or fear,
And marks the crest and gulf in station sink and rear,
And prophesies 'gainst trust in such a tide:
For he sometimes is prophet, heavenly taught,
Whose message is that he sees only nought.
  Nathless, discern'd may be,
By listeners at the doors of destiny,
The fly-wheel swift and still
Of God's incessant will,
Mighty to keep in bound, tho' powerless to quell,
The amorous and vehement drift of man's herd to hell.

XX

'LET BE!'

Ah, yes; we tell the good and evil trees
By fruits: But how tell these?
Who does not know
That good and ill
Are done in secret still,
And that which shews is verily but show!
How high of heart is one, and one how sweet of mood:
But not all height is holiness,
Nor every sweetness good;
And grace will sometimes lurk where who could guess?
The Critic of his kind,
Dealing to each his share,
With easy humour, hard to bear,
May not impossibly have in him shrined,
As in a gossamer globe or thickly padded pod,
Some small seed dear to God.
Haply yon wretch, so famous for his falls,
Got them beneath the Devil-defended walls
Of some high Virtue he had vow'd to win;
And that which you and I
Call his besetting sin
Is but the fume of his peculiar fire
Of inmost contrary desire,
And means wild willingness for her to die,
Dash'd with despondence of her favour sweet;
He fiercer fighting, in his worst defeat,
Than I or you,
That only courteous greet
Where he does hotly woo,
Did ever fight, in our best victory.

Another is mistook
Through his deceitful likeness to his look!
Let be, let be:
Why should I clear myself, why answer thou for me?
That shaft of slander shot
Miss'd only the right blot.
I see the shame
They cannot see:
'Tis very just they blame
The thing that's not.

XXI

'FAINT YET PURSUING'

Heroic Good, target for which the young
Dream in their dreams that every bow is strung,
And, missing, sigh
Unfruitful, or as disbelievers die,
Thee having miss'd, I will not so revolt,
But lowlier shoot my bolt,
And lowlier still, if still I may not reach,
And my proud stomach teach
That less than highest is good, and may be high.
An even walk in life's uneven way,
Though to have dreamt of flight and not to fly
Be strange and sad,
Is not a boon that's given to all who pray.
If this I had
I'd envy none!
Nay, trod I straight for one
Year, month or week,
Should Heaven withdraw, and Satan me amerce
Of power and joy, still would I seek
Another victory with a like reverse;
Because the good of victory does not die,
As dies the failure's curse,
And what we have to gain
Is, not one battle, but a weary life's campaign.
Yet meaner lot being sent
Should more than me content;
Yea, if I lie
Among vile shards, though born for silver wings,
In the strong flight and feathers gold
Of whatsoever heavenward mounts and sings

I must by admiration so comply
That there I should my own delight behold.
Yea, though I sin each day times seven,
And dare not lift the fearfullest eyes to Heaven,
Thanks must I give
Because that seven times are not eight or nine,
And that my darkness is all mine,
And that I live
Within this oak-shade one more minute even,
Hearing the winds their Maker magnify.

XXII

VICTORY IN DEFEAT

Ah, God, alas,
How soon it came to pass
The sweetness melted from thy barbed hook
Which I so simply took;
And I lay bleeding on the bitter land,
Afraid to stir against thy least command,
But losing all my pleasant life-blood, whence
Force should have been heart's frailty to withstand.
Life is not life at all without delight,
Nor has it any might;
And better than the insentient heart and brain
Is sharpest pain;
And better for the moment seems it to rebel,
If the great Master, from his lifted seat,
Ne'er whispers to the wearied servant 'Well!'
Yet what returns of love did I endure,
When to be pardon'd seem'd almost more sweet
Than aye to have been pure!
But day still faded to disastrous night,
And thicker darkness changed to feebler light,
Until forgiveness, without stint renew'd,
Was now no more with loving tears imbued,
Vowing no more offence.
Not less to thine Unfaithful didst thou cry,
'Come back, poor Child; be all as 'twas before.'
But I,
'No, no; I will not promise any more!
Yet, when I feel my hour is come to die,
And so I am secured of continence,
Then may I say, though haply then in vain,

"My only, only Love, O, take me back again!"'
Thereafter didst thou smite
So hard that, for a space,
Uplifted seem'd Heav'n's everlasting door,
And I indeed the darling of thy grace.
But, in some dozen changes of the moon,
A bitter mockery seem'd thy bitter boon.
The broken pinion was no longer sore.
Again, indeed, I woke
Under so dread a stroke
That all the strength it left within my heart
Was just to ache and turn, and then to turn and ache,
And some weak sign of war unceasingly to make.
And here I lie,
With no one near to mark,
Thrusting Hell's phantoms feebly in the dark,
And still at point more utterly to die.
O God, how long!
Put forth indeed thy powerful right hand,
While time is yet,
Or never shall I see the blissful land!
Thus I: then God, in pleasant speech and strong,
(Which soon I shall forget):
'The man who, though his fights be all defeats,
Still fights,
Enters at last
The heavenly Jerusalem's rejoicing streets
With glory more, and more triumphant rites
Than always-conquering Joshua's, when his blast
The frighted walls of Jericho down cast;
And, lo, the glad surprise
Of peace beyond surmise,
More than in common Saints, for ever in his eyes.

XXIII

REMEMBERED GRACE

Since succour to the feeblest of the wise
Is charge of nobler weight
Than the security
Of many and many a foolish soul's estate,
This I affirm,
Though fools will fools more confidently be:
Whom God does once with heart to heart befriend,
He does so till the end:
And having planted life's miraculous germ,
One sweet pulsation of responsive love,
He sets him sheer above,
Not sin and bitter shame
And wreck of fame,
But Hell's insidious and more black attempt,
The envy, malice, and pride,
Which men who share so easily condone
That few ev'n list such ills as these to hide.
From these unalterably exempt,
Through the remember'd grace
Of that divine embrace,
Of his sad errors none,
Though gross to blame,
Shall cast him lower than the cleansing flame,
Nor make him quite depart
From the small flock named 'after God's own heart,'
And to themselves unknown.
Nor can he quail
In faith, nor flush nor pale
When all the other idiot people spell
How this or that new Prophet's word belies

Their last high oracle;
But constantly his soul
Points to its pole
Ev'n as the needle points, and knows not why;
And, under the ever-changing clouds of doubt,
When others cry,
'The stars, if stars there were,
Are quench'd and out!'
To him, uplooking t'ward the hills for aid,
Appear, at need display'd,
Gaps in the low-hung gloom, and, bright in air,
Orion or the Bear.

XXIV

VESICA PISCIS

In strenuous hope I wrought,
And hope seem'd still betray'd;
Lastly I said,
'I have labour'd through the Night, nor yet
Have taken aught;
But at Thy word I will again cast forth the net!'
And, lo, I caught
(Oh, quite unlike and quite beyond my thought,)
Not the quick, shining harvest of the Sea,
For food, my wish,
But Thee!
Then, hiding even in me,
As hid was Simon's coin within the fish,
Thou sigh'd'st, with joy, 'Be dumb,
Or speak but of forgotten things to far-off times to come.'

BOOK II

I

TO THE UNKNOWN EROS

What rumour'd heavens are these
Which not a poet sings,
O, Unknown Eros? What this breeze
Of sudden wings
Speeding at far returns of time from interstellar space
To fan my very face,
And gone as fleet,
Through delicatest ether feathering soft their solitary beat,
With ne'er a light plume dropp'd, nor any trace
To speak of whence they came, or whither they depart?
And why this palpitating heart,
This blind and unrelated joy,
This meaningless desire,
That moves me like the Child
Who in the flushing darkness troubled lies,
Inventing lonely prophecies,
Which even to his Mother mild
He dares not tell;
To which himself is infidel;
His heart not less on fire
With dreams impossible as wildest Arab Tale,
(So thinks the boy,)
With dreams that turn him red and pale,
Yet less impossible and wild
Than those which bashful Love, in his own way and hour,
Shall duly bring to flower?

O, Unknown Eros, sire of awful bliss,

What portent and what Delphic word,
Such as in form of snake forebodes the bird,
Is this?
In me life's even flood
What eddies thus?
What in its ruddy orbit lifts the blood,
Like a perturbed moon of Uranus,
Reaching to some great world in ungauged darkness hid,
And whence
This rapture of the sense
Which, by thy whisper bid,
Reveres with obscure rite and sacramental sign
A bond I know not of nor dimly can divine;
This subject loyalty which longs
For chains and thongs
Woven of gossamer and adamant,
To bind me to my unguess'd want,
And so to lie,
Between those quivering plumes that thro' fine ether pant,
For hopeless, sweet eternity?
What God unhonour'd hitherto in songs,
Or which, that now
Forgettest the disguise
That Gods must wear who visit human eyes,
Art Thou?
Thou art not Amor; or, if so, yon pyre,
That waits the willing victim, flames with vestal fire;
Nor mooned Queen of maids; or, if thou'rt she,
Ah, then, from Thee
Let Bride and Bridegroom learn what kisses be!
In what veil'd hymn
Or mystic dance
Would he that were thy Priest advance
Thine earthly praise, thy glory limn?
Say, should the feet that feel thy thought
In double-center'd circuit run,
In that compulsive focus, Nought,
In this a furnace like the sun;
And might some note of thy renown

And high behest
Thus in enigma be expressed:
'There lies the crown
Which all thy longing cures.
Refuse it, Mortal, that it may be yours!
It is a Spirit, though it seems red gold;
And such may no man, but by shunning, hold.
Refuse it, till refusing be despair;
And thou shalt feel the phantom in thy hair.'

II

THE CONTRACT

Twice thirty centuries and more ago,
All in a heavenly Abyssinian vale,
Man first met woman; and the ruddy snow
On many-ridgëd Abora turn'd pale,
And the song choked within the nightingale.
A mild white furnace in the thorough blast
Of purest spirit seem'd She as she pass'd;
And of the Man enough that this be said,
He look'd her Head.
Towards their bower
Together as they went,
With hearts conceiving torrents of content,
And linger'd prologue fit for Paradise,
He, gathering power
From dear persuasion of the dim-lit hour,
And doubted sanction of her sparkling eyes,
Thus supplicates her conjugal assent,
And thus she makes replies:
'Lo, Eve, the Day burns on the snowy height,
But here is mellow night!'
'Here let us rest. The languor of the light
Is in my feet.
It is thy strength, my Love, that makes me weak;
Thy strength it is that makes my weakness sweet.
What would thy kiss'd lips speak?'
'See, what a world of roses I have spread
To make the bridal bed.
Come, Beauty's self and Love's, thus to thy throne be led!'
'My Lord, my Wisdom, nay!
Does not yon love-delighted Planet run,
(Haply against her heart,)

A space apart
For ever from her strong-persuading Sun!
O say,
Shall we no voluntary bars
Set to our drift? I, Sister of the Stars,
And Thou, my glorious, course-compelling Day!'
  'Yea, yea!
Was it an echo of her coming word
Which, ere she spake, I heard?
Or through what strange distrust was I, her Head,
Not first this thing to have said?
Alway
Speaks not within my breast
The uncompulsive, great and sweet behest
Of something bright,
Not named, not known, and yet more manifest
Than is the morn,
The sun being just at point then to be born?
O Eve, take back thy "Nay."
Trust me, Beloved, ever in all to mean
Thy blissful service, sacrificial, keen;
But bondless be that service, and let speak—'
  'This other world of roses in my cheek,
Which hide them in thy breast, and deepening seek
That thou decree if they mean Yea or Nay.'
  'Did e'er so sweet a word such sweet gainsay!'
  'And when I lean, Love, on you, thus, and smile
So that my Nay seems Yea,
You must the while
Thence be confirm'd that I deny you still.'
  'I will, I will!'
  'And when my arms are round your neck, like this,
And I, as now,
Melt like a golden ingot in your kiss,
Then, more than ever, shall your splendid word
Be as Archangel Michael's severing sword!
Speak, speak!
Your might, Love, makes me weak,
Your might it is that makes my weakness sweet.

'I vow, I vow!'
'And are you happy, O, my Hero and Lord;
And is your joy complete?'
'Yea, with my joyful heart my body rocks,
And joy comes down from Heaven in floods and shocks,
As from Mount Abora comes the avalanche.'
'My Law, my Light!
Then am I yours as your high mind may list.
No wile shall lure you, none can I resist!'
Thus the first Eve
With much enamour'd Adam did enact
Their mutual free contract
Of virgin spousals, blissful beyond flight
Of modern thought, with great intention staunch,
Though unobliged until that binding pact.
Whether She kept her word, or He the mind
To hold her, wavering, to his own restraint,
Answer, ye pleasures faint,
Ye fiery throes, and upturn'd eyeballs blind
Of sick-at-heart Mankind,
Whom nothing succour can,
Until a heaven-caress'd and happier Eve
Be join'd with some glad Saint
In like espousals, blessed upon Earth,
And she her Fruit forth bring;
No numb, chill-hearted, shaken-witted thing,
'Plaining his little span,
But of proud virgin joy the appropriate birth,
The Son of God and Man.

III

ARBOR VITÆ

With honeysuckle, over-sweet, festoon'd;
With bitter ivy bound;
Terraced with funguses unsound;
Deform'd with many a boss
And closed scar, o'ercushion'd deep with moss;
Bunch'd all about with pagan mistletoe;
And thick with nests of the hoarse bird
That talks, but understands not his own word;
Stands, and so stood a thousand years ago,
A single tree.
Thunder has done its worst among its twigs,
Where the great crest yet blackens, never pruned,
But in its heart, alway
Ready to push new verdurous boughs, whene'er
The rotting saplings near it fall and leave it air,
Is all antiquity and no decay.
Rich, though rejected by the forest-pigs,
Its fruit, beneath whose rough, concealing rind
They that will break it find
Heart-succouring savour of each several meat,
And kernell'd drink of brain-renewing power,
With bitter condiment and sour,
And sweet economy of sweet,
And odours that remind
Of haunts of childhood and a different day.
Beside this tree,
Praising no Gods nor blaming, sans a wish,
Sits, Tartar-like, the Time's civility,
And eats its dead-dog off a golden dish.

IV

THE STANDARDS

That last,
Blown from our Sion of the Seven Hills,
Was no uncertain blast!
Listen: the warning all the champaign fills,
And minatory murmurs, answering, mar
The Night, both near and far,
Perplexing many a drowsy citadel
Beneath whose ill-watch'd walls the Powers of Hell,
With armed jar
And angry threat, surcease
Their long-kept compact of contemptuous peace!
Lo, yonder, where our little English band,
With peace in heart and wrath in hand,
Have dimly ta'en their stand,
Sweetly the light
Shines from the solitary peak at Edgbaston,
Whence, o'er the dawning Land,
Gleam the gold blazonries of Love irate
'Gainst the black flag of Hate.
Envy not, little band,
Your brothers under the Hohenzollern hoof
Put to the splendid proof.
Your hour is near!
The spectre-haunted time of idle Night,
Your only fear,
Thank God, is done,
And Day and War, Man's work-time and delight,
Begun.

Ho, ye of the van there, veterans great of cheer,
Look to your footing, when, from yonder verge,
The wish'd Sun shall emerge;

Lest once again the Flower of Sharon bloom
After a way the Stalk call heresy.
Strange splendour and strange gloom
Alike confuse the path
Of customary faith;
And when the dim-seen mountains turn to flame
And every roadside atom is a spark,
The dazzled sense, that used was to the dark,
May well doubt, 'Is't the safe way and the same
By which we came
From Egypt, and to Canaan mean to go?'
But know,
The clearness then so marvellously increas'd,
The light'ning shining Westward from the East,
Is the great promised sign
Of His victorious and divine
Approach, whose coming in the clouds shall be,
As erst was His humility,
A stumbling unto some, the first bid to the Feast.
  Cry, Ho!
Good speed to them that come and them that go
From either gathering host,
And, after feeble, false allegiance, now first know
Their post.
Ho, ye
Who loved our Flag
Only because there flapp'd none other rag
Which gentlemen might doff to, and such be,
'Save your gentility!
For leagued, alas, are we
With many a faithful rogue
Discrediting bright Truth with dirt and brogue;
And flatterers, too,
That still would sniff the grass
After the 'broider'd shoe,
And swear it smelt like musk where He did pass,
Though he were Borgia or Caiaphas.
Ho, ye
Who dread the bondage of the boundless fields

Which Heaven's allegiance yields,
And, like to house-hatch'd finches, hop not free
Unless 'tween walls of wire,
Look, there be many cages : choose to your desire!
Ho, ye,
Of God the least beloved, of Man the most,
That like not leaguing with the lesser host,
Behold the invested Mount,
And that assaulting Sea with ne'er a coast.
You need not stop to count!
  But come up, ye
Who adore, in any way,
Our God by His wide-honour'd Name of YEA.
Come up; for where ye stand ye cannot stay.
Come all
That either mood of heavenly joyance know,
And, on the ladder hierarchical,
Have seen the order'd Angels to and fro
Descending with the pride of service sweet,
Ascending, with the rapture of receipt!
Come who have felt, in soul and heart and sense,
The entire obedience
Which opes the bosom, like a blissful wife,
To the Husband of all life!
Come ye that find contentment's vèry core
In the light store
And daisied path
Of Poverty,
And know how more
A small thing that the righteous hath
Availeth than the ungodly's riches great.
Come likewise ye
Which do not yet disown as out of date
That brightest third of the dead Virtues three,
Of Love the crown elate
And daintiest glee!
Come up, come up, and join our little band.
Our time is near at hand.
The sanction of the world's undying hate

Means more than flaunted flags in windy air.
Be ye of gathering fate
Now gladly ware.
Now from the matrix, by God's grinding wrought,
The brilliant shall be brought;
The white stone mystic set between the eyes
Of them that get the prize;
Yea, part and parcel of that mighty Stone
Which shall be thrown
Into the Sea, and Sea shall be no more.

V

SPONSA DEI

What is this Maiden fair,
The laughing of whose eye
Is in man's heart renew'd virginity;
Who yet sick longing breeds
For marriage which exceeds
The inventive guess of Love to satisfy
With hope of utter binding, and of loosing endless dear despair?
What gleams about her shine,
More transient than delight and more divine!
If she does something but a little sweet,
As gaze towards the glass to set her hair,
See how his soul falls humbled at her feet!
Her gentle step, to go or come,
Gains her more merit than a martyrdom;
And, if she dance, it doth such grace confer
As opes the heaven of heavens to more than her,
And makes a rival of her worshipper.
To die unknown for her were little cost!
So is she without guile,
Her mere refused smile
Makes up the sum of that which may be lost!
Who is this Fair
Whom each hath seen,
The darkest once in this bewailed dell,
Be he not destin'd for the glooms of hell?
Whom each hath seen
And known, with sharp remorse and sweet, as Queen
And tear-glad Mistress of his hopes of bliss,
Too fair for man to kiss?
Who is this only happy She,
Whom, by a frantic flight of courtesy,

Born of despair
Of better lodging for his Spirit fair,
He adores as Margaret, Maude, or Cecily?
And what this sigh,
That each one heaves for Earth's last lowlihead
And the Heaven high
Ineffably lock'd in dateless bridal-bed?
Are all, then, mad, or is it prophecy?
'Sons now we are of God,' as we have heard,
'But what we shall be hath not yet appear'd.'
O, Heart, remember thee,
That Man is none,
Save One.
What if this Lady be thy Soul, and He
Who claims to enjoy her sacred beauty be,
Not thou, but God; and thy sick fire
A female vanity,
Such as a Bride, viewing her mirror'd charms,
Feels when she sighs, 'All these are for his arms!'
A reflex heat
Flash'd on thy cheek from His immense desire,
Which waits to crown, beyond thy brain's conceit,
Thy nameless, secret, hopeless longing sweet,
Not by-and-by, but now,
Unless deny Him thou!

VI

LEGEM TUAM DILEXI

The 'Infinite.' Word horrible! at feud
With life, and the braced mood
Of power and joy and love;
Forbidden, by wise heathen ev'n, to be
Spoken of Deity,
Whose Name, on popular altars, was 'The Unknown,'
Because, or ere It was reveal'd as One
Confined in Three,
The people fear'd that it might prove
Infinity,
The blazon which the devils desired to gain;
And God, for their confusion, laugh'd consent;
Yet did so far relent,
That they might seek relief, and not in vain,
In dashing of themselves against the shores of pain.
Nor bides alone in hell
The bond-disdaining spirit boiling to rebel.
But for compulsion of strong grace,
The pebble in the road
Would straight explode,
And fill the ghastly boundlessness of space.
The furious power,
To soft growth twice constrain'd in leaf and flower,
Protests, and longs to flash its faint self far
Beyond the dimmest star.
The same
Seditious flame,
Beat backward with reduplicated might,
Struggles alive within its stricter term,
And is the worm.
And the just Man does on himself affirm

God's limits, and is conscious of delight,
Freedom and right;
And so His Semblance is, Who, every hour,
By day and night,
Buildeth new bulwarks 'gainst the Infinite.
For, ah, who can express
How full of bonds and simpleness
Is God,
How narrow is He,
And how the wide, waste field of possibility
Is only trod
Straight to His homestead in the human heart,
And all His art
Is as the babe's that wins his Mother to repeat
Her little song so sweet!
What is the chief news of the Night?
Lo, iron and salt, heat, weight and light
In every star that drifts on the great breeze!
And these
Mean Man,
Darling of God, Whose thoughts but live and move
Round him; Who woos his will
To wedlock with His own, and does distil
To that drop's span
The atta of all rose-fields of all love!
Therefore the soul select assumes the stress
Of bonds unbid, which God's own style express
Better than well,
And aye hath, cloister'd, borne,
To the Clown's scorn,
The fetters of the threefold golden chain:
Narrowing to nothing all his wordly gain;
(Howbeit in vain;
For to have nought
Is to have all things without care or thought!)
Surrendering, abject, to his equal's rule,
As though he were a fool,
The free wings of the will;
(More vainly still;

For none knows rightly what 'tis to be free
But only he
Who, vow'd against all choice, and fill'd with awe
Of the ofttimes dumb or clouded Oracle,
Does wiser than to spell,
In his own suit, the least word of the Law!)
And, lastly, bartering life's dear bliss for pain;
But evermore in vain;
For joy (rejoice ye Few that tasted have!)
Is Love's obedience
Against the genial laws of natural sense,
Whose wide, self-dissipating wave,
Prison'd in artful dykes,
Trembling returns and strikes
Thence to its source again,
In backward billows fleet,
Crest crossing crest ecstatic as they greet,
Thrilling each vein,
Exploring every chasm and cove
Of the full heart with floods of honied love,
And every principal street
And obscure alley and lane
Of the intricate brain
With brimming rivers of light and breezes sweet
Of the primordial heat;
Till, unto view of me and thee,
Lost the intense life be,
Or ludicrously display'd, by force
Of distance; as a soaring eagle, or a horse
On far-off hillside shewn,
May seem a gust-driv'n rag or a dead stone.
Nor by such bonds alone—
But more I leave to say,
Fitly revering the Wild Ass's bray,
Also his hoof,
Of which, go where you will, the marks remain
Where the religious walls have hid the bright reproof.

VII

TO THE BODY

Creation's and Creator's crowning good;
Wall of infinitude;
Foundation of the sky,
In Heaven forecast
And long'd for from eternity,
Though laid the last;
Reverberating dome,
Of music cunningly built home
Against the void and indolent disgrace
Of unresponsive space;
Little, sequester'd pleasure-house
For God and for His Spouse;
Elaborately, yea, past conceiving, fair,
Since, from the graced decorum of the hair,
Ev'n to the tingling, sweet
Soles of the simple, earth-confiding feet,
And from the inmost heart
Outwards unto the thin
Silk curtains of the skin,
Every least part
Astonish'd hears
And sweet replies to some like region of the spheres;
Form'd for a dignity prophets but darkly name,
Lest shameless men cry 'Shame!'
So rich with wealth conceal'd
That Heaven and Hell fight chiefly for this field;
Clinging to everything that pleases thee
With indefectible fidelity;
Alas, so true
To all thy friendships that no grace
Thee from thy sin can wholly disembrace;

Which thus 'bides with thee as the Jebusite,
That, maugre all God's promises could do,
The chosen People never conquer'd quite;
Who therefore lived with them,
And that by formal truce and as of right,
In metropolitan Jerusalem.
For which false fealty
Thou needs must, for a season, lie
In the grave's arms, foul and unshriven,
Albeit, in Heaven,
Thy crimson-throbbing Glow
Into its old abode aye pants to go,
And does with envy see
Enoch, Elijah, and the Lady, she
Who left the roses in her body's lieu.
O, if the pleasures I have known in thee
But my poor faith's poor first-fruits be,
What quintessential, keen, ethereal bliss
Then shall be his
Who has thy birth-time's consecrating dew
For death's sweet chrism retain'd,
Quick, tender, virginal, and unprofaned!

VIII

'SING US ONE OF THE SONGS OF SION'

How sing the Lord's Song in so strange a Land?
A torried waste of water-mocking sand;
Oases of wild grapes;
A dull, malodorous fog
O'er a once Sacred River's wandering strand,
Its ancient tillage all gone back to bog;
A busy synod of blest cats and apes
Exposing the poor trick of earth and star
With worshipp'd snouts oracular;
Prophets to whose blind stare
The heavens the glory of God do not declare,
Skill'd in such question nice
As why one conjures toads who fails with lice,
And hatching snakes from sticks in such a swarm
As quite to surfeit Aaron's bigger worm;
A nation which has got
A lie in her right hand,
And knows it not;
With Pharaohs to her mind, each drifting as a log
Which way the foul stream flows,
More harden'd the more plagued with fly and frog!
How should sad Exile sing in such a Land?
How should ye understand?
What could he win but jeers,
Or howls, such as sweet music draws from dog,
Who told of marriage-feasting to the man
That nothing knows of food but bread of bran?
Besides, if aught such ears
Might e'er unclog,
There lives but one, with tones for Sion meet.
Behoveful, zealous, beautiful, elect,

Mild, firm, judicious, loving, bold, discreet,
Without superfluousness, without defect,
Few are his words, and find but scant respect,
Nay, scorn from some, for God's good cause agog.
Silence in such a Land is oftenest such men's speech.
O, that I might his holy secret reach;
O, might I catch his mantle when he goes;
O, that I were so gentle and so sweet,
So I might deal fair Sion's foolish foes
Such blows!

IX

DELICIÆ SAPIENTIÆ DE AMORE

Love, light for me
Thy ruddiest blazing torch,
That I, albeit a beggar by the Porch
Of the glad Palace of Virginity,
May gaze within, and sing the pomp I see;
For, crown'd with roses all,
'Tis there, O Love, they keep thy festival!
But first warn off the beatific spot
Those wretched who have not
Even afar beheld the shining wall,
And those who, once beholding, have forgot,
And those, most vile, who dress
The charnel spectre drear
Of utterly dishallow'd nothingness
In that refulgent fame,
And cry, Lo, here!
And name
The Lady whose smiles inflame
The sphere.
Bring, Love, anear,
And bid be not afraid
Young Lover true, and love-foreboding Maid,
And wedded Spouse, if virginal of thought;
For I will sing of nought
Less sweet to hear
Than seems
A music in their half-remember'd dreams.
The magnet calls the steel:
Answers the iron to the magnet's breath;
What do they feel
But death!

The clouds of summer kiss in flame and rain,
And are not found again;
But the heavens themselves eternal are with fire
Of unapproach'd desire,
By the aching heart of Love, which cannot rest,
In blissfullest pathos so indeed possess'd.
O, spousals high;
O, doctrine blest,
Unutterable in even the happiest sigh;
This know ye all
Who can recall
With what a welling of indignant tears
Love's simpleness first hears
The meaning of his mortal covenant,
And from what pride comes down
To wear the crown
Of which 'twas very heaven to feel the want.
How envies he the ways
Of yonder hopeless star,
And so would laugh and yearn
With trembling lids eterne,
Ineffably content from infinitely far
Only to gaze
On his bright Mistress's responding rays,
That never know eclipse;
And, once in his long year,
With præternuptial ecstasy and fear,
By the delicious law of that ellipse
Wherein all citizens of ether move,
With hastening pace to come
Nearer, though never near,
His Love
And always inaccessible sweet Home;
There on his path doubly to burn.
Kiss'd by her doubled light
That whispers of its source,
The ardent secret ever clothed with Night,
Then go forth in new force
Towards a new return,
Rejoicing as a Bridegroom on his course!

This know ye all;
Therefore gaze bold,
That so in you be joyful hope increas'd,
Thorough the Palace portals, and behold
The dainty and unsating Marriage-Feast.
O, hear
Them singing clear
'Cor meum et caro mea' round the 'I am,'
The Husband of the Heavens, and the Lamb
Whom they for ever follow there that kept,
Or losing, never slept
Till they reconquer'd had in mortal fight
The standard white.
O, hear
From the harps they bore from Earth, five-strung, what music springs,
While the glad Spirits chide
The wondering strings!
And how the shining sacrificial Choirs,
Offering for aye their dearest hearts' desires,
Which to their hearts come back beatified,
Hymn, the bright aisles along,
The nuptial song,
Song ever new to us and them, that saith,
'Hail Virgin in Virginity a Spouse!'
Heard first below
Within the little house
At Nazareth;
Heard yet in many a cell where brides of Christ
Lie hid, emparadised,
And where, although
By the hour 'tis night,
There's light,
The Day still lingering in the lap of snow.
Gaze and be not afraid
Ye wedded few that honour, in sweet thought
And glittering will,
So freshly from the garden gather still
The lily sacrificed;
For ye, though self-suspected here for nought,

Are highly styled
With the thousands twelve times twelve of undefiled.
Gaze and be not afraid
Young Lover true and love-foreboding Maid.
The full noon of deific vision bright
Abashes nor abates
No spark minute of Nature's keen delight.
'Tis there your Hymen waits!
There where in courts afar, all unconfused, they crowd,
As fumes the starlight soft
In gulfs of cloud,
And each to the other, well-content,
Sighs oft,
"'Twas this we meant!'
Gaze without blame
Ye in whom living Love yet blushes for dead shame.
There of pure Virgins none
Is fairer seen,
Save One,
Than Mary Magdalene.
Gaze without doubt or fear
Ye to whom generous Love, by any name, is dear.
Love makes the life to be
A fount perpetual of virginity;
For, lo, the Elect
Of generous Love, how named soe'er, affect
Nothing but God,
Or mediate or direct,
Nothing but God,
The Husband of the Heavens:
And who Him love, in potence great or small,
Are, one and all,
Heirs of the Palace glad,
And inly clad
With the bridal robes of ardour virginal.

X

THE CRY AT MIDNIGHT

The Midge's wing beats to and fro
A thousand times ere one can utter 'O!'
And Sirius' ball
Does on his business run
As many times immenser than the Sun.
Why should things not be great as well as small,
Or move like light as well as move at all?
St. Michael fills his place, I mine, and, if you please,
We will respect each other's provinces,
I marv'lling not at him, nor he at me.
But, if thou must go gaping, let it be
That One who could make Michael should make thee.
O, foolish Man, meting things low and high
By self, that accidental quantity!
With this conceit, Philosophy stalks frail
As peacock staggering underneath his tail.
Who judge of Plays from their own penny gaff,
At God's great theatre will hiss and laugh;
For what's a Saint to them
Brought up in modern virtues brummagem?
With garments grimed and lamps gone all to snuff,
And counting others for like Virgins queer,
To list those others cry, 'Our Bridegroom's near!'
Meaning their God, is surely quite enough
To make them rend their clothes and bawl out, 'Blasphemy!'

XI

AURAS OF DELIGHT

Beautiful habitations, auras of delight!
Who shall bewail the crags and bitter foam
And angry sword-blades flashing left and right
Which guard your glittering height,
That none thereby may come!
The vision which we have
Revere we so,
That yet we crave
To foot those fields of ne'er-profaned snow?
I, with heart-quake,
Dreaming or thinking of that realm of Love,
See, oft, a dove
Tangled in frightful nuptials with a snake;
The tortured knot,
Now, like a kite scant-weighted, flung bewitch'd
Sunwards, now pitch'd,
Tail over head, down, but with no taste got
Eternally
Of rest in either ruin or the sky,
But bird and vermin each incessant strives,
With vain dilaceration of both lives,
'Gainst its abhorred bond insoluble,
Coveting fiercer any separate hell
Than the most weary Soul in Purgatory
On God's sweet breast to lie.
And, in this sign, I con
The guerdon of that golden Cup, fulfill'd
With fornications foul of Babylon,
The heart where good is well-perceiv'd and known,
Yet is not will'd;
And Him I thank, who can make live again,

The dust, but not the joy we once profane,
That I, of ye,
Beautiful habitations, auras of delight,
In childish years and since had sometime sense and sight,
But that ye vanish'd quite,
Even from memory,
Ere I could get my breath, and whisper 'See!'
But did for me
They altogether die,
Those trackless glories glimps'd in upper sky?
Were they of chance, or vain,
Nor good at all again
For curb of heart or fret?
Nay, though, by grace,
Lest, haply, I refuse God to His face,
Their likeness wholly I forget,
Ah, yet,
Often in straits which else for me were ill,
I mind me still
I *did* respire the lonely auras sweet,
I *did* the blest abodes behold, and, at the mountains' feet,
Bathed in the holy Stream by Hermon's thymy hill.

XII

EROS AND PSYCHE

'Love, I heard tell of thee so oft!
Yea, thrice my face and bosom flush'd with heat
Of sudden wings,
Through delicatest ether feathering soft
Their solitary beat.
Long did I muse what service or what charms
Might lure thee, blissful Bird, into mine arms;
And nets I made,
But not of the fit strings.
At last, of endless failure much afraid,
To-night I would do nothing but lie still,
And promise, wert thou once within my window-sill,
Thine unknown will.
In nets' default,
Finch-like me seem'd thou might'st be ta'en with salt,
And here—and how thou mad'st me start!—
Thou art.'
'O Mortal, by Immortals' cunning led,
Who shew'd you how for Gods to bait your bed?
Ah, Psyche, guess'd you nought
I craved but to be caught?
Wanton, it was not you,
But I that did so passionately sue;
And for your beauty, not unscath'd, I fought
With Hades, ere I own'd in you a thought!'
'O, heavenly Lover true,
Is this thy mouth upon my forehead press'd?
Are these thine arms about my bosom link'd?
Are these thy hands that tremble near my heart,
Where join two hearts, for juncture more distinct?
By thee and by my maiden zone caress'd,

What dim, waste tracts of life shine sudden, like moonbeams
On windless ocean shaken by sweet dreams!
Ah, stir not to depart!
Kiss me again, thy Wife and Virgin too!
O Love, that, like a rose,
Deckest my breast with beautiful respose,
Kiss me again, and clasp me round the heart,
Till fill'd with thee am I
As the cocoon is with the butterfly!
—Yet how 'scape quite
Nor pluck pure pleasure with profane delight?
How know I that my Love is what he seems!
Give me a sign
That, in the pitchy night,
Comes to my pillow an immortal Spouse,
And not a fiend, hiding with happy boughs
Of palm and asphodel
The pits of hell!'
  ''Tis this:
I make the childless to keep joyful house.
Below your bosom, mortal Mistress mine,
Immortal by my kiss,
Leaps what sweet pain?
A fiend, my Psyche, comes with barren bliss,
A God's embraces never are in vain.'
  'I own
A life not mine within my golden zone.
Yea, how
'Tis easier grown
Thine arduous rule to don
Than for a Bride to put her bride-dress on!
Nay, rather, now
'Tis no more service to be borne serene,
Whither thou wilt, thy stormful wings between.
But, Oh,
Can I endure
This flame, yet live for what thou lov'st me, pure?'
  'Himself the God let blame
If all about him bursts to quenchless flame!
My Darling, know

Your spotless fairness is not match'd in snow,
But in the integrity of fire.
Whate'er you are, Sweet, I require.
A sorry God were he
That fewer claim'd than all Love's mighty kingdoms three!'
  'Much marvel I
That thou, the greatest of the Powers above,
Me visitest with such exceeding love.
What thing is this?
A God to make me, nothing, needful to his bliss,
And humbly wait my favour for a kiss!
Yea, all thy legions of liege deity
To look into this mystery desire.'
  'Content you, Dear, with them, this marvel to admire,
And lay your foolish little head to rest
On my familiar breast.
Should a high King, leaving his arduous throne,
Sue from her hedge a little Gipsy Maid,
For far-off royal ancestry bewray'd
By some wild beauties, to herself unknown;
Some voidness of herself in her strange ways
Which to his bounteous fulness promised dainty praise;
Some power, by all but him unguess'd,
Of growing king-like were she king-caress'd;
And should he bid his dames of loftiest grade
Put off her rags and make her lowlihead
Pure for the soft midst of his perfumed bed,
So to forget, kind-couch'd with her alone,
His empire, in her winsome joyance free;
What would he do, if such a fool were she
As at his grandeur there to gape and quake,
Mindless of love's supreme equality,
And of his heart, so simple for her sake
That all he ask'd, for making her all-blest,
Was that her nothingness alway
Should yield such easy fee as frank to play
Or sleep delighted in her Monarch's breast,
Feeling her nothingness her giddiest boast,
As being the charm for which he loved her most?
What if this reed,

Through which the King thought love-tunes to have blown,
Should shriek, "Indeed,
I am too base to trill so blest a tone!
Would not the King allege
Defaulted consummation of the marriage-pledge,
And hie the Gipsy to her native hedge?'
  'O, too much joy; O, touch of airy fire;
O, turmoil of content; O, unperturb'd desire,
From founts of spirit impell'd through brain and blood!
I'll not call ill what, since 'tis thine, is good,
Nor best what is but second best or third;
Still my heart fails,
And unaccustom'd and astonish'd, quails,
And blames me, though I think I have not err'd.
'Tis hard for fly, in such a honied flood,
To use her eyes, far more her wings or feet.
Bitter be thy behests!
Lie like a bunch of myrrh between my aching breasts.
Some greatly pangful penance would I brave.
Sharpness me save
From being slain by sweet!'
  'In your dell'd bosom's double peace
Let all care cease!
Custom's joy-killing breath
Shall bid you sigh full soon for custom-killing death.
So clasp your childish arms again around my heart:
'Tis but in such captivity
The unbounded Heav'ns know what they be!
And lie still there,
Till the dawn, threat'ning to declare
My beauty, which you cannot bear,
Bid me depart.
Suffer your soul's delight,
Lest that which is to come wither you quite:
For these are only your espousals; yes,
More intimate and fruitfuller far
Than aptest mortal nuptials are;
But nuptials wait you such as now you dare not guess.'
  'In all I thee obey! And thus I know
That all is well:

Should'st thou me tell
Out of thy warm caress to go
And roll my body in the biting snow,
My very body's joy were but increased;
More pleasant 'tis to please thee than be pleased.
Thy love has conquer'd me; do with me as thou wilt,'
And use me as a chattel that is thine!
Kiss, tread me under foot, cherish or beat,
Sheathe in my heart sharp pain up to the hilt,
Invent what else were most perversely sweet;
Nay, let the Fiend drag me through dens of guilt;
Let Earth, Heav'n, Hell
'Gainst my content combine;
What could make nought the touch that made thee mine!
Ah, say not yet, farewell!'
'Nay, that's the Blackbird's note, the sweet Night's knell.
Behold, Beloved, the penance you would brave!'
'Curs'd when it comes, the bitter thing we crave!
Thou leav'st me now, like to the moon at dawn,
A little, vacuous world alone in air.
I will not care!
When dark comes back my dark shall be withdrawn!
Go free;
For 'tis with me
As when the cup the Child scoops in the sand
Fills, and is part and parcel of the Sea.
I'll say it to myself and understand.
Farewell!
Go as thou wilt and come! Lover divine,
Thou still art jealously and wholly mine;
And this thy kiss
A separate secret by none other scann'd;
Though well I wis
The whole of life is womanhood to thee,
Momently wedded with enormous bliss.
Rainbow, that hast my heaven sudden spann'd,
I am the apple of thy glorious gaze,
Each else life cent'ring to a different blaze;
And, nothing though I be
But now a no more void capacity for thee,

'Tis all to know there's not in air or land
Another for thy Darling quite like me!
Mine arms no more thy restless plumes compel!
Farewell!
Whilst thou art gone, I'll search the weary meads
To deck my bed with lilies of fair deeds!
And, if thou choose to come this eventide,
A touch, my Love, will set my casement wide.
Farewell, farewell!
Be my dull days
Music, at least, with thy remember'd praise!'
  'Bitter, sweet, few and veil'd let be
Your songs of me.
Preserving bitter, very sweet,
Few, that so all may be discreet,
And veil'd, that, seeing, none may see.'

XIII

DE NATURA DEORUM

'Good-morrow, Psyche! What's thine errand now?
What awful pleasure do thine eyes bespeak,
What shame is in thy childish cheek,
What terror on thy brow?
Is this my Psyche, once so pale and meek?
Thy body's sudden beauty my sight old
Stings, like an agile bead of boiling gold,
And all thy life looks troubled like a tree's
Whose boughs wave many ways in one great breeze.'
'O Pythoness, to strangest story hark:
A dreadful God was with me in the dark—'
'How many a Maid—
Has never told me that! And thou'rt afraid—'
'He'll come no more,
Or come but twice,
Or thrice,
Or only thrice ten thousand times thrice o'er!'
'For want of wishing thou mean'st not to miss.
We know the Lover, Psyche, by the kiss!'
'If speech of honey could impart the sweet,
The world were all in tears and at his feet!
But not to tell of that in tears come I, but this:
I'm foolish, weak, and small,
And fear to fall.
If long he stay away, O frightful dream, wise Mother,
What keeps me but that I, gone crazy, kiss some other!'
'The fault were his! But know,
Sweet little Daughter sad,
He did but feign to go;
And never more
Shall cross thy window-sill,

Or pass beyond thy door,
Save by thy will.
He's present now in some dim place apart
Of the ivory house wherewith thou mad'st him glad.
Nay, this I whisper thee,
Since none is near,
Or, if one were, since only thou could'st hear,
That happy thing which makes thee flush and start,
Like infant lips in contact with thy heart,
Is He!'
  'Yea, this I know, but never can believe!
O, hateful light! when shall mine own eyes mark
My beauty, which this victory did achieve?'
  'When thou, like Gods and owls, canst see by dark.'
  'In vain I cleanse me from all blurring error—'
  'Tis the last rub that polishes the mirror.'
  'It takes fresh blurr each breath which I respire.'
  'Poor Child, don't cry so! Hold it to the fire.'
  'Ah, nought these dints can e'er do out again!'
  'Love is not love which does not sweeter live
For having something dreadful to forgive.'
  'Sadness and change and pain
Shall me for ever stain;
For, though my blissful fate
Be for a billion years,
How shall I stop my tears
That life was once so low and Love arrived so late!'
  'Sadness is beauty's savour, and pain is
The exceedingly keen edge of bliss;
Nor, without swift mutation, would the heav'ns be aught.'
  'How to behave with him I'd fain be taught.
A maid, meseems, within a God's embrace,
Should bear her like a Goddess, or, at least, a Grace.'
  'When Gods, to Man or Maid below,
As men or birds appear,
A kind 'tis of incognito,
And that, not them, is what they choose we should revere.'
  'Advise me what oblation vast to bring,
Some least part of my worship to confess!'
  'A woman is a little thing,

And in things little lies her comeliness.'
 'Must he not soon with mortal tire to toy?'
 'The bashful meeting of strange Depth and Height
Breeds the forever new-born babe, Delight;
And, as thy God is more than mortal boy,
So bashful more the meeting, and so more the joy.'
 'He loves me dearly, but he shakes a whip
Of deathless scorpions at my slightest slip.
Mother, last night he call'd me "Gipsy," so
Roughly it smote me like a blow!
Yet, oh,
I love him, as none surely e'er could love
Our People's pompous but good-natured Jove.
He used to send me stately overture;
But marriage-bonds, till now, I never could endure!'
 'How should great Jove himself do else than miss
To win the woman he forgets to kiss;
Or, won, to keep his favour in her eyes,
If he's too soft or sleepy to chastise!
By Eros, her twain claims are ne'er forgot;
Her wedlock's marr'd when either's miss'd:
Or when she's kiss'd, but beaten not,
Or duly beaten, but not kiss'd.
Ah, Child, the sweet
Content, when we're both kiss'd and beat!
—But whence these wounds? What Demon thee enjoins
To scourge thy shoulders white
And tender loins!'
 ''Tis nothing, Mother. Happiness at play,
And speech of tenderness no speech can say!'
 'How learn'd thou art!
Twelve honeymoons profane had taught thy docile heart
Less than thine Eros, in a summer night!'
 'Nay, do not jeer, but help my puzzled plight:
Because he loves so marvellously me,
And I with all he loves in love must be,
How to except myself I do not see.
Yea, now that other vanities are vain,
I'm vain, since him it likes, of being withal
Weak, foolish, small!'

'How can a Maid forget her ornaments!
The Powers, that hopeless doom the proud to die,
Unask'd smile pardon upon vanity,
Nay, praise it, when themselves are praised thereby.'
'Ill-match'd I am for a God's blandishments!
So great, so wise—'
'Gods, in the abstract, are, no doubt, most wise;
But, in the concrete, Girl, they're mysteries!
He's not with thee,
At all less wise nor more
Than human Lover is with her he deigns to adore.
He finds a fair capacity,
And fills it with himself, and glad would die
For that sole She.'
'Know'st thou some potion me awake to keep,
Lest, to the grief of that ne'er-slumbering Bliss,
Disgraced I sleep,
Wearied in soul by his bewildering kiss?'
'The Immortals, Psyche, moulded men from sods
That Maids from them might learn the ways of Gods.
Think, would a wakeful Youth his hard fate weep,
Lock'd to the tired breast of a Bride asleep?'
'Ah, me, I do not dream,
Yet all this does some heathen fable seem!'
'O'ermuch thou mind'st the throne he leaves above!
Between unequals sweet is equal love.'
'Nay, Mother, in his breast, when darkness blinds,
I cannot for my life but talk and laugh
With the large impudence of little minds!'
'Respectful to the Gods and meek,
According to one's lights, I grant
'Twere well to be;
But, on my word,
Child, any one, to hear you speak,
Would take you for a Protestant,
(Such fish I do foresee
When the charm'd fume comes strong on me,)
Or powder'd lackey, by some great man's board,
A deal more solemn than his Lord!
Know'st thou not, Girl, thine Eros loves to laugh?

And shall a God do anything by half?
He foreknew and predestinated all
The Great must pay for kissing things so small,
And ever loves his little Maid the more
The more she makes him laugh.'
  'O, Mother, are you sure?'
  'Gaze steady where yon starless deep the gaze revolts,
And say,
Seest thou a Titan forging thunderbolts,
Or three fair butterflies at lovesome play?
And this I'll add, for succour of thy soul:
Lines parallel meet sooner than some think;
The least part oft is greater than the whole;
And, when you're thirsty, that's the time to drink.'
  'Thy sacred words I ponder and revere,
And thank thee heartily that some are clear.'
  'Clear speech to men is mostly speech in vain,
Their scope is by themselves so justly scann'd,
They still despise the things they understand;
But, to a pretty Maid like thee, I don't mind speaking plain.'
  'Then one boon more to her whom strange Fate mocks
With a wife's duty but no wife's sweet right:
Could I at will but summon my Delight—'
  'Thou of thy Jewel art the dainty box;
Thine is the charm which, any time, unlocks;
And this, it seems, thou hitt'st upon last night.
Now go, Child! For thy sake
I've talk'd till this stiff tripod makes my old limbs ache.'

XIV

PSYCHE'S DISCONTENT

'Enough, enough, ambrosial plumed Boy!
My bosom is aweary of thy breath.
Thou kissest joy
To death.
Have pity of my clay-conceived birth
And maiden's simple mood,
Which longs for ether and infinitude,
As thou, being God, crav'st littleness and earth!
Thou art immortal, thou canst ever toy,
Nor savour less
The sweets of thine eternal childishness,
And hold thy godhead bright in far employ.
Me, to quite other custom life-inured,
Ah, loose from thy caress.
'Tis not to be endured!
Undo thine arms and let me see the sky,
By this infatuating flame obscured.
O, I should feel thee nearer to my heart
If thou and I
Shone each to each respondently apart,
Like stars which one the other trembling spy,
Distinct and lucid in extremes of air.
O, hear me pray——'
'Be prudent in thy prayer!
A God is bond to her who is wholly his,
And, should she ask amiss,
He may not her beseeched harm deny.'
'Not yet, not yet!
'Tis still high day, and half my toil's to do.
How can I toil, if thus thou dost renew
Toil's guerdon, which the daytime should forget?

The long, long night, when none can work for fear,
Sweet fear incessantly consummated,
My most divinely Dear,
My Joy, my Dread,
Will soon be here!
Not, Eros, yet!
I ask, for Day, the use which is the Wife's:
To bear, apart from thy delight and thee,
The fardel coarse of customary life's
Exceeding injucundity.
Leave me awhile, that I may shew thee clear
How Goddess-like thy love has lifted me;
How, seeming lone upon the gaunt, lone shore,
I'll trust thee near,
When thou'rt, to knowledge of my heart, no more
Than a dream's heed
Of lost joy track'd in scent of the sea-weed!
Leave me to pluck the incomparable flower
Of frailty lion-like fighting in thy name and power;
To make thee laugh, in thy safe heaven, to see
With what grip fell
I'll cling to hope when life draws hard to hell,
Yea, cleave to thee when me thou seem'st to slay,
Haply, at close of some most cruel day,
To find myself in thy reveal'd arms clasp'd,
Just when I say,
My feet have slipp'd at last!
But, lo, while thus I store toil's slow increase,
To be my dower, in patience and in peace,
Thou com'st, like bolt from blue, invisibly,
With premonition none nor any sign,
And, at a gasp, no choice nor fault of mine.
Possess'd I am with thee
Ev'n as a sponge is by a surge of the sea!
  'Thus irresistibly by Love embraced
Is she who boasts her more than mortal chaste!'
  'Find'st thou me worthy, then, by day and night,
But of this fond indignity, delight?'
  'Little, bold Femininity,
That darest blame Heaven, what would'st thou have or be?'

'Shall I, the gnat which dances in thy ray,
Dare to be reverent? Therefore dare I say,
I cannot guess the good that I desire;
But this I know, I spurn the gifts which Hell
Can mock till which is which 'tis hard to tell.
I love thee, God; yea, and 'twas such assault
As this which made me thine; if that be fault;
But I, thy Mistress, merit should thine ire
If aught so little, transitory and low
As this which made me thine
Should hold me so.'
'Little to thee, my Psyche, is this, but much to me!'
'Ah, if, my God, that be!'
'Yea, Palate fine,
That claim'st for thy proud cup the pearl of price,
And scorn'st the wine,
Accept the sweet, and say 'tis sacrifice!
Sleep, Centre to the tempest of my love,
And dream thereof,
And keep the smile which sleeps within thy face
Like sunny eve in some forgotten place!'

XV

PAIN

O, Pain, Love's mystery,
Close next of kin
To joy and heart's delight,
Low Pleasure's opposite,
Choice food of sanctity
And medicine of sin,
Angel, whom even they that will pursue
Pleasure with hell's whole gust
Find that they must
Perversely woo,
My lips, thy live coal touching, speak thee true.
Thou sear'st my flesh, O Pain,
But brand'st for arduous peace my languid brain,
And bright'nest my dull view,
Till I, for blessing, blessing give again,
And my roused spirit is
Another fire of bliss,
Wherein I learn
Feelingly how the pangful, purging fire
Shall furiously burn
With joy, not only of assured desire,
But also present joy
Of seeing the life's corruption, stain by stain,
Vanish in the clear heat of Love irate,
And, fume by fume, the sick alloy
Of luxury, sloth and hate
Evaporate;
Leaving the man, so dark erewhile,
The mirror merely of God's smile.
Herein, O Pain, abides the praise
For which my song I raise;

But even the bastard good of intermittent ease
How greatly doth it please!
With what repose
The being from its bright exertion glows,
When from thy strenuous storm the senses sweep
Into a little harbour deep
Of rest;
When thou, O Pain,
Having devour'd the nerves that thee sustain,
Sleep'st, till thy tender food be somewhat grown again;
And how the lull
With tear-blind love is full!
What mockery of a man am I express'd
That I should wait for thee
To woo!
Nor even dare to love, till thou lov'st me.
How shameful, too,
Is this:
That, when thou lov'st, I am at first afraid
Of thy fierce kiss,
Like a young maid;
And only trust thy charms
And get my courage in thy throbbing arms.
And, when thou partest, what a fickle mind
Thou leav'st behind,
That, being a little absent from mine eye,
It straight forgets thee what thou art,
And ofttimes my adulterate heart
Dallies with Pleasure, thy pale enemy.
O, for the learned spirit without attaint
That does not faint,
But knows both how to have thee and to lack,
And ventures many a spell,
Unlawful but for them that love so well,
To call thee back.

XVI

PROPHETS WHO CANNOT SING

Ponder, ye Just, the scoffs that frequent go
From forth the foe:
'The holders of the Truth in Verity
Are people of a harsh and stammering tongue!
The hedge-flower hath its song;
Meadow and tree,
Water and wandering cloud
Find Seers who see,
And, with convincing music clear and loud,
Startle the adder-deafness of the crowd
By tones, O Love, from thee.
Views of the unveil'd heavens alone forth bring
Prophets who cannot sing,
Praise that in chiming numbers will not run;
At least, from David until Dante, none,
And none since him.
Fish, and not swim?
They think they somehow should, and so they try
But (haply 'tis they screw the pitch too high)
'Tis still their fates
To warble tunes that nails might draw from slates.
Poor Seraphim!
They mean to spoil our sleep, and do, but all their gains
Are curses for their pains!'
Now who but knows
That truth to learn from foes
Is wisdom ripe?
Therefore no longer let us stretch our throats
Till hoarse as frogs
With straining after notes
Which but to touch would burst an organ-pipe.
Far better be dumb dogs.

XVII

THE CHILD'S PURCHASE

A PROLOGUE

As a young Child, whose Mother, for a jest,
To his own use a golden coin flings down,
Devises blythe how he may spend it best,
Or on a horse, a bride-cake, or a crown,
Till, wearied with his quest,
Nor liking altogether that nor this,
He gives it back for nothing but a kiss,
Endow'd so I
With golden speech, my choice of toys to buy,
And scanning power and pleasure and renown,
Till each in turn, with looking at, looks vain,
For her mouth's bliss,
To her who gave it give I it again.
Ah, Lady elect,
Whom the Time's scorn has saved from its respect,
Would I had art
For uttering this which sings within my heart!
But, lo,
Thee to admire is all the art I know.
My Mother and God's; Fountain of miracle!
Give me thereby some praise of thee to tell
In such a Song
As may my Guide severe and glad not wrong
Who never spake till thou'dst on him conferr'd
The right, convincing word!
Grant me the steady heat
Of thought wise, splendid, sweet,
Urged by the great, rejoicing wind that rings
With draught of unseen wings,

Making each phrase, for love and for delight,
Twinkle like Sirius on a frosty night!
Aid thou thine own dear fame, thou only Fair,
At whose petition meek
The Heavens themselves decree that, as it were,
They will be weak!
  Thou Speaker of all wisdom in a Word,
Thy Lord!
Speaker who thus could'st well afford
Thence to be silent;—ah, what silence that
Which had for prologue thy 'Magnificat?'—
O, Silence full of wonders
More than by Moses in the Mount were heard,
More than were utter'd by the Seven Thunders;
Silence that crowns, unnoted, like the voiceless blue,
The loud world's varying view,
And in its holy heart the sense of all things ponders!
That acceptably I may speak of thee,
Ora pro me!
  Key-note and stop
Of the thunder-going chorus of sky-Powers;
Essential drop
Distill'd from worlds of sweetest-savour'd flowers
To anoint with nuptial praise
The Head which for thy Beauty doff'd its rays,
And thee, in His exceeding glad descending, meant,
And Man's new days
Made of His deed the adorning accident!
Vast Nothingness of Self, fair female Twin
Of Fulness, sucking all God's glory in!
(Ah, Mistress mine,
To nothing I have added only sin,
And yet would shine!)
Ora pro me!
  Life's cradle and death's tomb!
To lie within whose womb,
There, with divine self-will infatuate,
Love-captive to the thing He did create,
Thy God did not abhor,
No more

That Man, in Youth's high spousal-tide,
Abhors at last to touch
The strange lips of his long-procrastinating Bride;
Nay, not the least imagined part as much!
Ora pro me!
My Lady, yea, the Lady of my Lord,
Who didst the first descry
The burning secret of virginity,
We know with what reward!
Prism whereby
Alone we see
Heav'n's light in its triplicity;
Rainbow complex
In bright distinction of all beams of sex,
Shining for aye
In the simultaneous sky,
To One, thy Husband, Father, Son, and Brother,
Spouse blissful, Daughter, Sister, milk-sweet Mother;
Ora pro me!
Mildness, whom God obeys, obeying thyself
Him in thy joyful Saint, nigh lost to sight
In the great gulf
Of his own glory and thy neighbour light;
With whom thou wast as else with husband none
For perfect fruit of inmost amity;
Who felt for thee
Such rapture of refusal that no kiss
Ever seal'd wedlock so conjoint with bliss;
And whose good singular eternally
'Tis now, with nameles peace and vehemence,
To enjoy thy married smile,
That mystery of innocence;
Ora pro me!
Sweet Girlhood without guile,
The extreme of God's creative energy;
Sunshiny Peak of human personality;
The world's sad aspirations' one Success;
Bright Blush, that sav'st our shame from shamelessness;
Chief Stone of stumbling; Sign built in the way
To set the foolish everywhere a-bray;

Hem of God's robe, which all who touch are heal'd;
To which the outside Many honour yield
With a reward and grace
Unguess'd by the unwash'd boor that hails Him to His face,
Spurning the safe, ingratiant courtesy
Of suing Him by thee;
Ora pro me!
  Creature of God rather the sole than first;
Knot of the cord
Which binds together all and all unto their Lord;
Suppliant Omnipotence; best to the worst;
Our only Saviour from an abstract Christ
And Egypt's brick-kilns, where the lost crowd plods,
Blaspheming its false Gods;
Peace-beaming Star, by which shall come enticed,
Though nought thereof as yet they weet,
Unto thy Babe's small feet,
The Mighty, wand'ring disemparadised,
Like Lucifer, because to thee
They will not bend the knee;
Ora pro me!
  Desire of Him whom all things else desire!
Bush aye with Him as He with thee on fire!
Neither in His great Deed nor on His throne—
O, folly of Love, the intense
Last culmination of Intelligence,—
Him seem'd it good that God should be alone!
Basking in unborn laughter of thy lips,
Ere the world was, with absolute delight
His Infinite reposed in thy Finite;
Well-match'd: He, universal being's Spring,
And thou, in whom art gather'd up the ends of everything!
Ora pro me!
  In season due, on His sweet-fearful bed,
Rock'd by an earthquake, curtain'd with eclipse,
Thou shar'd'st the rapture of the sharp spear's head,
And thy bliss pale
Wrought for our boon what Eve's did for our bale;
Thereafter, holding a little thy soft breath,
Thou underwent'st the ceremony of death;

And, now, Queen-Wife,
Sitt'st at the right hand of the Lord of Life,
Who, of all bounty, craves for only fee
The glory of hearing it besought with smiles by thee!
Ora pro me!
  Mother, who lead'st me still by unknown ways,
Giving the gifts I know not how to ask,
Bless thou the work
Which, done, redeems my many wasted days,
Makes white the murk,
And crowns the few which thou wilt not dispraise,
When clear my Songs of Lady's graces rang,
And little guess'd I 'twas of thee I sang!
  Vainly, till now, my pray'rs would thee compel
To fire my verse with thy shy fame, too long
Shunning world-blazon of well-ponder'd song;
But doubtful smiles, at last, 'mid thy denials lurk;
From which I spell,
'Humility and greatness grace the task
Which he who does it deems impossible!'

XVIII

DEAD LANGUAGE

'Thou dost not wisely, Bard.
A double voice is Truth's, to use at will:
One, with the abysmal scorn of good for ill,
Smiting the brutish ear with doctrine hard,
Wherein She strives to look as near a lie
As can comport with her divinity;
The other tender-soft as seem
The embraces of a dead Love in a dream,
These thoughts, which you have sung
In the vernacular,
Should be, as others of the Church's are,
Decently cloak'd in the Imperial Tongue.
Have you no fears
Lest, as Lord Jesus bids your sort to dread,
Yon acorn-munchers rend you limb from limb,
You, with Heaven's liberty affronting theirs!'
So spoke my monitor; but I to him,
'Alas, and is not mine a language dead?'

APPENDIX

1877

"Go up, thou Bald-pate!" (hark, the Children say):
"The dyke-vex'd waters, now the dyke is riven,
How harmlessly they play,
Caressing yon loose raft that swims their way!
Those garrulous clans, before the bright gale driven,
How orderly they troop across the sandy bay!"
Wait, Children, till they reach
The check that bids them stay,
Heaping their hearts there, at the beck of the Moon,
As they will soon.—
What makes that sudden uproar on the beach?
What from the blasted sea-wall spits at Heaven?

L'ALLEGRO

Felicity!
Who ope'st to none that knocks, yet, laughing weak,
Yield'st all to Love that will not seek,
And who, though won, wilt droop and die,
Unless wide doors bespeak thee free,
How safe's the bond of thee and me,
Since thee I cherish and defy!
Is't Love or Friendship, Dearest, we obey?
Ah, thou art young, and I am gray;
But happy man is he who knows
How well time goes,
With no unkind intruder by,
Between such friends as thou and I!
'Twould wrong thy favour, Sweet, were I to say,
'Tis best by far,
When best things are not possible,
To make the best of those that are;
For, though it be not May,
Sure, few delights of Spring excel
The beauty of this mild September day!
So with me walk,
And view the dreaming field and bossy Autumn wood,
And how in humble russet goes
The Spouse of Honour, fair Repose,
Far from a world whence love is fled
And truth is dying because joy is dead;
And, if we hear the roaring wheel
Of God's remoter service, public zeal,
Let us to stiller place retire
And glad admire
How, near Him, sounds of working cease
In little fervour and much peace;
And let us talk

Of holy things in happy mood,
Learnt of thy blest twin-sister, Certitude;
Or let's about our neighbours chat,
Well praising this, less praising that,
And judging outer strangers by
Those gentle and unsanction'd lines
To which remorse of equity
Of old hath moved the School divines.
Or linger where this willow bends,
And let us, till the melody be caught,
Harken that sudden, singing thought,
On which unguess'd increase to life perchance depends.
He ne'er hears twice the same who hears
The songs of heaven's unanimous spheres,
And this may be the song to make, at last, amends
For many sighs and boons in vain long sought!
Now, careless, let us stray, or stop
To see the partridge from the covey drop,
Or, while the evening air's like yellow wine,
From the pure stream take out
The playful trout,
That jerks with rasping check the struggled line;
Or to the Farm, where, high on trampled stacks,
The labourers stir themselves amain
To feed with hasty sheaves of grain
The deaf'ning engine's boisterous maw,
And snatch again,
From to-and-fro tormenting racks,
The toss'd and hustled straw;
Whilst others tend the shedded wheat
That fills yon row of shuddering sacks,
Or shift them quick, and bind them neat,
And dogs and boys with sticks
Wait, murderous, for the rats that leave the ruin'd ricks;
And, all the bags being fill'd and rank'd fivefold, they pour
The treasure on the barn's clean floor,
And take them back for more,
Until the whole bared harvest beauteous lies
Under our pleased and prosperous eyes.
Then let us give our idlest hour

To the world's wisdom and its power;
Hear famous Golden-Tongue refuse
To gander sauce that's good for goose,
Or the great Clever Party con
How many grains of sifted sand,
Heap'd, make a likely house to stand,
How many fools one Solomon.
Science, beyond all other lust
Endow'd with appetite for dust,
We glance at where it grunts, well-sty'd,
And pass upon the other side.
Pass also by, in pensive mood,
Taught by thy kind twin-sister, Certitude,
Yon puzzled crowd, whose tired intent
Hunts like a pack without a scent.
And now come home,
Where none of our mild days
Can fail, though simple, to confess
The magic of mysteriousness;
For there 'bide charming Wonders three,
Besides, Sweet, thee,
To comprehend whose commonest ways,
Ev'n could that be,
Were coward's 'vantage and no true man's praise.

KING COPHETUA THE FIRST

Said Jove within himself one day,
'I'll make me a mistress out of clay!
These ninefold spheres of chiming quires,
Though little things and therefore sweet,
Too Godlike are for my desires:
My pleasure still is incomplete.
The gust of love is mystery,
Which poorly yet the heavens supply.
Now where may God for mystery seek
Save in the earthly, small, and weak?
My work, then, let me crown and end
With what I ne'er shall comprehend!'
And so the unfathomable Need,
Hell's mock, Heaven's pity, was decreed.
And, with perversity immense
As all his other affluence,
Jove left his wondering Court behind
And Juno's almost equal mind,
On low and little Earth to seek
That vessel infinitely weak,
(The abler for the infinite honour
He hugely long'd to put upon her,)
And, in a melancholy grove,
Found sighing his predestined Love,
A pretty, foolish, pensive maid,
The least of heaven-related things,
Of every boy and beast afraid,
But not of him, the King of Kings.
He look'd so measurelessly mild,
And so he flatter'd her, poor child,
By lifting with respect her hand
To his salute benign and grand,
That, when he spoke, and begged to be
Instructed in her wishes, she,

Having a modest minute tarried,
Lisp'd, 'I should like, Sire, to be married.'
But, when he smiling ask'd, 'Whom to?'
She blush'd and said, she scarcely knew.
Then Jove named Shepherds, Lords, and Kings
To her free choice; for all such things
Were his and his to give; but these
She shook her curls at. 'Hard to please
Is my small Cousin, but my nod
Shall call from heaven some splendid God—'
'Ah, Maker mine, no God will do
That's not as great a God as you!'
Thereat Jove laugh'd: 'As least of things
Alone can sate the King of Kings,
So the least thing, it seems, that I
Alone of Gods can satisfy!'
And, fading in her flushing arms,
He blazed for ever from her charms.
Thenceforth the maiden sang and shone,
Admired by all and woo'd by none,
For, though she said she was a sinner,
'Twas clear to all that Jove was in her,
And, but for that deep pagan night,
She would have been a Carmelite.

NOTES
ON POEMS OF
COVENTRY PATMORE

THE WEDDING SERMON

Date of Publication: Macmillan's Magazine, vol. V. (Dec. 1861). Revised and enlarged, it was first published in book form in 1863.

Versions Compared: Changes made in the final version as compared with the original version in *Macmillan's Magazine* are indicated in the notes.

Significance and Importance in Patmore's Poetry: Standing as it does at the end of Patmore's epic of human love, and coming before the odes, "The Wedding Sermon" is the fruit of all that precedes it and the seed of what is to come. It is really a summary of Patmore's philosophy of love. As Mr. Burdett expresses it: "It is the middle point of rest to which either the epic or the odes, when considered separately, must be referred." (p. 98) Written, moreover, just a few years before he became a Catholic, it is an epitome of his philosophy of love as he conceived and expressed it during that period of his life. "It has been with a sense of wonder," we find in Patmore's Autobiography, "that I have since read many passages of that poem, passages in which, when I was writing them, I fancied I was making audacious flights into the regions of unknown truth, but in which I have since found that I have given exact expression to some of what may be called the more esoteric doctrines of the Catholic faith." (Champneys II, p. 51)

It is true that the philosophy of the *Angel in the House* and *Victories of Love* is not unlike the philosophy of the odes. But it were difficult to conceive the same ideas more differently expressed than they are in the poetry that found its inspiration in Patmore before and after his conversion. The truths of "The Wedding Sermon" are cold and measured and restrained. The same truths in the odes are warm with passion, intense, and poured forth with the abandon that marks all great lyric poetry. In all English poetry there is no more interesting example than Patmore to prove that the intensest poetic emotion may find its most authentic inspiration and its most successful lyric expression in Catholic truths. In the odes we see the consummation of the re-marriage of Religion and Poetry whose divorce effected by the Reformation, is so poignantly described by Francis Thompson in his essay on Shelley.

1. Originally:

"Dear children, God is love, and love
Is everything. The truths thereof
Are as the waters of the sea."

[Resume text, l. 2.]

1–2. The sea, symbol of the mysteriousness, purity, and truth of nuptial love, is singularly appropriate in these opening lines. But it is notably restrained when compared with the ardent symbols we find in the odes.

4. *Maiden and Youth,* originally, "senses and soul."

7. *full spirit,* originally, "true spirit."

12–13. Conjugal love is the visible, human expression of divine love. This particularization of the general truth in ll. 139–40, is the chief inspiration of Patmore's work.

15. *of the height,* originally, "of its height."

16–17. Originally, the following passage was inserted between these lines:

"That good which does itself not know,
Scarce is. Old families are so,
Less through their coming of good kind,
Than having borne it well in mind,
And this does all from honor bar,
The ignorance of what they are!
In the heart of the world, alas, for want
Of knowing that which light souls taunt
As lightness, and which God has made
Such that, for even its feeble shade,
Evoked by falsely fair ostents
And soiling of its sacraments,
Great Statesmen, Poets, Warriors, Kings,
(The World's Beloved), all other things
Gladly having counted nothing, what
Fell fires of Tophet burn forgot!"

[Resume text, l. 17.]

19. Originally: "The appointed course and bound assigned."

17–20. The passion of love is God's gift to man. If in the enjoyment of that passion man observes the restraints of God's law, its clear waters will flow back to God, its source, as a virtue meriting the reward of eternal life. Even if it violates God's law, the defiled waters of human love must flow back to Him, a sin, deserving eternal punishment. This same thought transcendent in the fuller light of faith and the fire of intenser love is found in "Legem Tuam Dilexi," ll. 79–95, where Patmore treats the joys of the higher restraints of the vow of obedience.

20–22. From the context here and in ll. 59–65, it is clear that *desire* means sheer carnal love, sinful because it fails to keep *the course assign'd* by God. Edmund Burke uses the word in this sense in his essay, "Origin of Our Ideas on the Sublime and Beautiful": "beauty and the passion caused by beauty, which I call love, is different from desire." (III, i)

Benevolence here signifies lofty, spiritualized love, a virtue because it keeps *the course assign'd.*

23–25. When the Pharisee, learned in the law, asked Our Blessed Savior, tempting Him: "Master, which is the great commandment in the law?" (St. Matthew XXII, 36) he received as his answer the words of the Old Testament which he dared not deny: "Thou shalt love the Lord thy God with thy whole heart, and with thy whole soul, and with thy whole mind." (Deuteronomy VI, 5) Then immediately Jesus added: "This is the greatest and the first commandment. And the second is like to this," and again quoting from the Old Testament, concluded: "Thou shalt love thy neighbour as thyself." (Leviticus XIX, 18)

25. His Poor, His Proxies: "Amen I say to you, as long as you did it to one of these my least brethren, you did it to me." (St. Matthew XXV, 40)

26–27. "And God is faithful, who will not suffer you to be tempted above that which you are able: but will make also with temptation issue, that you may be able to bear it." (1 Corinthians X, 13)

28–35. Sanctity in married life will be attained by those whose lives are a blend of the active and contemplative virtues typified by Martha and Mary. (Cf. St. Luke X, 38–42.)

32. To the claims, originally, "to claims."

36–48. In the time of prayer the soul is sensibly aware of God's presence, but in the external activities of the day it sometimes happens that sensible consolations are withdrawn so that even acts of virtue seem a mockery. At such times the soul must fall back upon faith alone and be content with a veiled vision of God and a suprasensible conviction of His presence. Similarly, in the ways of nuptial love, husband and wife must be content with their love of each other, when, in the exercise of external duties, the sensible delights and attractions of their love are lessened.

Apropos of the withdrawal of sensible devotion even in the time of prayer, we find this advice in the writings of Marie Lataste, attributed to Our Lord Himself: "You are mistaken if you think you do not love Me because you are unable to pray with attention, because your mind is distracted and in a state of dryness, because your heart does not feel any tenderness for Me. When you find yourself in this state, remember what I said when I was on earth:

'He who loves Me keeps My commandments'; for love is shown more by acts than by feelings. Feelings do not always depend upon yourself; sometimes I am pleased to withdraw from a soul to try it; but I do not prevent it from fulfilling My law and being faithful to My commandments. If sometimes a soul cannot testify its affective love, it can always testify its effective love. Thus, daughter, provided you do not wish to separate yourself from Me by sin, provided that you desire to remain always united to Me by the observance of My precepts, provided that you pray because you know your own misery and My goodness, be calm and tranquil, and you will thus prove your love for Me in a sufficient manner." (Vol. I, p. 266) (Cf. Psyche Odes, *passim.*)

48–49. Originally, the following passage was inserted between these lines:

"Leaving Christ's right and left in Heaven
To be to them, unenvied, given
For whom it is prepared. Let us,
Who are but babes in Christ, think thus
(Admiring them whose skill it suits
To adore, unscathed, God's attributes),
That all ambition bears a curse;
And none, if height metes error, worse
Than his who sets his hope on more
Godliness than God made him for.
At least, leave distant worlds alone
Till you are native to your own!"

[Resume text, l. 49.]

49–50. The motive prompting acts of Christian charity should be our power to help our neighbor, rather than our neighbor's indigence. This is one way in which supernatural charity differs from mere humanitarianism.

51–54. Many truths of life are mysteries when looked at in the light of *cold faith,* but in the warm light of love they are completely understood. (Cf. "De Natura Deorum," ll. 2–7.)

51. *fathom well,* originally, "fathom first."

52. *In loves,* originally, "In dues."

54. Originally: "To many Bible mysteries."

55–57. Nuptial love takes precedence over all other natural loves. "Wherefore a man shall leave father and mother and shall cleave to his wife." (Genesis II, 24) "Let every one of you in particular love his wife as himself." (Ephesians V, 33)

56. *All other kinds,* originally, "all special kinds."

57–59. Though nuptial love is the most perfect love of one human being for another, it is *not so high* as the direct love of God in a Religious who,

> *Heaven with single eye*
> *Considers.*

Marie Lataste writes that once during prayer she received the following instruction on this subject from Our Lord Himself: "Marriage, My daughter, is a holy state instituted by God: consequently there is nothing in it opposed to purity or chastity and neither chastity nor purity is lost in the state of marriage where there is fear and love of God. This is why Heaven counts so many saints, both men and women who have sanctified themselves in the married state, and who consequently have not lost their purity. Virginity, it is true, is a more perfect state, a state of much greater purity and chastity, but it is not the natural state of men, it is that of the angels whom one who observes it comes to resemble. Hence this state cannot be recommended to everyone; it can be the state only of the few." (Vol. II, p. 177)

Originally these lines read:

> "As being, though not so saintly high
> As what seeks Heaven with single eye,
> Sole perfect."

59–63. In nuptial love *benevolence* and *desire* are perfectly balanced and completely fused. (Cf. *supra,* ll, 20–22.)

64–70. The elements of *self-seeking* and *self-sacrifice* are fused and exalted by love. In marriage today it is *self-seeking* divorced from *self-sacrifice* that has given us those plausible perversions of love, such as birth-control.

64. *And, both,* originally, "And, each."

71–77. Nuptial love is the chief and most sensitive abode of God's love, because in it God's infinite, intangible love is confined within bounds and made tangible. (Cf. "Legem Tuam Dilexi" ll. 1–33.)

73. *all that the,* originally, "all the."

78–84. In this, nuptial love is like a prosperous State. It does not become less worthy of praise or smaller in itself, because it yields its common land to private owners, *To fence about and cultivate.*

85–88. The position of these two couplets was originally reversed. *Nay,* l. 85, was originally, "And." *And,* l. 87, was originally, "Nay."

85–86. The *infinite* in man (God's love within him) is not lost by reason of its bounds. It is *found,* rather, in man's encountering these bounds when the infinite longings of his soul strive to pass them. (Cf. "Legem Tuam Dilexi.")

87–88. If a brook overflows its banks the result is a morass, symbol of lust. If it keeps within bounds, the waters of pure human love may rise and fall, but in the end they will join the clear, mysterious waters of the sea, symbol of love that is divine because it is mysterious, pure, and true. (Cf. *supra* ll. 1–2: 86–86, *etc.*) Saint Bernard makes use of the same figure in speaking of man's love of himself for his own sake: "But truly if this love, as is its wont, begins to be too precipitate or too lavish and is not at all satisfied with the river-bed of necessity, overflowing rather widely it will be seen to invade the fields of pleasure. At once its overflow is held in check by the commandment that opposes itself to it: *Thou shalt love thy neighbor as thyself.*" (St. Matthew XXII, 39) (*De Diligendo Deo,* §23; Translation, p. 37.)

89–92. Without divine revelation and the example of Christ, human reason alone would never have dreamed of the heights to which God has raised human love in the sacrament of matrimony.

89–90. These two lines stand for the following three lines of the original version:

"The Word of God alone can lure
Belief to the snowy tops obscure
Of marriage truth. What wildest guess"

[Resume text, l. 91.]

91. Originally: "E'er dared to dream of its own height,"

92. *Heaven's bold sun-gleam:* The sun as symbol of Christ is a constantly recurring figure in Francis Thompson's poetry. The most notable instance is the "Ode to the Setting Sun." Marie Lataste gives divine approval to this symbol in the following words ascribed to private revelation:

"Fitly is the Son of Man likened to the sun which enlightens the world, for I am the true sun which sheds its beams of light upon men, blesses them with its vivifying heat, and governs and directs them by its movements. I am the sun of the world, the supernatural world, the world made for eternity. . . . I am the sun, not only the light and heat of the world, but the sun full of action which made the world and vivifies it. . . .

"The material sun enlightens and sustains life; the true sun of justice, which is the Son of Man, transforms into its own light and imparts its life. The material sun scorches when it approaches too near the earth; the true sun of justice, which is the Son of Man, transforms into itself in proportion as it is more nearly approached. The material sun is reflected in the ocean, but always appears distinct from that which reflects it; the true sun of justice, which is the Son of Man, not only is reflected in the Christian soul, but inhabits it and transforms it into itself." (Vol. I, pp. 70–71.)

92–97. Originally this passage read:

"Till that bold sun-gleam quenched the night,
Showing Heaven's chosen symbol where
The torch of Psyche flash'd despair;
Proclaiming love, in things divine,
Still to be male and feminine;
Foretelling, in the Song of Songs,
Which time makes clear as it prolongs,
Christ's nuptials with the Church, (far more,
My children, than a metaphor!)
And still, by names of Bride and Wife,
Husband and Bridegroom, Heaven's own life
Picturing, so proving their's to be
The Earth's unearthliest sanctity.
"But, dear my children, heights are heights
And hardly scaled."

[Resume text l. 98.]

93–94. In his "Sermons on the *Canticle of Canticles*" Saint Bernard shows what literal truth there is in speaking of the Church as the Spouse of Christ. (Cf. also Ephesians V, 22–23.)

95–96. Divine revelation in showing us Christ the Lover and the human soul His beloved, has made nuptial love a symbol of supernatural hope, whereas, in pagan times, the merely natural light of mythological eroticism in Eros and Psyche, *flash'd despair*. This is the theme of such essays as Patmore's "Ancient and Modern Ideas of Purity," Francis Thompson's "Paganism Old and New," and of such poems as Chesterton's "Ballad of the White Horse." (Cf. "Eros and Psyche.")

97–106. Ideal love is difficult. (Cf. "Faint Yet Pursuing.") Its *best delights,* rarely attained even by *the most perfect* souls, cause those who attain them, to long with a sort of celestial nostalgia for the ultimate union of the soul with God, of which the delights of human love are the foreshadowing.

107–118. The innermost sweetness of nuptial love lies in *the doctrine of virginity*. Were lovers to gratify their passion incontinently, they would kill *the bliss which they intend,* for the joyousness of love is a consequence of obedience to the higher laws governing nuptial union, laws which curb and direct the yearnings of sense. Such prenuptial longings have their place in the divine economy of love, for they provide lovers with that which they must sacrifice *on the high altar of true love,* to feel the joy which sacrifice alone can give to love. (Cf. "The Contract.")

Originally this passage read as follows:

"God's truth, when most it thwarts our wills
In show, then most in fact fulfills.
Love's nuptial highest, wherefore, see
In the doctrine of virginity!
For what's the virgin's special crown
But that which Love in faith lays down,
Transmuted, without shade of loss,
By the mere contact of the Cross,
To what love nuptial oft makes vow
With sighs to be, but knows not how!"

[Resume text, line 109.]

114. *which dream that they,* originally, "which fancy they."

116. *sacrifice,* originally, "costly gifts."

118. *with tears,* originally, "in hours." *To move,* originally, "Men move."

118–127. In those who, like comets, seek love's bliss, the revulsions no less than the attractions they experience are a perversion of the love-delights of those planet-like souls who keep their divinely appointed paths and receive a two-fold reward—the joy of *full sight,* and the *pathos of hopeless want* with which it alternates. Instead of these rewards, incontinent lovers know only the pride of *unreal victory* and the remorse of *unreal defeat.* (Cf. "Deliciae Sapientiae," ll. 49–71.)

119. *to our bliss,* originally, "to their bliss."

120. *that we always,* originally, "that they always."

120–121. Originally the following couplet was inserted between these lines:

"And this perpetual, fond mistake,
Which love will n'er learn not to make,"

[Resume text, l. 121.]

121. *And so,* originally, "On earth."

127–132. Originally this passage read:

"And plaint of an unreal defeat,
Languor and passion.

Misconceit
May also be of vestal life.
The Virgin's self was Joseph's Wife,
And bridal promises are still
The goal that glads the virgin will,
Whose nature doth indeed subsist
There where the outward forms are missed,"

128–138. No less dangerous than the false idea of love found in the unrestraint of incontinent lovers is the Manichean and Puritanical misconception of its nature found sometimes in virginal lovers in whose *'due benevolence'* is found the essence of nuptial sweetness born of perpetually seeking another's joy through self-restraint and the sacrifice of *desire*. (Cf. *supra*, l. 60.)

133. *In those,* originally, "In all."

136. *selfish thought,* originally, "selfishness."

139–140. These lines contain the essence of Patmore's doctrine of love. "Plato's cave of shadows is the most profound and simple statement of the relation of the natural to the spiritual life ever made. Men stand with their backs to the Sun, and they take the shadows cast by it upon the walls of their cavern for realities . . . . If we want fruition we must turn our backs on the shadows, and gaze on their realities in God." (*Knowledge and Science* XV) It need hardly be said that although he here adopts the figurative language of Plato's 'Allegory of the Cave,' Patmore rejects Plato's Theory of Knowledge which the allegory was used to illustrate. (Cf. *Republic* VII, 514, and *supra,* ll. 12–13.)

140–144. These lines express a general principle derived from the preceding lines of this stanza,—those who fly from love by sacrificing sheer *desire,* will find themselves pursued by love's sweet benevolence. (Cf. "The Unknown Eros," ll. 71–75.)

144–145. Originally, the following passage was inserted between these lines:

"But each must learn that Christ's Cross is
Safety, ere he can find it bliss.
The powers that nature's powers can stem
Must come to us, not we to them.
The heavenward soul no measure keeps,
But, lark-like, soars by wayward leaps;
And highest achievements here befall,
As elsewhere, expectations small."

[Resume text, l. 145.]

145–148. Wisdom dictates that the aspirations of lovers must not be too high. Rather, they should make *sweet and regular use* of the good in their human natures. (Cf. 'Faint Yet Pursuing.')

149–154. Nature and Grace should move in harmony, as a man whose steps beat time with music. For, nature bursts the bonds of laws that do it violence. (Cf. "The Precursor," Saint Bernard's *De Diligendo Deo,* chap. XV, and odes: "Deliciae Sapientiae," and "Sponsa Dei," *etc., passim.*)

154–155. Originally the following passage was inserted between these lines:

"And those who conquer her are they
Who comprehend her and obey;
Which let your one ambition be;
For pride of soaring sanctity
Revolts to hell; and that which needs
The world's high places, and succeeds,
Suffers as if a level shock'd
The upstepping foot. Be ye not mocked:"

[Resume text, l. 155.]

155–160. In a *life* that is both joyous and just, duty becomes a joy and life blossoms forth in the flowers of the freedom of obedience and heaven rejoices at the sight of actions that go beyond the essential requirements of the law.

161–162. Let this be your rule: judge the morality of the law by the delight you experience in acting according to it.

161. *Be this your rule,* originally, "This still observe."

163–168. It is possible to do much that is contrary to God's will, but there is none of the enjoyment of love in such disobedience. The delights of love draw their vigor from control. (Cf. "Legem Tuam Dilexi.")

168. *They take,* originally, "they get."

169–188. A man who observes the *indispensable first precepts* of the Church is, in matrimony, freed from the awesome observance of the restraints imposed upon an unmarried lover. And even, *for his spouse,* the Church urges him no longer to observe God's law *in its extremer sense* — i.e., as it applies to those who are not married — and bids him enjoy the *exuberant liberty* of his new state with *untroubled heart.*

169. *A man need only,* originally, "Wherefore, dear Children."

172. *Nay, more, she bids him,* originally, "Nay, bids a man leave."

174. *His immaculate law,* originally, "her, his Mother's law."

180. *In the,* originally, "In their."

181–182. These two lines stand for the following three lines of the original:

> "Happy who in their lives are seen
> At all times in the golden mean,
> Who having learn'd and understood"
> [Resume text, l. 182.]

182. *Central Good,* originally, "central good."

184–185. Originally the following passage was inserted between these lines:

> "Nor loves outlast the thorn's brief flame,
> Unless God burns within the same,
> Can yet, with no proud disesteem
> Of mortal love's prophetic dream,"
> [Resume text, l. 185.]

185. Originally, "Take in its innocent pleasures part."

187. *And faith that, straight,* originally, "And faith that oft."

189–214. Lovers on the day of their marriage think that the perfection of their new state will consist in sustaining the delight of their *spousal hour.* But if they remain true to each other, time will reveal to them that in their *spousal hour* they were merely *unwrought material* that was to be brought to perfection through the succeeding years of matrimony. Moreover, the love of the *spousal hour* is far from perfection without the discipline and awe imposed by the laws which govern marriage. Often, even, it happens that those who enter into marriage without really loving each other, will be blest with that love as time goes on, if they are faithful to the obligations of their state. On the other hand, love which is not bound by marriage-vows seldom imposes upon itself the restraint that is needed to save it from the ruin of unblessed liberty. Married lovers who have grown old, know well that it was their voluntary submission to the obligations of their state that kept them faithful to each other through agonizing doubts and fears about the wisdom of their irrevocable choice.

"Love is a recent discovery and requires a new law. Easy divorce is the vulgar solution. The true solution is some undiscovered security for true marriage." (*Aurea Dicta* CXXXV)

Such love is as far removed from the romantic love of Victorian novels where they married and lived happily ever afterwards, as it is from the love in modern literature where they live unhappily ever afterwards.

188–189. Originally the following passage was inserted between these lines:

"Of wedlock's perils all the worst
By ignorance are bred and nurst."

[Resume text, l. 189]

192. *delighted gain,* originally, "completed gain."

194. Originally: "Fulfil what is that hour foreshewn."

212. *Or love,* originally, "And love."

215–235. Lovers who meet by chance and enter into matrimony *without pretence of insight or experience,* have nothing to fear. God has drawn them together and if they place their trust in Him, He will surely bless their *ignorance* and *blind election* more surely than if their union had been the result of cold deliberation prompted by human prudence. The particular *choice* in marriage does not matter, provided the wife is and has been true to the ideals of Christian womanhood and the husband, in pre-nuptial days, has been *loyal to his future wife.*

228. *never,* originally, "rarely."

229. *helpless,* originally, "hopeless."

231. *choice not matters much.* In the matter of one's vocation Patmore held the relative unimportance of the choice deliberately made by the individual. If, humanly speaking, a person in good faith were to make a mistake in his choice and enter into an indissoluble state such as matrimony, God would give him grace to persevere, Patmore held. And in this he was in perfect agreement with most moral theologians of today. In *Victories of Love,* Bk. I, Patmore develops this theme and shows how the ill-mated Frederick and Jane finally triumph over the difficulties consequent upon their choice of each other. In the end this marriage proves no less happy than that of Felix and Honoria in Bk. II, in which nature and grace blent harmoniously from the very beginning.

236–240. Past folly destroys the vigor of true love and its universal penalty is that, later, it will mock even the pure love of matrimony. This is one of the penalties of rejecting the stern admonition of Ecclesiastes, XII, I: "Remember thy Creator in the days of thy youth."

238. *all,* originally, "an."

241–248. Even though both were the perfect *unwrought material* of nuptial bliss, in marriage the real woman must succeed to the ideal woman of courtship days. If the happiness of nuptial love is to survive such a crisis the man must realize that the disappointment he has experienced is a practical proof of the fact that in his wife he must look for the human semblance of love, only, not for the perfection of the Reality itself. Forgetfulness of this fact in either party will *perturb the happiest pact.*

241. Originally: "Howbeit, tho' both be true, that she."

249–264. The only law which will effectively control this new situation is this: *leave ill alone!* The man must not try to *mend his wife.* She knows his desires better than he does himself and she aspires to meet them,

> *With perfect zeal, and a deep wit*
> *Which nothing helps but trusting it.*

264. *but trusting it,* originally, "but faith in it."

265–277. He must overlook all imperfections and act as if the perfection which love strives ever to attain had already been realized. For, deeds are honorable only when looked at in the light of the future perfection towards which they tend. Moreover, it were wrong to say that such deeds, though imperfect, are not honorable. For honor is the mould which gives beauty of form to the molten gold of deeds performed with good intention. It is,

> *the prop*
> *That lifts to the sun the earth-drawn crop*
> *Of human sensibilities.*

265. *loyally o'erlooking,* originally, "handsomely ignoring."

271. *our best,* originally, "mortal."

272. *honour to deny,* originally, "honour here to scant."

275. *the prop,* originally, "the stay."

276. Originally: "That leads aloft the ivy stray."

279–310. The husband who thus honors his wife will be happiest if he hedges his love about with *obvious prudencies,* neither debasing love by too great familiarity, nor vulgarizing it by bad manners, nor chilling it by uxoriousness. For, a woman can only half love a man who has no higher interest than herself. That husband is safest who relies on *time,* on the instinctive *love-wisdom* of his wife, and on their *mutual aid* in sharing *affliction and delight.*

It is in the realm of humility that is taught by the heart rather than by the head that love thrives. Love for their children far more than their love for each other will strengthen their union and intensify their yearning for the perfect Love of eternity,

> *While others with their use decay.*

288. *warm,* originally, "frank."

299–302. These lines were not in the original version.

303. *hearts have account,* originally, "hearts keep account."

307–310. Conjugal love is man's preparatory communion for his eternal communion with God. (Cf. *infra,* ll. 350–365.)

311–319. The primary end of marriage is the procreation of children, who, like the *sleeping centre* of a wheel transmit energy to all contained within the family circle. Such love is itself the *noblest offspring* and the chief *sanction* of marriage. Finally, mutual *help and sympathy* in man and wife transmute the consequences of venial sin in each, *to blessings*. (Cf. "Psyche's Discontent," l. 89.)

311. *true marriage,* originally, "love-nuptial."

320–49. During this time a man should surrender himself to grace allowing his wife to grow more and more his opposite, while he himself learns to admire all others through and in her, and delights in the seeming monotony of their relationship and forgetfulness of self.

333–334. Originally the following passage was inserted between these lines:

"That, whereas, in its earlier day
The least flaw threaten'd love's decay,
No crime could now, on either's part,
Do more than make the other start,
And, full of pity, say, 'It is
'I, some how I, who have done this;'"
[Resume text, l. 334.]

334. *That,* originally, "And."

335. *lust of,* originally, "taste for."

345. *doom desire,* originally, "doom, desire,"

Narcissus' doom: Narcissus "rejected the love of the Nymph Echo and Aphrodite punished him for this by inspiring him with a passion for the reflexion of himself which he saw in the water of a fountain. He pined away in desire for it." (*Dictionary of Classical Antiquities.*)

350–365. The love of youth does not return in after-years, but it is transcended by another which no more regrets the earlier love than a sparrow with her brood of young regrets the loss of her eggs. This love in mature years, however, does not altogether fulfil the fond hopes of youth. For, love's best part is service and the bliss of service is dulled by use because the home of love is not here. Even in love's *fullest pleasure* there is the pathos of a sigh that betrays a longing for its true home in eternity.

In Francis Thompson's essay, "Paganism Old and New," we read: "Not in marriage is the fulfilment of Love, though its earthly and temporal fulfilment may be therein; for how can Love, which is the desire of soul for soul, attain satisfaction in the conjunction of body with body? Poor indeed if this were all the promise which Love unfolded to us—the encountering light of two flames from within their close-shut lanterns. Therefore sings Dante, and sing all noble poets after him, that Love in this world is a pilgrim and a wanderer, journeying to the New Jerusalem: not here is the consummation of his yearnings, in that mere knocking at the gates of union which we christen marriage, but beyond the pillars of death and the corridors of the grave, in the union of spirit to spirit within the containing spirit of God."

This same consummation awaits those who strive to love God directly in the state of consecrated virginity. Marie Lataste attributes these words to Our Lord Himself: "My daughter, make your life a sojourn like the Limbo of the just souls: let your soul find its own Limbo in your body. Let it be always sighing after Me: let it await the hour of My coming, no longer through My death but through your own. Live in such wise that after your death our separation will not last any longer, but rather that we may be immediately united forever." (Vol. I, p. 91.) (Cf. essay, "Love and Poetry," and odes: "De Natura Deorum" and "Deliciae Sapientiae.")

351. *That joy,* originally, "Love's youth."

358. *say I the fruit,* originally, "say, the fruit."

366–380. Be grateful for love in the spirit of supernatural faith because through love we learn to give praise to God, which is *the end of mortal happiness.*

379. *disappoint with bliss,* originally, "disappoint with joy."

381. *The heart,* originally, "The sight."

382–385. To the theological difficulty in regard to marriage in Heaven proposed to Our Blessed Savior by the Saducees, He answered: "For in the resurrection they shall neither marry nor be married: but shall be as the Angels of God in heaven." (St. Matthew, XXII, 30) Patmore discusses this question at length in *Victories of Love,* Book II, Letters vii and viii. The only certain answer there given is in Letter x, ll. 27–29, quoted *infra,* ll. 406–411. Patmore's own solution seems to be that when the soul comes into the presence of Love Himself to whom every soul is woman, the semblance (*the name*) of love in this life, will be exchanged for the reality (*the thing*).

386–393. These lines savor more of poetry than of exegesis. The best commentary upon them is the following passage from the essay, "Dieu et ma Dame:"—"Theology teaches that a characteristic of all the angelic orders is the capacity of assuming a double aspect. They can turn their gaze directly upon God, a state which St. Thomas Aquinas describes as the 'Morning Joy,' or they can turn to God in his creature, which is said to be the 'Evening Joy.' . . . In this duplicate order, each angelic entity represents and contains the Divine Fatherhood for the entity next below, and the womanhood, its 'glory' for that next above; a fact which Milton seems to have discerned, without the aid of Catholic theology, when he wrote

'Spirits at will
Can either sex assume.'"

In speaking of man Patmore develops an analogous idea in another passage: "The woman is 'homo' as well as the man, though one element, the male, is suppressed and quiescent in her, as the other, the female, is in him; and thus he becomes the Priest and representative to her of the original Fatherhood, while she is made to him the Priestess and representative of that original Beauty which is 'the express image and glory of the Father,' each being equally, though not alike, a manifestation of the Divine to the other." (*Ibid*)

394–398. In this life we mould our souls to the spiritual stature that will be ours for eternity. Even *a careless word* will have its effect forever. "But I say unto you that every idle word that men shall speak, they shall render an account for it in the day of judgment. For by thy words thou shalt be justified and by thy words thou shalt be condemned." (St. Matthew XII, 36–37)

398–405. If that be so, can it be possible that the tremendous soul-effects of marriage will not endure for eternity? Will this tree of life, *king of all the forest,* be the only one that will not fulfil the words of Ecclesiastes: "If the tree fall to the south, or to the north, in what place soever it shall fall, there shall it be." (XI, 3)

406–411. The fear that nuptial love might not endure in heaven is voiced by Jane in *Victories of Love,* Bk. II, Letter vii, ll. 10–14:

"A horrible fear within me grew,
That since the preciousness of love
Went thus for nothing, mine might prove
To be no more, and heaven's bliss
Some dreadful good which is not this."

Ultimately, Jane calms her own fears and settles her own doubts:

"Our union is,
You know 'tis said, 'great mystery.'
Great mockery, it appears to me;
Poor image of the spousal bond
Of Christ and Church, if loosed beyond
This life!"

(*Ibid,* ll. 96–101.)

And Frederick writes to Honoria with profound faith in *what* will be true in heaven, but frankly confesses that he does not see *how* it will be done:

"All I am sure of heaven is this:
Howe'er the mode, I shall not miss
One true delight which I have known."

(*Ibid.* Letter x, ll. 27–29.)

In this Frederick agrees with the common teaching of theologians: "We are created for love and friendship, for indissoluble union with our friends. At the grave of those we love our heart longs for a future reunion. This cry of nature is no delusion. A joyful and everlasting reunion awaits the just man beyond the grave." (*Catholic Encyclopedia: Heaven*) (Cf. supra, ll. 382–385.)

406. *unflagging flame,* originally, "most quenchless flame."

408. *in fury,* originally, "like torch, the."

409. *darkness,* formerly, "nothing."

410. *glows,* originally, "burns."

411–412. Originally the following passage was inserted between these lines:

"In the keen air beyond the grave,
The air love gasps for, sickening here
Out of its native atmosphere?
  It cannot be! The Scripture tell
Only what's inexpressible,
And 'gainst each word, to make it right,
Themselves propound the opposite."

[Resume text, l. 412.]

412–420. Fiends delight in the partial profession of God's law, for God will not suffer men, unpunished, to make His doctrine *more pure* than He has made it, as did the Manacheans. Nor will He permit men on earth to tune any other lyre to sing His praises than the one He has decreed they will play upon in heaven.

417. *the five-string'd lyre,* may suggest the five senses. (Cf. "Deliciae Sapientiae," l. 86.) One of Patmore's favorite themes is the part the body and its faculties play in working out the soul's salvation. (Cf. "To the Body.")

419. *of him who,* originally, "of whomsoever."

421–430. Beware the doctrines of unbalanced idealists that lure men to lofty soul-flights, unmindful of their bodily nature tainted by the consequences of original sin, the *solid adamant* of life, as it were, which confers upon the *ether* of the spirit the power to sustain the wings of angels; which *makes and measures height;* which exceeds all other things as the Earth itself exceeds all else in visible creation.

421. *of Darkness and,* originally, "and Princedoms of."

422. Originally: "Which make of none effect man's hope."

425. Originally: "Its counter poising adamant."

426. *That strengthens,* originally, "Which strengthens."

429. *such,* originally, "like."

430–435. Does this doctrine seem *too dark* in reminding man of his sinful inclinations; *too high* in urging him to spiritual flights? Have you never seen a butterfly in all its pride and beauty (symbol of the presumptuous flights of man's spirit), slain by *a bird's beak* (symbol of sin)? Straightway its *frail wings* (symbol of man's lofty nature of the spirit), *drop.*

431. *aught too dark,* originally, "aught that's dark."

435. Originally: "Wanting the weight that made them soar."

436–441. Man's soul and the lofty aspirations of his spirit are the wings of human nature and yet those wings are as nothing, without the weight of man's lower nature, his body and his senses. Whereas his lower nature in itself, without the wings of the spirit, is at least something, though it be only *a maggot,* a pupa within its chrysalis. When the butterfly emerges, its *maggot*-form is still retained although it has been transformed in beauty and winged for lofty flights. This is an appropriate symbol of man as he embarks in *honour and delight* upon the high adventures of the spirit, confident with Saint Paul: "I can do all things in Him who strengtheneth me" (Philipians IV, 13), and humble with the humility born of Christ's warning to his disciples: "Without Me you can do nothing." (St. John XV, 5)

This is merely a corollary to the great paradox of man's nature recorded in Holy Scripture: "Thou hast made him a little less than the angels, thou hast crowned him with glory and honour, and hast set him over the works of thy hand," (Psalm VIII, 6–7) and "dust thou art, and into dust thou shalt return." (Genesis III, 19) Francis Thompson has made this the theme of "Any Saint." (ll. 165–172) and Patmore expresses it in *Magna Moralia* IV. (Cf. "The Child's Purchase," ll. 58–59.)

The butterfly is frequently used as a symbol of Catholic mysticism as opposed to those types of false mysticism that attempt the Illuminative and Unitive Ways without first having tread the difficult paths of the Purgative Way. Dom S. Louismet, O.S.B. makes an effective use of the butterfly-symbol in *Mysticism True and False,* pp. 40–41.

442–to the end. This passage, is not in the original version as printed in *Macmillan's Magazine,* nor is it found in the first edition of

Victories of Love, Bk. II, published, according to Champneys (I, p. 173), in 1863. But the American edition published in Boston by T. O. H. P. Burnham bears the date, 1862.

442–453. If there are any who have never experienced the romance of love, let them remember that *few wed whom they would.* But even this, *like all God's laws, is good,* for it enables nuptial love to grow with the years. Intense first love, however, is glorious and in its light all other things appear as strange as the shadows cast by the sun at noon and evening. (Cf. "Wind and Wave," ll. 7–13.)

When Patmore was a boy at school at St. Germains he used to spend his Sundays at Mrs. Charles Gore's. "I was very much in love with her daughter," he wrote, "afterwards Lady Edward Thynne. I was a very shy boy, and she used to snub me unmercifully." (Champneys I, p. 36) He thus records the incident in his Autobiography: "At St. Germains I entertained a passion of a kind not uncommon in youths; a passion which neither hoped nor cared much for a return. On this occasion I remember praying more than once with torrents of tears that the young lady might be happy, especially in marriage, with whomsoever it might be." (*Ibid.* II, p. 42) Patmore, then only sixteen, seems thus early to have realized that *few wed whom they would.* And his life proved the truth of his words: *Glorious for light is the earliest love.* For, "Years afterwards he found a picture which seemed to resemble Miss Gore, and had it set in a frame with shutters. It used to hang in the drawing-room of the house in which he lived with his first wife, and, if visitors were curious to know what was behind the shutters, Patmore would tell them that it was 'the very first Angel.'" (*Ibid.* I, p. 42.)

In *Magna Moralia* XXIII, we read: "Who knows but that the greatest Cross in life, the knowledge that the only Dear One is for another's arms, may be changed, by fulness of sympathy, into fulness of fruition. 'His law is exceeding broad,' and let us not limit our eternal faculties by a temporal denial of their possibilities. In such case 'let our will have no word to say.' Let us be content with His promise that 'He will fulfil all our desires,' we know not how."

448–453. "The whole of after-life depends very much upon how life's transient transfiguration in youth by love is subsequently regarded; and the greatest of all the functions of the poet is to aid in his readers the fulfilment of the cry, which is that of nature as well as religion, 'Let not my heart forget the things mine eyes have seen.' The greatest perversion of the poet's function is to falsify the memory of that transfiguration of the senses and to make light of its sacramental character." ("Love and Poetry.")

454–486. According to Heaven's impartial law, however, even if first love is lacking, marriage will prove happy if the husband is a true man and the *woman's womanly*. Even if such a wife is not beautiful to look upon and the man still remembers one whom he loved more ardently but failed to win, if he is faithful he will find that *God's ordinance is mightier* than the attractive graces of beauty and it will manifest its power by revealing to him that even the external union of matrimony, will, in time, engender and foster within him real love and devotion. If, after five years of wedded life a man still finds that his wife is not fair let him blame himself, for nuptial love is like the sun, it *makes beauty abound, where all seems dead.*

465. *Eshcol grapes.* It took two men to carry a single cluster. (Cf. Numbers XIII, 24.)

487–498. It were wrong to demand that the prelude to every marriage should be such first-love as sees in one woman the ideal of all. But to those who experience it, it brings present *honour* and is a pledge of *future bliss.* For, who that has known the *height* and *depth* of such delight, can ever be content with the mediocre bliss of love that lies midway?

THE UNKNOWN EROS SEQUENCE

Date of Publication: In April, 1866, under the simple title, *Odes,* Patmore printed nine of the present sequence. They were printed for private circulation, without titles and anonymously. Although the introduction was signed C.P., the initials meant nothing to the general reader at that time. Identified according to the titles later given them the odes are: I. "Prophets Who Cannot Sing." II. "Felicia" ("Beata" in later editions). III. "Tired Memory." IV. 'Faint Yet Pursuing.' V. "Pain." VI. "The Two Deserts." VII. "Deliciae Sapientiae de Amore." VIII. "Dead Language." IX. "1867."

In 1877 a sequence of thirty-one odes including the original nine was published anonymously under the title, *The Unknown Eros and Other Odes* (*Odes* I–XXXI). Of these, six had already appeared in the *Pall Mall Gazette.* (Cf. Champneys I, p. 246.) And two other poems not in the sequence were included in the volume—"The Rosy Bosom'd Hours" and "The After-Glow."

In 1878 sixteen new odes including the three *Psyche Odes,* were added to the sequence as it had been published in the previous year, and one ode, "1877" was omitted. The title was *The Unknown Eros* (*Odes* I–XLVI).

In an undated edition of *Poems,* probably published in 1879, the fourth volume, *The Unknown Eros,* contained forty-two odes and the arrangement of them retained in subsequent editions. In this edition the Proem was strictly a *proem* instead of Ode I as in previous editions of the sequence. Three odes of the 1878 edition were now excluded from the sequence but included among the other poems. They were: "Psyche" (now called "Mignonne"), "Semele," and "Alexander and Lycon."

Circumstances of Composition: I. The *Nine Odes:* After the death of Patmore's first wife and his subsequent loneliness; after the fearful spiritual unrest that resulted in his conversion to Catholicism and the consequent peace it brought him and after the bitter struggle of conflicting loyalties that terminated in his second marriage. A short time before, in 1865, he had resigned from the Britism Museum because of ill health and retired to his estate, Heron's Ghyll, in Sussex.

II. The *Thirty-one Odes:* After his disappointment at the reception given the *Nine Odes;* after his favorite daughter had entered the convent; after his long-delayed inspiration had returned when he was finally settled in the Mansion, Hastings, and very shortly after his memorable pilgrimage to Lourdes. (Cf. "The Child's Purchase.")

Title: Its origin may have been Robert Waring's *"Amoris Effigies,"* published in 1648. As early as 1856 Patmore had acknowledged this work as the inspiration of parts of *The Espousals.* In Morris' translation, which Patmore used, we read: "But, O Cupid, the least of Gods, and greatest of Deities, I should think it less than your Deserts (if yet there could be anything greater) that you are Deifi'd by those bold Philosophers the Poets. You have this Property of a God, to be unknown, and to receive Homage from Men." (p. 57) Moreover conjugal love, the peculiar symbol used throughout the Odes, was almost completely *unknown* as the theme of profane lyric poetry, and even more *unknown* when made the type and symbol of divine love. Patmore was well aware of this as is evident from an entry made in his diary shortly after his first wife's death: "The relation of the soul to Christ *as His betrothed wife* is a mine of undiscovered joy and power." Another element of Patmore's theme that was *unknown* before his time is suggested by Mr. Burdett: "Patmore remembered one fact which Plato had forgotten, namely, that Eros, the divine child is *par excellence* the Domestic Deity." (p. 126)

It is true that in the *Angel in the House,* Patmore had not neglected the divine element in human love but the human element was his chief concern. In the Odes, however, he finds his inspiration in the divine element of human love. Appropriately enough, he chose as the personification of this love, a pagan god who fell in love with a human being. (Cf. "Eros and Psyche.") Eros (ἔρως), according to Hesiod was "the fairest of all the deities, and subdued the hearts of gods and men. He was born from Chaos at the same time as the Earth and Tartarus, and was the comrade of Aphrodite from the moment of her birth. Hesiod conceived Eros not merely as the god of sensual love, but as a power which forms the world by inner union of the separated elements.

"According to a later and commoner notion Eros was the youngest of the gods, generally the son of Aphrodite by Ares or Hermes. Anteros, the god of mutual love, is his brother, and his companions are Pathos and Himeros, the personification of longing and desire, with Peitho (Persuasion), the Muses, and the Graces." (*Dictionary of Classical Antiquities*) It was Hesiod's version rather than the later one that interested Patmore.

Theme: It is a development and an illumination of the *Angel in the House* and *Victories of Love,* as epitomized in "The Wedding Sermon." (Cf. *supra, Circumstances of Composition: Title.*)

As Champneys expresses it: "Though to the casual reader there will appear to be as great a gulf in thought as in form between the 'Angel' and the 'Odes,' no one will have understood the inner meaning of the former who has failed to find in it the same essential idea which is more fully and more exclusively conveyed in the latter . . . . The metal is the same in both cases; but in the latter work it is free from alloy." (Introduction to *Poems,* pp. xxxii and xxxv.)

The greater emotional intensity of the Odes when compared with Patmore's earlier work is easily understood if we remember that he believed that the passion of love is purest when it is most intense. This makes Eros a peculiarly appropriate personification of Patmore's ideal, because in Greek ἔρως means love that is intensely passionate.

Throughout the sequence Patmore is not reflecting an indirect approach to the love of God through the love of visible creatures, although he had a keen awareness of the hierarchy of visible creation as we have seen. He even spoke of an invisible hierarchy: "What hinders then, that there should be many kinds of substance, each more subtle than that below it, as ether is more subtle than matter; and why not correspondent ranges of being, until you reach the absolute and underivative substance, God?" (*Knowledge and Science,* XXIX.)

But in the odes of Book II, Patmore writes as one who views human love from the heights of those who have attained to God's love. "My work," he wrote, "is mainly that of the Poet, bent only upon discovering and reporting how the 'loving hint' of doctrine has 'met the longing guess' of the souls of those who have so believed in the Unseen that it has become visible, and who have thenceforward found their existence to be no longer a sheath without a sword, a desire without fulfilment." (*The Rod, the Root and the Flower, Preface.*) And again: "I only report the cry which certain 'babes in Christ' have uttered: 'Taste and see that the Lord is sweet.' And far be it from me to pose as other than a mere reporter, using the poetic intellect and imagination so as in part to conceive those happy realities of life which in many have been and are an actual and abiding possession; and to express them in such a manner that thousands who lead beautiful and substantially Catholic lives, whether outside or within the visible Church, may be assisted in the only true learning, which is to know better that which they already know." (*Ibid.*)

In a more particularized passage he writes: "The external womanhood is a superfluity and even a hindrance to the Saint. He sees in her only the projected shadow of one half of his own personality, and she is an obstacle to his peace and well being in the society of the reality." Then humbly tempering this lofty view as one who has more of desire than actual attainment he concludes: "But this thought need not trouble us, who are not Saints, in our domestic felicities." (*Homo,* XIII.)

The theme of the entire sequence may briefly be expressed as the human soul's attainment of union with God through love. (Cf. Sequence, *infra.*) It is foreshadowed in the words of Divine Wisdom spoken in the text quoted on the title-page: *"Deliciae meae esse cum filiis hominum*—My delights *were* to be with the children of men." (*Proverbs* VIII, 31.)

For Patmore the most perfect consummation of these divine delights was to be found in love—*or mediate or direct*—as it exists between the soul and God.

Symbolism: In Patmore's day as in our own, there were those who objected to so literal and vivid a use of conjugal love as a symbol of the divine. An apology for it is suggested in the notes prefatory to the *Psyche Odes.* (Cf. *Theme.*)

Sequence: The casual reader will scarcely discern any sequence of thought or development in the Odes. But to the student of Patmore it is as clear as it is fundamental. Perhaps the following outline will best indicate how the sequence develops in the transition from one Ode to another.

Bk. I. The part that Nature plays in the soul's approach to God.
- i. Odes of EXTERNAL NATURE: They describe the Seasons of external nature, symbols of the Seasons of natural love.

"St. Valentine's Day"—Spring, symbol of pre-nuptial love. "Wind and Wave"—Summer, symbol of love developed and transformed by grace.

"Winter"—The season is symbol of love's attainment of *plentitude of peace* (l. 6), before the breaking of Spring Eternal.

("L'Allegro" treats of Autumn as a symbol of spiritual solitude and rest. Cf. appendix.)

ii. Odes of HUMAN LOVE: They present the reality of human love as a parable and premonition of divine love.

LOVE'S DELIGHTS: "Beata," and "The Day after To-morrow."

LOVE'S SORROWS and SACRIFICES: "The Toys," "The Azalea," "Departure," "Eurydice," 'If I Were Dead,' "A Farewell," "Tired Memory," and "Tristitia."

iii. POLITICAL. Odes: They give us the reactions of human love to problems of state as they affect the individual: "1867," "Peace," and "1880–1885." For "1877," cf. appendix.

iv. PHILOSOPHICAL. Odes: With a power of penetration born of his faith Patmore here reveals the absurdity of the political mouthings and popular fallacies of his day. He also voices his bitter hatred of democracy and his adoration of aristocracy. All this is interpreted in the light of God's will that must inevitably prevail: "Magna est Veritas," "The Two Deserts," and "Crest and Gulf."

v. Odes of SPIRITUAL PREPARATION: Passing from the nature of human love and its reactions to domestic and public life, we now see the soul's fortitude in enduring pain and suffering that issue in the preparative purgation required for union with God in contemplation: 'Let Be!", 'Faint Yet Pursuing,' "Victory in Defeat," "Remembered Grace," and "Vesica Piscis."

Bk. II. A description of the workings and manifestations of grace as it supplements nature in effecting the mystical union of the soul with God.

i. The first mysterious and uncomprehended stirrings of divine love in the soul: "To the Unknown Eros."

ii. Sacrifice comprehended as an essential of the soul's love of God: "The Contract."

iii. The Catholic Church, the soul's infallible guide in her love of God: "Arbor Vitae," and "The Standards."

iv. The intrinsic nature of the soul's love of God: "Sponsa Dei."

v. The nature of the restraints which the law of God imposes upon the soul who loves Him: "Legem Tuam Dilexi."
vi. The soul's love of God, rooted in the flesh: "To the Body."
vii. England, a strange land, deaf to the soul's song of God's love: 'Sing Us One of the Songs of Sion.'
viii. The virginal element in the soul's love of God: "Deliciae Sapientiae de Amore."
ix. God known through faith, not Man known through philosophy, the measure of Man's achievement in his love of God: "The Cry at Midnight."
x. Even in desolation, God sustains the soul that loves Him: "Auras of Delight."
xi. The mystical union of the soul with God, effected and sustained through God's gratuitous grace, not through the soul's own efforts: "Eros and Psyche."
xii. Through the revelation granted her in mystical union with God, the soul comprehends to a degree, the nature of her love of God: "De Natura Deorum," "Psyche's Discontent," and "Pain."
xiii. Man's song of God's love should be lofty as his theme: "Prophets Who Cannot Sing."
xiv. In Mary, the Mother of God, was accomplished the perfection of the human soul's love of God: "The Child's Purchase."
xv. A modern Ezekiel's lament over the world's rejection of his song of God's love: "Dead Language."

Mysticism: Today when poetry that is deliberately vague, obscure and unintelligible is often accepted as mystical, it is well to understand what we mean by mysticism, before we attempt to form a judgment concerning the mystical element of Patmore's work. The "mystical experience" in its strictest sense is the soul's immediate perception of God's presence, without the aid of the senses or the use of the discursive reasoning. This perception may be acquired from actual experience, as in the case of Saint John of the Cross, or it may be known through study and analogous personal experiences as in the case of Patmore. It was through the analogous personal experience narrated in his Autobiography and from his study of Saint Thomas Aquinas, St. John of the Cross, Saint Bernard and Marie Lataste that Patmore acquired the speculative knowledge of genuine mysticism which is the very substance of his odes, especially those of Book II, culminating in the Psyche Odes. (Cf. Psyche Odes, *Theme.*) In this matter Patmore was no pretender. "Far be it from me," he wrote, "to pose as other than a mere reporter, using the poetic intellect and imagination so as in part to conceive those happy realities of life which in many have been and are an actual and abiding possession." (*Rod, Root, and Flower,* Preface.)

Technique: The metrical scheme of the odes, like their subject-matter, is merely a development of Patmore's early work. He was as much a poet of one metre as of one theme. But as Arthur Symons has written: "Never was a development in metre so spiritually significant." When, in the *Athenaeum,* Symons had alluded to the "dinner-table domesticities of the 'Angel in the House,'" Patmore wrote him a letter protesting: "I think that you have been a little misled—as almost everybody has been—by the differing characters of the metres of the 'Angel' and 'Eros.' The meats and wines of the two are, in very great part, almost identical in character; but in one case, they are served on the deal table of the octo-syllabic quatrain, and, in the other, they are spread on the fine, irregular rock of the free tetrameter." (*Figures of Several Centuries,* Symons, p. 364.)

For a complete understanding of the metre of the odes, one must study Patmore's theory expressed in the "Essay on English Metrical Law," and read his preface in the third edition of the *Unknown Eros.* It will be enough here to explain Patmore's terminology and give the essentials of his metrical theory—a theory to which A. E. Housman attributes great importance in his lecture, "The Name and Nature of Poetry." Speaking of the artifice of versification he says: "A few pages of C. Patmore and F. Myers contain all, so far as I know, or all of value, which has been written on such matters."

When he refers to his work as "Catalectic Verse," Patmore takes the name from his free use of the pause. "Nearly all English metres," he explains, "owe their existence as metres to 'catalexis,' or pause, for the time of one or more feet, and, as a rule, the position and amount of catalexis are fixed." But the verse in which the odes are written, "is catalectic *par excellence,* employing the pause (as it does the rhyme) with freedom only limited by the exigencies of poetic passion."

In speaking of his work as "Free Tetrameter," Patmore stresses the fact that his verse is not conditioned by stanzas, hence, "free." It is "tetrameter" because, following the Greeks, he makes the dipode the elementary measure or integer of verse. And his verse is always iambic. This explains his meaning when he says: "All English verses in common cadence [iambic] are therefore dimeters, trimeters, or tetrameters, and consist when *full, i.e.,* without catalexis, of eight, twelve, or sixteen syllables." Regarding the length of individual verses he tells us: "Every verse proper contains two, three or four of these 'metres', or as with a little allowance they may be called, 'dipodes.'" His tetrameter line has the "time of eight iambics, when expressive of an exalted strain." When less exalted: "It is allowable to vary the tetrameter ode by the introduction of passages in either or both of these inferior measures [trimeter or dimeter], but not by the use of any other."

To Patmore the most important elements of his technique are rhythm and time. And an essential of these is the pause—the pause within the line or at the end. The extreme to which he carried his theory can best be deduced from his readiness to admit "almost *unlimited catalexis*" in the tetrameter line of the "iambic ode," erroneously called the "irregular ode," according to Patmore. In such a tetrameter he would allow pauses varying "from the time of two to fourteen syllables." This, we are told, "is justified by the analogy of the pauses, or stops, in a similar style of music." But this free use of catalexis is never to be indulged for its own sake, but only: "to suit the variations of the high and stately lyrical feeling which can alone justify the use of this measure."

On the one hand, Patmore constantly stresses the necessity of poetry that is subject to law. "The quality of all emotion which is not ignoble," he held, "is to boast of its allegiance to law." This law admitted inflection, but not infraction. "The best poet," he insists, "is not he whose verses are the most easily scanned, and whose phraseology is the commonest in its materials and the most direct in its arrangement; but rather he whose language combines the greatest imaginative accuracy with the most elaborate and sensible metrical organization, and who, in his verse, preserves everywhere the living sense of metre, not so much by invarying obedience to, as by innumerable small departures from, its *modulus*. The over-smooth and 'accurate' metre of much of the eighteenth century poetry, to an ear able to appreciate the music of Milton and the best parts of Coleridge, is almost as great a defect as the entire dissolution of metre displayed by some of the writers of our own century." Strange words from the pen of one who is frequently mentioned as the precursor of Free Verse! Like Mrs. Meynell, he believed that the liberty of English metre is, "The rooted liberty of flowers in breeze." And from the paragraph just quoted it is evident how completely he concurred in her disdain of Free Verse. Toward the end of her life she wrote in the *Dublin Review*: "Those who have nothing to say clamor for large license in which to say it, and hence *vers libre*. Those who have something to say cling to the order and discipline of bonds valuing that voluntary obedience which is the force of art, literature, morals, religion and politics."

In his essay Patmore cites with enthusiastic approval the following sentences from Hegel: "It is false that versification offers any obstacle to the free outpouring of poetic thought. True genius disposes with ease of sensible materials, and moves therein as in a native element, which, instead of depressing or hindering, exalts and supports its flight." Then Patmore concludes: "Art, indeed, must have a body as well as a soul; and the higher and purer the spiritual, the more powerful and unmistakable should be the corporeal element;—in other words, the more vigorous and various the life, the more stringent and elaborate must be the law by obedience to which life expresses itself."

In his use of rhyme as of metre, Patmore's innovations are those of inflection, not infraction. "The license to rhyme at indefinite intervals," he explains, "is counterbalanced by unusual frequency in the recurrence of the same rhyme."

PROEM

Publication: As Ode I among Odes I–XXXI, 1877.

2. *The beast who talk'd:* Balaam's ass. (Cf. Numbers XXII, 28–33.)

3–4. To the council of Chief Priests and Pharisees gathered together to discuss the most effective means of protecting themselves from the consequences of Christ's teaching, Caiphas said: "It is expedient for you that one man should die for the people, and that the whole nation perish not." (St. John XI, 50.)

5–8. The chief offender among poets was Swinburne, according to Patmore. As Mr. Shane Leslie expresses it: "The flaming content of Patmore's *Unknown Eros* left Swinburne panting in his gilded brothel." Offenders in other fields are described in the Political Odes.

8–14. Nearly ten years elapsed between the printing of the Nine Odes and the publication of the *Unknown Eros.* Deep depression of spirit had followed the cold reception given the Odes by those who had admired the poet's early work. And there ensued one of the darkest periods of Patmore's life. He felt himself a rejected prophet. Peace of soul and fresh stirrings of poetic inspiration came to him only after his removal to Hastings and his memorable pilgrimage to Lourdes. (Cf. "Dead Language.")

16–26. Here we have Patmore's lyrical description of those essentials of all poetry—thought, emotion, insight and expression.

29. Cf. 'Sing Us One of the Songs of Sion.'

31–34. According to the nodal phenomenon of history the great poets of succeeding cultures of the world have appeared at the *eclipse* of their respective civilizations. This was true, certainly, of Homer, Virgil, Dante, and Chaucer.

38–52. The *ancient beauty* of England's regime which Patmore loved, is here contrasted with its feverish restlessness in the pursuit of the democratic ideal which he loathed. In the following passage from Patmore's essay, "Thoughts on Knowledge, Opinion, and Inequality," the same idea is expressed with even greater vividness and realism: "The other day, walking in a country lane, I saw what appeared at a little distance to be a dying animal. On closer view it proved to be the carcass of a sheep which had in great measure been actually transformed into a mass of the soft, white, malodorous grubs known to anglers by the name of gentles. The struggles of these creatures to get at the food which they concealed produced a strong and regular pulsation throughout the whole mass, and gave it a ghastly semblance of breathing. The ordered state of England, according to its ideal, which for many generations has been more or less realised, compared with the sort of democracy to which we are fast drifting and have well-nigh attained, is much like the animal in which myriads of individual organs, nerves, veins, tissues and cells formed subordinated parts of one living thing, compared with this pulsating mass of grubs, each one of which had no thought but of its just share of carrion."

53–74. The poet finds solace in the thought that in centuries to come, when the present history of his country will have grown dim, it will be transfigured by the remembered wisdom of its poets and will shed something of the lustre derived from them, upon *nations yet unborn.*

74–84. Patmore's realization that his song would fall upon deaf ears is best expressed in "Dead Language."

85–102. These lines remind us of Milton's petition to the Heavenly Muse in the opening lines of *Paradise Lost.* But beyond the power of Milton, Patmore here expresses the spiritual cleansing of repentance in a nation as in a soul.

102. The humility and strength of this paradoxical line is characteristic of Patmore.

ST. VALENTINE'S DAY

Composition: Written under the same circumstances as "L'Allegro." Champneys says: "It is no doubt founded on the close observation of nature which country life developed, and for which he never had elsewhere quite the same advantages, at any rate in his later days." (I, p. 362.)

Publication: It first appeared in the sequence of Odes I–XLVI, 1878.

Theme: This is the first of four nature odes which find their inspiration in the seasons of the year. The others are: "Wind and Wave." "L'Allegro," and "Winter." Here the coming of Spring is made the symbol of pure prenuptial love. This description of first-love, by inference and by symbol, may be compared with the explicit description in "Tamerton Church-Tower; or First Love." Such a comparison will show how greatly Patmore improved in his later treatment of an earlier theme. In his essay, "Religio Poetae" Patmore expresses the function of a poet which he exemplifies in his Nature Odes. "The Poet is not more singular for the delicacy of his spiritual insight, which enables him to see celestial beauty and substantial reality where all is blank to most others, than for the surprising range and alertness of vision, whereby he detects, in external nature, those likenesses and echoes by which spiritual realities can alone be rendered credible and more or less apparent, or subject to 'real apprehension,' in persons of inferior perceptive powers. Such likenesses, when chosen by the imagination, not the fancy, of the true Poet, are *real* words—the only real words; for 'that which is unseen is known by that which is seen,' and natural similitudes often contain and are truly the visible *ultimates* of the unseen. . . . The Poet, again, has, like Newton, a special *calculus*—a doctrine of infinite series, whereby he attains to unveil the infinite and express it in credible terms of the finite, showing it, if not as actually apprehensible, yet as possible, and even certainly so, to orders of intellect which are probably only a continuation and development of our own."

1–5. The feast of St. Valentine, martyr, is February 14th. These lines seem at variance with the medieval tradition expressed by Chaucer in the "Parliament of Foules":

"For this was Seynt Valentyne's day
When every foul cometh ther to choose his mate."

2. *Vestal February* is a symbol of that element of virginity that must surrender to *the exceeding sweet of dear Desire* (ll. 37–38) in the consummation of conjugal love. In *Amoris Effigies* (p. 11) we read: "The Virginal Love is no sooner unloos'd, but there succeeds another Knot, which like the Gordian one, may perhaps be cut asunder, but never unty'd." For the elements of virginity that survive and are intensified in matrimony, cf. "The Contract."

11–13. In his Preface to "Sister Songs," Thompson acknowledges an unconscious plagiarism of these lines in his own:

"For Spring leaps in the womb of the young year!"
("Sister Songs," Proem, l. 15.)

"Finding I could not disengage it without injury to the passage in which it is embedded," wrote Thompson, "I have preferred to leave it, with this acknowledgment to a poet rich enough to lend to the poor."

14–36. The mood of *praevernal* time here so beautifully described is seldom the subject of poetic treatment.

35–36. Here, by gentle inference, is Patmore's doctrine of sacrifice in love, a doctrine objectively stated in the "Wedding Sermon," ll. 107–27, and developed with fierce literalness in later odes of the sequence. In the essay, "Love and Poetry," we read of nuptial love: "Its felicity consists in a perpetual conversion of phase from desire to sacrifice, and from sacrifice to desire."

37–57. Here Patmore applies to inanimate nature his philosophy of human love and urges the nuptials of the hesitating Earth and May.

37–38. The sweetness and joyousness of sacrifice here only lightly foreshadowed, are the explicit themes of later odes. (Cf. "The Contract.")

44–53. These lines descriptive of youth's rash vows of innocence, later annulled in the wisdom of maturity, are in perfect agreement with Patmore's views. They remind us of the personal experience of his second wife who had been bound by "a formal religious promise never to marry," a promise from which she was dispensed in order to marry him.

44–50. We find the same idea in Thompson's "From the Night of Forebeing," ll. 87–92:

> "O Earth, unchilded, widowed Earth, so long
> Lifting in patient pine and ivy-tree
> Mournful belief and steadfast prophecy,
> Behold how all things are made true!
> Behold your bridegroom cometh in to you,
> Exceeding glad and strong."

WIND AND WAVE

Composition: Cf. "L'Allegro" and "Saint Valentine's Day."

Publication: In sequence of Odes I–XXXI, 1877.

Theme: The fruition, in Summer, of the consummated nuptials of May and the hesitating Earth (Cf. "Saint Valentine's Day," ll. 37–57), symbol of human love, sacramentally divine, in which all that is *sensitively good is sought and understood* (ll. 11–12). This second of the nature-odes makes the summer sea a symbol of first-love, grown mature, transfigured by grace and consummated sacramentally. (Cf. "Saint Valentine's Day," and "Winter," *Theme.*)

1–6. The aimlessness of *wedded light and heat* until they bring forth from the earth flowers and the luxuriant growth of plant life clearly suggests the contrast between the futility of human love when misdirected and the greatness of its consummation according to the law of God in matrimony.

7–13. "Every 'Bride of Christ' who is also a pure and ardent lover discerns, when his eyes are first opened, as by a deific flash, to the feminine splendour, that 'Dieu et ma Dame' is no irreverent or hyperbolic legend for his double but not divided worship. The ideal womanhood, which only one woman has realised fully, but which every woman seems to be capable of more or less representing to some man for at least one moment in his life, is the photosphere of God, the light and joy of the universe, 'Regina Mundi,' as the glory of nature, and 'Regina Coeli' when she shall have become nature glorified." ("Dieu et ma Dame.") (Cf. "Sponsa Dei," ll. 38–56.)

7–9. 'The bliss which woman's charms bespeak,
I've sought in many, found in none!'
'In many 'tis in vain you seek
What can be found in only one,'
(*The Angel in the House,* Bk. II, Canto ix, Prelude 3.)

9. Cf. "Legem Tuam Dilexi" and "Beata."

10–13. "I loved her in the name of God,
And for the ray she was of Him."
(*The Angel in the House,* Bk. I, Canto x, ll. 35–36.)

14–37. This imaginative description of how love transfigures life is as delicate as it is beautiful. (Cf. "The Wedding Sermon," ll. 448–53.) The peaceful ecstasy of first-love (ll. 14–17) is followed by intenser alternations of love and discontent (ll. 18–21), but so long as this great human passion is curbed and directed according to God's law, it tends one way, toward happiness that is at first *unguess'd* and only gradually realized as it comes to the soul through the delights of the senses that have God's blessing. And then comes the ultimate glory of such love in the little children begotten of it (ll. 35–37). The part that children play in human love is more explicitly described in "The Wedding Sermon," ll. 304–16.

23. Cf. "De Natura Deorum," ll. 8–9 for the symbolic expression of the opposite state of soul.

25–37. Champneys in his introduction to *Poems* (p. xliii) calls attention to these last lines as "a splendid movement expressive of the action of the waves approaching the shore."

WINTER

Composition: Cf. "L'Allegro" and "Saint Valentine's Day."

Publication: In sequence of Odes I–XLVI, 1878.

Theme: Chronologically this is the last of the four nature odes. In "L'Allegro," contemplating Autumn the poet saw a symbol of *The Spouse of Honour, fair Repose* (l. 24), that state of spiritual solitude and rest that follows the soul's attainment of the *Certitude* and *Felicity* of "Saint Valentine's Day" and "Wind and Wave." In the present ode winter is a symbol of the highest reaches of the sacramental love of man and woman—the attainment of a *plenitude of peace* that is a prelude to Spring Eternal.

Throughout all the odes, as here, Patmore continues to use parables, symbols and metaphors for the purpose set down in his essays: "Parables and symbols are the only possible modes of expressing realities which are clear to perception though dark to the understanding." ("Love and Poetry.") "Symbols and parables and metaphors—which are parables on a small scale—are the only means of adequately conveying, or rather hinting, super-sensual knowledge. 'He spake not without a parable.' Hebrew, Greek, Indian and Egyptian religions all spoke in parables . . . simply because there is no other vehicle for what they have to say." ("Seers, Thinkers, and Talkers.")

We find a more sublime application of this truth in St. Bernard: "When suddenly and as it were with the speed of a flash of lightning something divine becomes clearly manifest to the mind when the soul is raised in ecstasy, straightway—though I know not whence they come—there are present to the mind certain imaginative pictures of lower [earthly] things, either to temper a splendor that is too intense or to be used in teaching [others the nature of what has been seen]. They are appropriately adapted to the thoughts divinely infused, and by them that most pure and dazzling ray of truth is, as it were, toned down so that it becomes more bearable to the mind and more capable of being imparted to whomsoever we will." (Sermons on the *Canticle of Canticles,* Sermon XLI, § 3; Translation, p. 163.) (Cf. "Saint Valentine's Day," *Theme.*)

It is interesting to compare the significance of winter as a symbol in this ode with its significance in Thompson's "From the Night of Forebeing."

5. *Trophonian pallor:* The oracle of Trophonius at Lebadea in Beotia was a subterranean chamber into which inquirers descended

to receive a variety of revelations. "The descent into the cave and the sights which there met the eye were so awe-inspiring that the popular belief was that no one who visited the cave ever smiled again." (*Dictionary of Classical Antiquities,* Seyffert.)

6. *plentitude of peace:* "Peace is the indwelling of God and the habitual possession of all our desires." ("Emotional Art.") "Peace is no negative quality. It does not consist in the mere absence of disturbance by pain or pleasure. It is the peace of which St. Thomas says 'perfect joy and peace are identical, (I. ii, q. 270, art. 3), and is the atmosphere of a region in which smiles and tears are alike impertinences. . . . ' Peace," says again the writer above quoted, 'is the tranquility of order and has its seat in the will.' (*Ibid.*) This peace, which is the common character of all true art and of all true life, involves, in its fullest perfection, at once the complete subdual and the glorification of the senses and the 'ordering of all things strongly and sweetly from end to end!" ("Peace in Life and Art.") "The peace which is 'identical with perfect joy' in life and its expression in art, is also identical with purity, which is so far from being, as is commonly supposed, a negative quality, that it is the unimpeded ardour of ordered life in all its degrees, and is as necessary to the full delight of the senses as it is to the highest felicity of the spirit." (*Ibid.*)

6–12. The poetic imagery of these lines is too notable to be passed over in silence. But their meaning is too clear to need explanation. Any Christian knows that as Winter conceals the potential vitality of Spring beneath the appearances of death, so, to the eyes of faith, physical death conceals life eternal and the resurrection that is to come.

17–38. In one of Patmore's essays, "December in Garden and Field," we have a prose expression of these lines: "To the close observation which is given by a love of nature, the year is never dead. . . . The old year does not sink into its grave until it has seen the new year smiling in its lap. Even before autumn has fairly set in, the buds of next year's blossom are large and full upon the rhododendron and the azalea; and if at this time you break them open, you discover all the parts of the flower which far-off June is to divulge, not only perfectly formed but distinctly touched with colour. The flower of the tall white lily is no sooner dropped than the roots put forth their full complement of new leaves for the summer after that which is not yet ended. The buds of the horse-chestnut are black and viscous, and as big as hazel-nuts, almost before the first winter storm has blown away the last rusty leaf; and there is scarcely a tree or shrub the withering leaf of which does not hold in its armpit a little knob, black, brown, red, or green, which is the infant form of the new spray. The laurustinus, arbutus, and gorse will even yield their full blossom in winter; and the yucca mostly chooses the time of the first snow to surprise the eye with the sudden apparition of its great flower-spear, clothed with tender pink scales. The primrose in December sends up a crop of little sturdy crimped leaves from the midst of the large, lank, and prostrated growth of the past summer; three or four mild days will be too much for the patience of the next year's blossoms themselves; and a touch of tenderest perfume and blue, from the snail-eaten violet-bed, will come to you with a pathos and sweetness such as May and June know nothing of."

17–45. This passage is notable for its poetical description of the commonplaces of early Spring.

18. *shaw:* copse or grove.

32. *gorse:* a spiny shrub with yellow flowers.

33. *Jason's fleece:* The fleece sought by Jason and the Argonauts was the *golden* fleece of the ram given to Nephele by Mercury.

46–54. There is a note of subtle poignancy in making *Winter's sometime smiles* spring from *infancy ineffable.*

BEATA

Publication: One of the original Nine Odes of 1868.

Theme: The next ten odes, exclusive of "Magna Est Veritas" and the three Political Odes, form a sequence in which the poet turns from external nature as a parable of love, and contemplates human love directly in its double aspect—a reality in itself and a parable of divine love. In "Beata" and "The Day After Tomorrow" Patmore presents love's delights. The remaining odes of the sequence describe love's losses. (Cf. "The Toys," *Theme.*)

It is, really, an instance of Patmore's escape from the awfulness of infinity, which he so feared. (Cf. "Legem Tuam Dilexi.") The boundless rays of Heaven's infinity striking *a diamond stalactite* in the black cavern of earth are a symbol of God's infinite attributes, made finite for man in the woman whom he loves. As we read in "Dieu et ma Dame": "Woman is the last and lowest of all spiritual creatures; made 'a little lower than the angels' to be 'crowned with the glory and honour' of being the final and visible reflection of the beauty of God, which in itself no eye shall ever see." (Cf. "Wind and Wave," ll. 7–13.)

We find the same idea in St. Bernard's "Sermons on the *Canticle of Canticles*" (Sermon XXXI, § § 1–3; Translation p. 135): "The Word Who is the Bridegroom often appears to zealous minds, and not under one form. Why? Because He is not yet seen *as He is.* . . . Such a vision is not for the present life but it is reserved for our final state—for those, at least, who can say: *We know that when He shall appear we shall be like to Him, because we shall see Him as He is.* (1 St. John III, 2.) And now, even, He appears to whom He will; but as He wills, not as He is. No man of wisdom, no saint, no prophet can see Him as He is, or ever could see Him in this mortal body. But he who will be considered worthy will be able to see Him, in a body that is immortal. But that will be hereafter. Meanwhile so great a variety of forms and so great a number of *species* in created things—what are they but rays of the Sun of Divinity, as it were, showing indeed that He truly *is* from whom they derive their being, but not defining *what* He is! . . . This manner of seeing is common to all men. For it is easy, according to the Apostle, for everyone with the use of reason to see clearly the invisible things of God, *being understood by the things that are made.*" (Romans I, 20.)

So purely spiritual is the love revealed in this ode that its immediate inspiration might easily be Our Lady. But it is really the poet's wife. The particular attribute of this love here stressed is the ever-recurring strain of Patmore's poetry—its power to transfigure life. (Cf. "Sponsa Dei," ll 45–56.)

1–15. The entire ode is a singularly beautiful and effective use of the symbol of white light refracted from a prism and broken up into its constituent colors. It is *viewless* to the eye until thus refracted. Similarly the infinite attributes of God such as *Reason Power and Love* become most clearly visible when they are reflected in a woman. Then the *deadening might* and the *withering white* of infinite perfections become a source of quickening delight to the soul. (Cf. "The Child's Purchase," ll. 79–81.)

Thompson makes a slightly different use of the same symbol in "Lines for a Drawing of Our Lady of the Night":

"She bears on her front's lucency
The starlight of her purity:

For as the white rays of that star
The union of all colors are,

She sums all virtues that may be
In her sweet light of purity."

In Patmore's essay "Dieu et ma Dame," we read: "Woman, that opaque surface in which the rays of Deity end, and from which they are reflected in all the multiplied splendors which they have gathered by being transmitted through the prismatic and refractive spheres that intervene." And in the *Angel in the House,* Bk. I, Canto x, ll. 35–36 we read:

> "I loved her in the name of God,
> And for the ray she was of Him."

THE DAY AFTER TOMORROW

Publication: Among Odes I–XXXI, 1877.

Title: By implication, *today* and *tomorrow* are symbols of time. *The Day after Tomorrow* is eternity.

Theme: The sensible delights of love are delicately and chastely described as a reality and as a parable of things divine. The *lives* of human lovers *shall be fulfill'd* (l. 15), not here on earth in the sacrament of matrimony, but in Heaven. This is, I believe, the theme of this ode—Patmore's own answer to the question of the survival of conjugal love in eternity. (Cf. "Wedding Sermon," ll. 382–385.) But as Mrs. Meynell has written: "It is not readily understood to refer to reunion after death." And yet it is in this sense that she herself understood it, as is clear from her own words: "Coventry Patmore does not always capture terror for such purposes of eternal sadness [as he does in "Eurydice"]; he is able to marry terror to joy in the magnificent ode of reunion, *The Day after Tomorrow.*" (*Second Person Singular,* p. 97.)

2. *coming pleasure:* the joy of reunion after death.

6. *heaving Sea:* the sea of time bounded by the day of her death and the future day of his own. (Cf. *infra* ll 39–41.)

16–38. "No other are the Joys of Heaven than to *Love* and to be *Lov'd,* no other are the Joys of Earth. That Divine *Ardor* which makes the *Empyreal* Heaven to be what it is, and wherein will consist the Happiness of the future Life, must be the only Solace of this." (*Amoris Effigies,* Translation p. 34.)

15. Here as in l. 35 and ll. 62–64 is Patmore's view that the perfect consummation of conjugal love is in Heaven. "Nothing more clearly proves that love between man and woman is 'a great sacrament' than the sense of infinite non-desert and infinite poverty of capacity for its whole felicity, which those who are most deserving and most capable of its joy, feel in the presence of its mysteries." (*Homo,* VI.) (Cf. "Deliciae Sapientiae," l. 115.)

the third day: *The Day after Tomorrow,* Eternity.

16. *all has been before:* here on earth.

34. Life that is bounded by time finds its fulfilment in conjugal love, but life eternal finds its fulfilment in the Beatific Vision.

38. *peace:* Cf. "Winter," l. 6.

62–64. These lines remind us of St. Paul's immortal lines to the Romans VIII, 37–39, quoted in the notes on "Eros and Psyche," ll. 157–166.

In *Amoris Effigies* we read: "We confess there is something in *Love* more Powerful than Calamities, more Magnificent than Honour, more splendid than Riches, more Charming than Pleasures, for whose sake we contemn all these, yea for whose sake we do not contemn them but have them in the greater Veneration." (Translation, p. 34.)

70. *honied peace:* the peace of eternity. (Cf. "Winter," l. 6.)

TRISTITIA

Publication: Among Odes I–XXXI, 1877.

Title: It is clear that Patmore uses the word in the theological sense of *sadness* or *melancholy* which is the result of spiritual sloth. (Cf. ll. 23–24; 26.) This is its meaning in the writings of St. Thomas, Cassian, St. Gregory, St. Bernard and others. (Cf. *Studies in Dante,* Edward Moore, Second Series, pp. 183–208.)

Theme: In *The Angel in the House* Patmore wrote: *The death of nuptial joy is sloth* (Bk. II. Canto xi, l. 53.) In this ode he applies the same idea to the soul's spiritual joy in its love of God.

1–5. Hope grows weak when a lover looks forward to the inconceivable delights of love and he can only be sustained by the rememebrance of the actual attainment of past delights that in prospect seemed unattainable. The same is true in the purely supernatural order. As Patmore expresses it: "The fulfilment of God's promises even in this life, to those 'who so believe that there shall be a fulfilment of the things which have been promised,' are so beyond hope and beyond and unlike all previous imagination of those promises, that they are more incredible than were the promises themselves; and the difficulty of faith is thenceforward that of believing our own eyes and senses, and of accepting the self-evident." (*Homo* XXXI.)

1. *Darling:* Patmore's second wife.

6–28. If you should win heaven and I should fail, do not mar your happiness by thinking of the sufferings I bear and the joy I lack. Else, I shall be condemned to tortures beyond those inflicted by divine justice.

It need hardly be remarked that in the supposition underlying these lines there is more of lyricism than theology. The stern truth is that the happiness of the blessed in Heaven will not be dimmed by the just condemnation of those they loved on earth, and the punishments of those condemned will be in the hands of God alone.

St. Bernard concludes his treatise *On the Love of God* with this description of Heaven: "In that native land no suffering or sadness will be allowed to enter in, even as it is sung thereof: *The dwelling in thee is as it were of all rejoicing* (Psalm LXXXVI, 7), and again: *everlasting joy shall be unto them* (Isaias LXI, 7). Finally, how shall one be mindful of mercy where the justice of God alone will be remembered? Just so, where now there will be no place for misery or occasion for pity, surely there can be no feeling of compassion."

St. Thomas says: "The Blessed in glory will have no compassion upon the damned." (*Summa* III, Suppl. q. 94, art. 2.) And this same view is expressed by Patmore himself in *Magna Moralia* XXI: "You do not truly 'love God and keep His commandments' by insisting, in desire, upon anything, even the salvation of your dearest and nearest. If you believe in and love God, you will effectually believe that He loves all who are capable of His love far better than you do, and you will be heartily sure that you will give, when you know all, a joyful consent to decrees which may seem to you now most hard and terrible."

16–24. This passage suggests Dante's description of hell. In the first terrace are those condemned for carnal sin and in the other terraces of "Outer Hell" that lead to the steel wall beyond which lies the City of Dis, or "Inner Hell," are those guilty of other forms of incontinence. In the successive terraces of the City of Dis are heretics, those guilty of physical violence, suicides, blasphemers, the fraudulent and betrayers. The sin for which Patmore imagines himself condemned is one of incontinence, the *gracious-seeming sin* of *loving too much* (ll. 9–10), for which God's justice would condemn him to the first terrace of Outer Hell, *the mild borders of the banish'd world* (l. 19). There the consciousness that his loved-one in heaven grieved for him would condemn him to the intenser sufferings of the souls in the city of Dis, where dwell those guilty of *pride, fraud, envy, cruel lust, or hate* (l. 22).

25–26. *such as these:* incontinent sinners in whom there is less guilt than the others—even they are condemned to *loss without measure, sadness without end!*

29–31. Should you grieve for me, your grief would appear black in the light of heaven, though on earth it might appear as *light* dimmed by *mortality.*

32–33. "Whither shall I go from Thy spirit? or whither shall I flee from Thy face? If I ascend into heaven, Thou are there; If I descend into hell, Thou are present," (Psalm CXXXVIII, 7–8.) Commenting upon the last part of this text Patmore once wrote: "That is, the Heavenly Love is there also [*i.e.* in hell], and can in some degree be apprehended as Love, or it would be false to say that it was 'there.'" (Champneys II, p. 87.) God's love is apprehended by the blessed in heaven for their weal. In hell it is apprehended by the damned for their woe. (Cf. ll. 48–53.) In Marie Lataste we read: " 'There is no God!'—he has spoken truly; for that man there shall be no God, the Supreme Happiness and Bliss; there shall be no God, the Sovereign of everlasting goodness and love; but to him there shall be a God eternally angry, eternally terrible, eternally just, a God who is the everlasting avenger of the offense committed against Him." (Vol. I, p. 21.)

34–43. It requires the robust faith of Dante to include Love among the divine attributes that reared the Gates of Hell above which he saw written:

> "I owe my being to the Power Divine
> Highest Wisdom, Primal Love did me ordain."
> (*Inferno* III, ll. 5–6, Eleanor V. Murray, translator.)

God's infinite love is made manifest by this punitive sanction of His law, so terrible that we often remain faithful to Him through fear when the motive of love fails to sustain us. But in these lines Patmore seems to say that in hell God conceals his love. Thus he mitigates the sufferings of the damned by killing their remorse for God's love which they have lost and then no longer remember. If this be what the poet means, he is clearly at variance with Catholic doctrine.

44–57. This is a further description of the souls in Hell referred to in ll. 19–26. [Line 45 is a repetition of l. 19 and l. 47 is a repetition of l. 26.] But the description here suggests Dante's limbo more than his hell.

48. *since:* since the time of their loss. If *since* is interpreted as causal, what follows becomes an anacoluthon.

48–53. It is difficult to reconcile the tender consolation these souls feel, with the doctrine of the Church concerning the sufferings of those who are the objects of God's wrath. "The damned are confirmed in evil; every act of their will is evil and inspired by hatred of God. . . . And according to theologians the pain of loss and the pain of sense constitute the very essence of hell, the former being by far the most dreadful part of eternal punishment. . . . Just as the blessed in heaven are free from all pain, so, on the other hand, *the damned never experience even the least real pleasure.* In hell the separation from the blissful influence of Divine love has reached its consummation." (*Catholic Encyclopedia.*)

49. *ineffectual fervour of regret:* This savors more of Ernest Dowson's "Cynara" than of Patmore's inspiration in the great bulk of his work. (Cf. *infra,* ll. 48–53.)

58–60. It is difficult to imagine from what words of *Doctors and Saints* Patmore has derived this doctrine. Personally, I can see no possible interpretation of it that would be consistent with Catholic teaching.

60–63. Among Patmore's *Aphorisms and Extracts* is one in which he cites an unnamed priest, a friend of his, as saying: "*Tristitia* or *melancholy*—a state of mind which many poets and musicians exalt as full of secret sweetness—is the *hell* of those who, not having fallen into mean and malignant sins, are not visited with malignant pains. . . . (Cf. *supra* ll. 48–53.)

"When I asked Fr. ——— why he and others did not preach the *love* of God more, he answered that if he dwelt too much on that, and so destroyed the hard thoughts which his congregation have of God, they would all be living in mortal sin before the end of the week. That might indeed be the *first* effect, but the power of the idea would grow upon and gradually change them, in a way that no preaching of God's wrath could ever do. A person who has rightly apprehended the love of God—as so few have—may fail in many and great things through frailty, and may very well be condemned to everlasting *Tristitia,* but he or she can never be mean or malignant or become subject to the vulgar tortures which a true instinct (which milksops would call vindictiveness) foresees and *craves* for such persons." (Champneys II, p. 87.) (Cf. "Dead Language," ll. 5–6.)

Instinct whether of milksops or of the orthodox such as Patmore, is not a safe guide in matters of dogma, as is proved by the prose passage just quoted. And the false interpretation of the *arcanum fidei* attributed to Fr. ——— finds its completest refutation in the widespread movement in the Church today to teach and preach the love of God.

It is true, according to Catholic teaching, that the pains of hell—the pain of loss as well as the pain of sense—differ in degree according to demerit. But in his application of this teaching in this poem, Patmore has followed his instinct rather than the positive teaching of the Church, and his instinct has proved as fastidious as his conclusions are false.

66. *Tristitia:* Cf. supra, *Title,* ll. 60–63, *etc.*

67–80. Here again Patmore seems clearly at variance with the teaching of the Church concerning the tortures of the damned. In these lines the lover condemned to hell finds solace and pleasure in the realization that his beloved has attained to heavenly bliss. (Cf. *supra,* ll. 48–53, *etc.*)

AZALEA

Publication: First included in sequence in Odes I–XLVI, 1878.

Theme: It may best be expressed by the Latin *desiderium*—the longing of the human heart for some beloved object which is absent. Here it is the poet's dead wife. The inspirational incident was one of those strange psychological phenomena, a dream within a dream. It occurred about six weeks after his first wife's death and is thus recorded by Patmore in his diary, August 23, 1862: "Last night I dreamt that she was dying: awoke with unspeakable relief to find that it was a dream; but a moment after, to remember that she was dead." (Champneys I, p. 146.) This is the prosaic statement of the experience which in the ode Patmore expresses with a poignancy as intense as he ever achieved.

24–25. Even in expressions of human love so tender as this, Patmore is intimately aware of God's love: "He (the Divine Lover) requires in her (the elect Soul), as a mortal lover does, that amount of 'vanity,' as the world calls it, which sees and rejoices in her own beauty; for it is only her knowledge of her own loveliness in His eyes which makes His love credible to her, and it is only her belief in His love which enables her to give that perfect response of feeling which is love's fruition, and causes her beauty to brighten more and more in the joy of His flatteries, making her *sweet to herself who is so sweet to Him.*" ("Dieu et ma Dame.") (Cf. "Sponsa Dei," ll. 48–50.)

The Pythoness in "De Natura Deorum" (ll. 112–115) expresses a similar thought.

DEPARTURE

Publication: Among Odes I–XXXI, 1877.

Theme: The death of Patmore's first wife at Elm Cottage, Hampstead. During the last few days before the end he and his wife were alone. Their children had been sent to stay with friends. In the awfulness of this solitude the poet's soul was sensitive to the least detail of those last moments before the inevitable parting from her whom he so passionately loved as wife and mother of his children. Mrs. Meynell has written: "The extremity of grief without bitterness, the grief that kisses and says a conscious 'farewell, farewell', is in 'Departure.'" (*Second Person Singular,* p. 98.)

1–9. Commenting upon these lines and ll. 27–30 Gosse writes: "In the bewilderment of his distress it is not the endless bereavement that surprises him, but the discourtesy in one who never failed in the beauty of her manners before.

"It was not like your great and gracious ways! His wretchedness is concentrated for a moment upon the bitter disappointment that the only loveless look which she ever gave him should be that with which she leaves him." (pp. 231–232.)

4. Patmore's first wife died July 5, 1862.

17–18. These lines are redolent of the sentiments of "Winter." The *growing gloom of* human *love* in those last moments was presently dispelled by the blinding light of love divine.

19–22. This dissembling of deep and tragic emotions behind feigned happiness and trivialities is more harrowing than the literal expression of what is concealed. Here is Patmore's own realization of how true were the lines written several years before:

> "Love in tears too noble is
> For pity, save of love in smiles."
> (*Angel in the House,* Bk. I, Canto V, Prelude ii.)

25–30. It is to be doubted if the unspeakable experience that inspired these lines has ever been expressed in poetry with greater poignancy. (Cf. *supra,* ll. 1–9.)

EURYDICE

Publication: Among Odes I–XXXI, 1877.

Title: The Nymph Eurydice was married to Orpheus, the famous mythological poet. After her sudden and tragic death Orpheus descended into the lower world. There the music of his song so moved Persephone, Queen of the lower regions, that she allowed him to bring Eurydice back to the upper world on condition that he would not look round. Orpheus failed to observe the condition and Eurydice was forced to return to Hades forever. (Cf. *Georgics,* Virgil, IV, ll. 453–527.)

Theme: Patmore builds a spiritual allegory upon Orpheus' search for Eurydice in the realms of the dead. He draws a parallel between it and his own agonized dream-wanderings after his first wife's death, wanderings that bring him ever to her bedside, as so often he had gone during the last years of her life when she lay stricken with a mortal illness. "Not without profoundly conscious art," wrote Mrs. Meynell, "did he achieve the ultimate, the mortal pathos of such an ode as 'Eurydice.' He was ready to tell the secret which no others could use as he used it, however it might be guessed; and the secret of Eurydice was: 'After exceeding ill, a little good.' The slenderness of the good and the poignancy of the ill are mingled in this ode on dreams, with such closeness of fear as no other poet has ever endured. *Eurydice* is the dream of the mourner who night by night follows some dreary clue through labyrinths without hope, to find the dear dead living the thin, remote, neglected life that the dead do live in these intolerable dreams." (*Second Person Singular,* p. 97.) (Cf. *infra,* l. 43.)

1–9. Is this, my dream-wandering, such a *portent* as is the dying day and *a restless grave*—a portent of night and death, and the dawn and life that are to follow? Or is it such as we experience when the vast waters of the Spirit rise within us when the *world of awe,* reflection of the awesomeness of eternity, is in conjunction with the world in which we live.

8. *at unguess'd dates:* The high tides of the ocean recur at regular intervals when the moon is in conjunction with the earth. Not so the tides of the Spirit—"The Spirit breatheth where He will; and thou hearest His voice, but thou knowest not whence He cometh and whither He goeth." (St. John III. 8.)

11–13. These lines spring more from the exaggerations of humility than from literal truth. The sin of loving his wife *more than Heaven* is the *gracious-seeming sin* for which the poet imagines he may be eternally condemned, in "Tristitia," ll. 9–11.

15–37. It were difficult to surpass these lines in describing the awful dreams that harass the sleep of those whose grief is still fresh for a loved-one lost through death. The poignancy of the passage is deepened by the introduction of Orpheus' search along the avenue of Hades for his lost Eurydice.

26–29. There is bitterness in these lines if they refer to an actual lack of sympathy on the part of Patmore's *kith and kin,* for his inconsolable grief at the death of his first wife.

43. In a letter to Mrs. Meynell, December 5, 1885, Patmore wrote: "Shakespeare above all who ever lived knew the art of tempering extremities with extreme sweet, which is the secret of great pathos. Aristotle, who is worth fifty Platos, says that after exceeding ill a little good is the essence of pathos. I put that phrase, as you will

remember, into the Ode called 'Eurydice.' There is plenty of that in Shakespeare, but very little of it in any other poet." And in Patmore's essay entitled "Pathos" we read: "The author of the Rhetoric shows his usual incomparable subtilty of observation when he notes that a little good coming upon or in the midst of extremity of evil is a source of the sharpest pathos."

47. *here:* in this life.

THE TOYS

Publication: In the *Pall Mall Gazette,* Nov. 30, 1876, and later included among Odes I–XXXI, 1887.

Theme: It is really the love of God the Father for His children, and only apparently the love of a human father for his little son. In a letter to Buxton Forman, Oct. 26, 1888, Patmore referring to this poem wrote: "The poem . . . was not about Henry [he was two years old when his mother died] but my eldest, Milnes" (Champneys II, p. 271). Mr. Page is inclined to believe that this is not the case because Milnes was fourteen at the time of his mother's death and a cadet in the Navy. "Therefore," he concludes, "the poem is not, in all its circumstances, historical, and probably Frederick's." (*Patmore, A Study,* p. 110.) It is Mr. Page's theory that the characters in the Odes are a development of those found in Patmore's earlier writing. (Frederick is Honoria's rejected lover in *Victories of Love.*) It is true that Patmore even in his Autobiography is frequently unreliable in matters of detail. And it may be that in his letter to Forman he was mistaken in saying that the poem does not refer to Henry. But in view of Patmore's statement it does not seem likely that there was no such incident as the poem describes.

Significance: Commenting upon the poem Gosse writes: "It illustrates with more delicacy and truth of analysis than any biographer can hope to seize, the ceaseless oscillation of his spirit between severity and tenderness. It is a 'document' of the highest possible value to us in forming a just notion of the temperament of Patmore." (p. 117.)

Mrs. Meynell, with that originality so characteristic of her literary criticism, writes: "Why, of all these all-intelligible poems, is only one generally known, even with the relative generalness possible among the little minority that care for poetry? That one is, needless to say, *The Toys,* a very beautiful and tender poem, but one containing less essential poetry than any other page of the odes." (*Second Person Singular,* p. 103.)

TIRED MEMORY

Publication: One of the original Nine Odes, 1868.

Versions: The present version is considerably altered, chiefly by the omission of the last twenty-three lines of the original:

"I woo'd her with thy praises, and I won
With protestations of my love for thee;
And, by her answering kindness for the name
Of thee, her Rival, she became
Thine own.
Less kind than she could'st thou entreat her, Dear,
In thy expectant sphere,
If, loving thine and mine and thee and me,
There 'twere adjudged her right with us to be?
Twain is the mind of love, ev'n as the mood
Of stars is solitude.
And yet the learned lonely watcher views
A twofold, sometimes, or a triple star,
Strange in the crowd of shinings singular.—
But, oh, my Love,
No more will I amuse
My doubting heart with verse of vain excuse.
Let holy Law the theme be of all Song;
And let the seldom and excepted case,
If such it prove,
(That none, my way misquoting, travel wrong),
Walk silent, with veil'd face,
Contented best to be accounted base."

Other minor changes are indicated in the notes on particular lines. All these changes, it will be noticed, tend to soften the charge of *treason.*

Theme: It is literally a page of Patmore's spiritual biography—his soul-struggle in reconciling his love for his second wife, with fidelity to his first wife's memory. During the long illness before her death, Patmore's first wife urged him to marry again when she was gone and she prepared her children for the new mother that she would send them from Heaven. "Her will was found by Patmore in her desk in 1860 when the immediate danger [of her death] was passed. In it she says: 'I leave my wedding-ring to your second wife with my love and blessing . . . also, I leave you my grateful acknowledgement of your goodness and love to me, my last prayer that God may bless and console you, my first, last, and only love. If in a year or two you are able to marry again, do so happily, feeling that if my spirit can watch you, it will love her who makes you happy, and not envy her the reward of a part of your love, the best years of which I have had.' Patmore records that, 'scarcely comprehending the profundity of her self-abnegation in a matter in which he himself would have felt so differently,' he remonstrated with her, and that in answer she referred him to the Scriptural permission, adding, 'You cannot be faithful to God and unfaithful to me'; and in a letter written a year later, she says that as regards the children, in taking a second wife, 'there will be no change from one rule to the other, so fatal to discipline and good feeling. You will be able to help and advise with a freedom you could never do to a stranger, and your dear wife, whom you will love as a friend, will soon learn that her best way of expressing her love for you will be to watch tenderly over your little lambs—and surely she must have a hard heart who will not love such pretty and amiable children as ours . . . I have brought the children to look forward to your second marriage as a probable and desirable thing. They will not prejudice their new mother against them by giving her an ill reception. The two little ones will feel her to be their natural parent. May God bless you and keep you and direct you in this and all your steps.'" (Champneys I, pp. 133–34.)

Many of these details find almost literal expression in *Victories of Love,* Bk. II, Letter viii, From Jane to Frederick (ll. 131–45) in which Jane says to her husband:

"The only bond I hold you to
Is that which nothing can undo.
A man is not a young man twice;
And if, of his young years, he lies
A faithful score in one wife's breast,
She need not mind who has the rest.
In this do what you will, dear Love,
And feel quite sure that I approve.
And, should it chance as it may be,
Give her my wedding-ring from me;
And never dream that you can err
T'wards me by being good to her;
Nor let remorseful thoughts destroy
In you the kindly flowering joy
And pleasure of the natural life."

Despite all this, in trying to reconcile these two loves Patmore suffered as only they suffer in whom intensity of human affection is joined with a fierce determination to be faithful to God.

It may be that Patmore still remembered the following passage from *Amoris Effigies* in which the author speaks of conjugal love: "The *Love* does not dye with its departed Object . . . Nay even after the last Separation, his *ever, ever* surviving Friend shall live in his tenacious Memory, as if he were divided from him only by the little Intervals of Absence: And as often as he embraces his sweet Phantasm, he will not yield him dead. You do nothing, ye Fates, we still continue our Commerce, we are still a loving Couple; you have robb'd others of a Man, but me not so much as of a shadow. Before we had but one Soul betwixt us, but now but one Body. He is lodg'd in me as in his Star or Orb." (Translation, pp. 11–12.)

1–10. Here the poet describes how, after the freshness of his sorrow when he grieved equally in mind and heart, gradually his sorrow grew less and less. In *Victories of Love* (Bk. II, Letter viii, ll. 117–130), making Jane his mouthpiece in her letter to Frederick, Patmore had written:

"Oh, should the mournful honeymoon
Of death be over strangely soon,
And life-long resolutions, made
In grievous haste, as quickly fade,
Seeming the truth of grief to mock,
Think, Dearest, 'tis not by the clock
That sorrow goes! A month of tears
Is more than many, many years
Of common time. Shun, if you can,
However, any passionate plan.
Grieve with the heart; let not the head
Grieve on, when grief of heart is dead;
For all the powers of life defy
A superstitious constancy."

Here we have the poet's answer to his own question:

"Besides, where all things limp and halt,
Could I go straight, should I alone
Have kept my love without default
Pitch'd at the true and heavenly tone?"
(*Angel in the House,* Bk. II, Canto vii, ll. 61–64.)

11–15. Here is the poet's deliberate struggle against *all the* defiant *powers of life,* to maintain his *superstitious constancy.* It was then that he prayed with his head in *unfeeling prayer,* when he could no longer pray with his heart.

27–36. The power of love's sacrifice to quicken joy is one of Patmore's fondest themes.

37–38. Patmore's idealism is never unbalanced. His human love was an awful reality and it could not be satisfied by a dream—even by so beautiful a dream as he has just described.

40–52. Note the quickening power of sacrifice in that expression of divine love which we call prayer, when the poet is ready to accept the greatest sacrifice that can be asked of him:

bliss
Wherein She has no part.

45–49. There is a close parallel between this prayer and the prayer of Our Savior in Gethsemane: "Father, if Thou wilt, remove this chalice from me: but yet not my will but Thine be done." (St. Luke XXII, 42.)

49. *submit,* originally, "consent."

53–58. That the law of God permits re-marriage when one of the parties is dead, is clear from the tradition of the Church and from such scriptural texts as Romans VII, 2–3, and this from 1 Corinthians VII, 39: "A woman is bound by the law as long as her husband liveth; but if her husband die, she is at liberty: let her marry to whom she will; only in the Lord." (Cf. *supra, Theme.*)

53–54. Between these lines, originally, the following line was inserted:

"Another wears thy ring upon her hand."

55. *thy veiled mind,* originally, " 'twas thy command."

57. Originally this line read: "It is thy duty and thou canst not be."

65–88. His love for his second wife, intensified by her *delusive likeness* to his first wife, restored *sensitive delight* to his *poor brain* so that he *lived again.*

68–70. These lines do not appear in the original version. In their place we read:

"To her some tender heed
Unmeant by me
Unmeant by me, yet such" *etc.*

MAGNA EST VERITAS

Theme: The central idea is philosophical or theological as it is in "The Two Deserts," "Crest and Gulf," and "The Cry at Midnight." There can be little objection to what Patmore says in these odes but in some of them the manner in which he says it is, at times, too bitterly satirical to be convincing. But is is impossible to read them without being made increasingly aware of the ultimate triumph of the will of God and the futility of man's striving against it. For, whatever may have been Patmore's faults he was essentially humble. "It is not fit," he once wrote, "that men who hear these songs should not know that I am no better than themselves. May I so do my works that men seeing them may praise my Father and leave me from them,

Exempt
In the safe shadow of the world's contempt."
(Champneys II, p. 69.)

It would seem incredible that anyone could so misinterpret this poem as to write of it: "There are again poems . . . the pessimistic tone of which we find it hard to reconcile with any Christian creed. Such is the short poem, 'Magna est Veritas.'" (*Reviews and Essays,* D. C. Tovey, p. 166.) Far from being pessimistic, the poem is a stern expression of divine optimism. (Cf. "Saint Valentine's Day," *Theme;* "Crest and Gulf," ll. 33–36.)

2. The paradox of this line is characteristically Patmorean and exemplifies how little of quietism there was in his idea of *repose.* (Cf. "Winter," l. 6.)

4. The gladness of the ocean springs from seeming purposelessness which is really the purposeful though unconscious fulfilment of God's will. (Cf. "Legem Tuam Dilexi.")

5–6. Cf. "L'Allegro," ll. 42–49.

7–10. Here Patmore expresses the humility born of truth through the realization of how unnecessary we are, from God's side, in working out the divinely appointed purpose of the world—*For we can do nothing against the truth; but for the truth.* (2 Corinthians XIII, 8.) But St. Bernard remarks: "There is a humility which truth engenders in us and it has no warmth. And there is a humility which charity produces in us and sets on fire. One consists in affection; the other in knowledge . . . It is one thing for a man constrained by the light of truth, to have a lowly opinion of himself. It is quite another for him, assisted by the grace of charity, freely to *consent to the humble* (Romans XII, 16). The one is a matter of necessity. The other is a free act of the will." (Sermons on the *Canticle of Canticles:* Sermon XLII, §§ 6–7; translation pp. 165–66.)

The reconcilement of truth and untruth—good and evil—that has so vexed the poets and philosophers of the world is here effected by the ultimate and complete triumph of Truth. In Patmore's ideas on good and evil there is nothing of such obfuscations as Blake's in "The Marriage of Heaven and Hell."

9–10. In his discussion of the question, "Whether the Will of God is Always Fulfilled," St. Thomas quotes Psalm CXIII, 11: *God hath done all things whatsoever He would,* and then adds: "The will of God must needs always be fulfilled . . . Since the will of God is the universal cause of all things, it is impossible that the divine will should not produce its effect. Hence that which seems to depart from the divine will in one order, returns to it in another order; as does the sinner, who by sin falls away from the divine will as much as in him lies, yet falls back into the order of that will, when by its justice he is punished." (*Summa* I, q. 19, art. 6.) And again: "As Augustine says (*Enchir.* XI): *Since God is the highest good, He would not allow any evil to exist in His works unless His omnipotence and goodness were such as to bring good out of evil.* This is part of the infinite goodness of God, that He should allow evil to exist, and out of it produce good." (*Ibid.* q. 2, art. 3.)

1867

Publication: The last of the Nine Odes, 1868.

Title: 1867 was the year of the Second Reform Bill. The First Reform Bill, 1831, took power from the nobles and gave it to the middle classes; The Second, 1867, gave some power to workers and extended suffrage to nearly 3,000,000 voters; the Third, 1884, gave even more workmen the power to vote; but universal man-suffrage, later followed by woman-suffrage, was not granted until after the World War. Patmore seems to ignore the fact that the Reformed Parliament elected in 1833 had introduced many reforms in British affairs.

In the edition of Patmore's poems edited by Champneys we read the following note: "In this year [1867] the middle and upper classes were disenfranchised by Mr. Disraeli's Government, and the final destruction of the liberties of England by the Act of 1884 rendered inevitable." It were truer to say that in 1867 the upper and middle classes were merely deprived of their unjust monopoly of political power and in 1884 the liberties of England became actual realities instead of political mouthings.

Theme and Place in Sequence: After the Nature Odes (cf. "St. Valentine's Day," *etc.*) and the odes in which domestic love is treated (cf. "Beata," *etc.*) the poet turns in this and in two other

Political Odes, "Peace" and "1880–85," to *God's remoter service, public zeal.* This line from "L'Allegro" is the best explanation of Patmore's inclusion of the Political Odes in the sequence of *The Unknown Eros.*

Tone: It is acutely autobiographical as we learn from Patmore's preface to the Nine Odes: "I meant to have extended and developed this series of Odes until they formed an integral work expressing an idea which I have long had at heart; but feelings which are partly conveyed by the concluding piece have discouraged me from fulfilling my intention."

Strangely enough, as Champneys points out, Patmore's hopeless pessimism in things political existed simultaneously with an extreme optimism in matters of every day life. " 'His house was the only house in England he could have brought himself to live in, Henry's poems the best ever written at his age, Bertha's drawings the finest ever put on paper.' At the same time the political outlook was never less than desperate. No statesman on either side was to be relied on for a moment: the distinction between parties was only that between the various shades of black, and scarcely worth making; England, a corpse simulating life only by the exuberance of its corruption." (Vol. I, p. 360.) (Cf. Patmore's essay, "A 'Pessimist' Outlook.")

Political Views: Champneys establishes the following very interesting connection between Patmore's political views and his doctrine concerning the relationship between man and woman, in which woman's proper attitude was that of subordination to man. "It would, I think," writes Champneys, "be scarcely fanciful to trace his political convictions to the same essential ideas. It was, in his view, necessary that the weaker or more 'feminine' element in the state should be governed by the 'masculine' and strong, its emotional and thoughtless members, those who seek the mere gratification of the moment, by the wise and far-sighted who can apprehend more permanent interests. He had no belief whatever in the collective wisdom of the multitude—failed to see:

How many grains of sifted sand,
Heap'd make a likely house to stand,
How many fools one Solomon.
("L'Allegro," ll. 78–80.)

He held that according to eternal and irrefragable law, power should be exclusively in the hands of those who by birth and education were in a position to attain to political wisdom. That the material interests of the masses could be promoted only by their having a share in government was an argument which did not touch him. He cared not a jot for 'comfort,' holding that it had proved in no degree conducive to spiritual and moral growth, but rather the reverse; and this was the only kind of welfare for which he had the least regard. To him, a democratic constitution was not merely a house built with sand, but was further a direct violation of the eternal and immutable law by which, as with the sexes, the weak must always be, and find their true happiness in being, subordinate to the strong . . .

"It seems scarcely necessary to add that, if he was in such respects an 'aristocrat,' the term must not be taken in any social sense: no one could have been more free from any approach to snobbishness. The one exclusiveness which he showed was the desire to associate only with what seemed to him to be best in character, intellect and capacity for religious ideas; nor in such matters was he likely to accept any standard but that of his individual judgment." (Champneys II. pp. 14–16.)

We must take these facts into consideration in judging Patmore's views as expressed in this and the other Political Odes. It is not fair to attribute to him without qualification, the sentiments and tone of Sir Lob's statement in "Tamerton Church Tower":

I hate the herd that vulgar be
And, O, the stars are fair!

(Cf. *Reviews and Essays,* Rev. D. C. Tovey, pp. 160–166.)

And yet it is difficult to see any great difference between Sir Lob's views and Patmore's own view as expressed in the following sentence: "Democracy is only a continually shifting aristocracy of money, impudence, animal energy, and cunning, in which the best grub gets the best carrion; and the level to which it tends to bring all things is not a mountain tableland, as its promoters would have their victims think, but the unwholesome platitude of the fen and the morass, of which black envy would enjoy the malaria so long as all others shared it." ("Thoughts on Knowledge, Opinion and Inequality.")

Patmore was greatly indebted to the *Summa Theologica* of St. Thomas for many of his fundamental ideas and their corollaries. He would have improved his political ideals by adopting such views as this: "Two points are to be observed concerning the right ordering of rulers in a state or nation. One is that all should take some share in the government: for this form of constitution ensures peace among the people, commends itself to all, and is most enduring as stated in *Polit.* ii. The other point is to be observed in respect of the kinds of government, or the different ways in which the constitutions are established. For whereas these differ in kind, as the Philosopher states (*Polit.* iii), nevertheless the first place is held by the *kingdom,* where the power of government is vested in one; and *aristocracy,* which signifies government by the best, where the power of government is vested in a few. Accordingly, the best form of government is in a state or kingdom, wherein one is given the power to preside over all; while under him are others having governing powers: and yet a government of this kind is shared by all, both because all are eligible to govern, and because the rulers are chosen by all. For this is the best form of polity, being partly kingdom, since there is one at the head of all; partly aristocracy, in so far as a number of persons are set in authority; partly democracy, *i.e.,* government by the people, in so far as the rulers can be chosen from the people, and the people have the right to choose their rulers." (*Summa* II. i, q. 105, art. 1.)

2. *their Jew:* Disraeli who carried the Second Reform Bill. In his essay, "Courage in Politics," Patmore writes: "Disraeli had, indeed, many of the qualities required by a popular leader; but he had not the courage to throw up place rather than disembowel his Reform Bill of all that distinguished it from the Bill of the preceding Ministry, the principles of which he was called to the head of the Government expressly to oppose."

3–4. In 1860 and again in 1867 the Conservatives were pledged to oppose the Reform Bills and actually did oppose them until they saw the strength of the Liberals. Then they passed the Bills and slew the *Trust* they were *pledged to keep from wrong.*

6–7. On the authority of Champneys it appears that Patmore himself was unwilling to indicate the exact period of English history to which he here refers. "In vain did one endeavour to make him fix by date this *mild and almost mythic time of England's prime,* prepared to show, if one could, that wherever in time he placed it, it had, in the light of ordinary reason certain rather serious defects: in vain did one call attention to hopeful symptoms in the present." (Vol. I, p. 361.)

9–10. Patmore's aristocratic lament for the passing *freedom of the few* sounds strange to a people long accustomed to look upon democracy as a panacea for all social and political ills. But we must remember the reason for Patmore's views: "For material improvement, such as the social rise of the working-classes, he cared nothing, seeing that it did not appear to him to involve that spiritual and moral advance which was all he cared for." (Champneys I, p. 361.)

12–14. Cf. 'Sing Us One of the Songs of Sion' and "Prophets Who Cannot Sing."

15–21. This blend of regret for the passing of the old regime, and

Patmore's pessimistic prophecy concerning the new order is reminiscent of Wellington's feeling in 1832 when the First Reform Bill was passed.

22. *two daws,* originally, "jays twain."
daws, the common people.
swans, the aristocrats.

22–23. In the Nine Odes between these two lines we find the following:

"Harsh words and brief asks the dishonour'd Year!"

23. *outlaw'd Best:* the Aristocrats deprived of their monopoly of political power. (Cf. *supra, Political Views,* and "1880–85," l. 15.)

29. *the dark and selfish brood:* the masses.

34. *the plain:* the level of the common people. (Cf. *supra, Political Views.*)

35–39. It may have been *England's Law* that Aristocrats alone should reign. But it is at least doubtful that it is *Nature's* and *Heaven's.*

40–43. After the Napoleonic Wars the heavy taxes imposed upon English commerce tended to give more and more power to the money-making class, the *Traders.* Simultaneously the drop in food-prices tended to impoverish the land-holding class of Aristocrats, the *Best.*

40. *the sordid Trader:* the wealthy middle-class engaged in commerce and business, not the aristocratic land-owners.

42. *the Mechanic vain:* the working-man.

43. *the proud toy:* the power to vote which the working-man, in Patmore's opinion, was capable of using only as a vain *toy* of which he was *proud.*

44. *broke,* originally, "sapp'd."

45–49. The real *beauty* of the Aristocrats died with their honor when they surrendered their monopoly of power to the lower and middle classes. They retained only the external trappings of peerage—seats in the House of Lords, coronets, robes of state and coats of arms—all of which might lead them to dream that they were still the minor deities they once were when they possessed the power as well as the trappings of Olympus.

47. *not less,* originally, "no less."

51. *Masters:* the common people, *i.e.* the middle class and some of the workers. The proletariat was not granted suffrage until after the Great War.

67. *The great ship:* the Ship of State, a common metaphor from the time of Horace to our own Longfellow.

73–74. An adaptation of Our Lord's words: "the night cometh when no man can work." (St. John IX, 4.)

75. *Liberty in every Land lies slain.* Here Patmore probably re-

fers to the various political revulsions throughout Europe. The rebellion of Poland against Russian oppression in 1863 had been brutally crushed. In Turkey recent massacres of Bulgars and Armenians had made the lot of Christians insufferable. The contest over Schleswig-Holstein in Germany, had at first resulted in separating these two provinces from Denmark and finally in their annexation by Prussia under Bismark's autocratic rule. In the United States the North had been victorious at Appomattox in April, 1865, and to Englishmen of Patmore's sympathies this seemed a slaying of liberty. Maximilian of Austria had, with French assistance, converted the republic of Mexico into an empire which was overthrown in June, 1867, when Maximilian faced a firing squad. But there were other happenings in Europe to which Patmore's political pessimism seems to have blinded him. A constitutional, independent monarchy in Roumania had, in 1866, succeeded its despotic rule by Turkey. In 1867 a successful uprising of the Serbs had expelled the Turks from Serbia. And the Austrians, in 1867, made many concessions to the liberty of the Magyars in Hungary.

76. *the two Tyrannies:* probably the irreligion and democracy, so-called, of European revolutionists.

77–80. Our Lord foretold His coming on the Last Day, the signs that would precede it, and its bearing upon *the elect—the righteous few:* "For there shall be then great tribulation, such as hath not been from the beginning of the world until now, neither shall be . . . But for the sake of the elect those days shall be shortened." (St. Matthew XXIV, 21–22.) Patmore, like many during the World War, saw in the awful culmination of calamities in his day, the fulfilment of the signs foretold by Our Lord as an indication that the end of the world was near. The suspension of the prophecies, *At supplication of the righteous few,* is a reminder of Abraham's prayer for Sodom and Gomorrah. (Cf. Genesis, XVIII.)

82. *the Time of Grace:* the visible coming of Christ on the Last Day.

83. *Breathless be song,* originally, "Hush'd be all song."

84. *Christ's own:* the Elect.

86. *the gray secret lingering in the East:* the grey dusk visible in the East, amidst the surrounding darkness is precursive of the dawn, Christ's second coming: "For as lightning cometh out of the east, and appeareth even into the west: so shall also the coming of the Son of man be." (St. Matthew XXIV, 27.) Though the coming of this dawn is certain, the time is secret: "But of that day and hour no one knoweth, not the Angels of heaven, but the Father alone." (St. Matthew XXIV, 36.)

'IF I WERE DEAD'

Publication: First published in *The Pall Mall Gazette* Nov. 14, 1876, it was included in Odes I–XXXI, 1877.

Theme: The occasion which inspired this ode is not clear from known facts. But it would seem a safe conjecture that the first line was spoken by Patmore's first wife during her last illness. Here Patmore recalls it with the intensity that death brings to human love.

"Too soon, too soon comes Death to show
We love more deeply than we know."
(*Victories of Love,* Bk. II, Letter v, ll. 5–6.)

(cf. "Beata" and "Toys," *Theme.*)

Technique: It is difficult to justify Patmore's rhymes in this poem. They would seem to be more lawless than bold.

13–16. These lines did not appear in the first published version.

PEACE

Publication: First in the *Pall Mall Gazette,* Jan. 18, 1876, and included among Odes I–XXXI, in 1877.

Occasion: It was about 1874, three years after Patmore's visit to the chief battle-fields of the Franco-Prussian War. During his stay in Germany he had been strongly impressed by the strength and aggressiveness of its militarism. He was not proud of England by comparison. With unwarlike spirit she had stood aloof from the Franco-Prussian struggle, and with dishonorable methods of diplomacy she had launched her newly-adopted policy of colonial expansion. Yet England was not altogether a peaceful nation during this time, as is evident from Francis Thompson's poem, "The Nineteenth Century." And the apparent peace that she enjoyed was built upon the exactions of superior strength rather than upon justice. (Cf. Thompson's ode, "Peace.")

Theme: In the other two Political Odes, "1867" and "1880–85," Patmore finds his chief inspiration in *God's remoter service, public zeal* ("L'Allegro," l. 28), as it should be found in individual citizens and in particular political parties. Here, the theme is rather the reciprocal *public zeal* with which the nation should cherish and safeguard the national honor and thus protect the honor of its individual citizens. In the other Political Odes Patmore stresses the fact that for the individual there is no such thing as "good politics" and bad morality. Here, he emphasizes the same obligation as binding upon the national conscience. For the nation there can be no "good diplomacy" which is bad morality. With unfailing logic he applies to England the Nation, the principles that in "Pain," ll. 12–29, he applies to the individual. Marie Lataste does the same in the following passage: "Temporal peace is peace in the family, in cities, in empires; it comes from charity, because charity is the union of hearts, and the union of hearts is the peace of families, and the union of families is the peace of cities, and the union of cities is the peace of kingdoms and empires; for charity is the accord, the agreement, of two persons, of many persons, of many different peoples. Where there is no charity there is no peace." (Vol. II, pp. 58–59.)

Today it is difficult to share Patmore's enthusiasm for German militarism. But it were well if the nations of the world had a more sympathetic appreciation of the underlying principles of this ode. Clearly, they are as alien to the wrecklessness of Junkerism as they are to the irrational spinelessness of a Pacifism that is content with peace at any price. According to Patmore's ideal a war undertaken to preserve a nation's honor is often a necessity of fidelity to the dictates of the Nation's conscience. As Padraic Pearse expresses it: "War is a terrible thing, but war is not an evil thing. It is the things that make war necessary that are evil. The tyrannies that wars break, the lying formulae that wars overthrow, the hypocrisies that wars strip naked, are evil." ("Peace and the Gael.") And again: "Bloodshed is a cleansing and a sanctifying thing, and the nation which regards it as the final horror has lost its manhood." ("The Coming Revolution.")

Such sentiments as these can only be understood when referred to the Sacrifice of Calvary and the glory of Thabor—the common source of the inspiration of Pearse and Patmore, an inspiration which springs from the fearless application of the teaching and example of Christ, to the life of men and nations. This does not imply a lack of appreciation of the horrors of war, and it is perfectly consistent with unceasing efforts to prevent war by every honorable means. Patmore appreciated this fully. In *St. James Gazette,* March 23, 1887, he wrote: "If the world is not in the end either to explode like a bombshell or to become the appanage of a simple absolute despot, some means must be found before very long of lessening the risks of war or of stopping them altogether; and the reference by common consent of cases of war to an ultimate umpire, assisted in his decisions by arguments proposed, in open counsel, by the differing parties, seems to be the only conceivable mode of attaining this end." ("Courage in Politics and Other Essays," p. 24.) Patmore was too clear-sighted a prophet to fail to indentify the one person in the world who could effectively act as such an umpire—the Holy Father. Strangely enough he has been consistently excluded from all the international Peace Conferences that have been held from Patmore's day to our own—an eventuality unthinkable even to so great a pessimist as Patmore, as is clear from the following passage: "While, then, war is rapidly becoming a more and more devastating and intolerable evil, while hosts that count by millions are even now confronting each other with uplifted arms that 'mean no second blow,' the world seems to be growing ripe for a solution which has hitherto in its recent history been impossible. It may be a good while yet, and Europe may have to be deluged several times with blood, before the necessity is felt to be hard enough to enforce recourse in case of quarrel to an umpire; but, when that time comes, who will there be that can be qualified for that position but one? Who will be found sufficiently disencumbered of personal interests and political partialities, and at the same time possessed, by his position, of a guarantee of sufficient knowledge and statesmanship for the post?" (*Ibid.* pp. 26–27.)

1–14. Read Thompson's ode, "Peace," ll. 54–91.

4. This line is reminiscent of Our Savior's lament over Jerusalem: "If thou hadst known, and that in this thy day, the things that are to thy peace!" (St. Luke XIX, 42.)

5–7. The reconcilement of peace and conflict in Christ's ideal is thus briefly stated by St. Thomas in the *Summa* II. ii, q. 37: "Just as a man's will that adheres to God is a right rule, to disaccord with which is a sin, so too a man's will that is opposed to God is a perverse rule, to disaccord with which is good. Hence to cause a discord, whereby a good concord resulting from charity is destroyed, is a grave sin: wherefore it is written: *Six things there are, which the Lord hateth, and the seventh His soul detesteth,* which seventh is stated to be *him that soweth discord among brethren* (Proverbs VI, 16, 19). On the other hand, to arouse a discord whereby an evil concord (*i.e.* concord in an evil will) is destroyed, is praiseworthy. In this way Paul was to be commended for sowing discord among those who concorded together in evil, because Our Lord also said of Himself: *I came not to send peace, but the sword.*" (St. Matthew X, 34.)

5. *Honour is peace:* St. Thomas in his treatise on peace reminds us of the Psalmist's words: *Much peace have they that love Thy Law* (Psalm CXVIII, 165). Again: "Peace is the work of justice indirectly, in so far as justice removes the obstacles to peace: but it is

the work of charity directly, since charity, according to its very nature, causes peace." (*Summa* II. ii, q. 29, art. 3.) In the following passage St. Thomas (*ibid.* art. 2) clearly distinguishes false peace from true: "There can be no true peace except where the appetite is directed to what is truly good, since every evil, though it may appear good in a way, so as to calm the appetite in some respect, has, nevertheless many defects, which cause the appetite to remain restless and disturbed. Hence true peace is only in good men and about good things. The peace of the wicked is not a true peace but a semblance thereof, wherefore it is written: *Whereas they lived in a great war of ignorance, they call so many and so great evils peace.*" (Wisdom XIV, 22.)

7. In this line Patmore combines two paradoxical texts into one: "Peace I leave with you, My peace I give unto you," (St. John XIV, 27), and: "I came not to send peace, but the sword." (St. Matthew X, 34.)

8–10. That the very sacrifices which the soul fears in remote prospect are cherished when *confronted near,* is the theme of the last lines of Thompson's "The Hound of Heaven."

9. For Patmore as for St. Thomas the things which make for peace are *the things which make for joy.* (Cf. "Winter," l. 6 and "Pain," ll. 44–60.) Apropos of this subject Patmore once made a prophecy concerning England, which will interest us as Americans even if it does not please us: "In America, where it has been well said there is everywhere comfort but no joy . . . we probably have the mirror of our own very near future." ("A Modern Classic, William Barnes.")

11–12. The most notorious example of bribery in England's colonial expansion was that of Cecil Rhodes. (Cf. Thompson's ode, "Cecil Rhodes.")

14–15. This description of a sudden and unprovided death is notably Patmorean as are the lines that follow.

16–20. The very essence of the poem is here. The circumstances which inspired these lines are interesting: "Patmore was walking with his daughter Gertrude, on the Common near Tunbridge Wells, and had for a long time been silent and absorbed, when he suddenly asked her if she had a piece of paper with her. She had none, but gave him her linen cuff on which she found these lines—lines which must have been constantly present to the minds of those who know the Odes, during the last few months [at the time of the Boer War, 1899–1902] when most days have brought news of the heroic deaths of our soldiers." (Champneys I, pp. 241–42.)

18–20. The grace of justification may be obtained by Baptism of

Blood, *i.e.,* by suffering martyrdom for the faith. That is the teaching of the Catholic Church. But Patmore's adaptation of it in these lines is rather bold.

21–33. The austerity of these lines is a reminder of Mrs. Meynell's poem, "Length of Days," written amidst a general wail of regret for the young lives sacrificed in the Great War.

21. *home's bond:* Patmore may have intended to play upon the meaning attributed to this expression by a popular etymology according to which, *husband* is derived from *house-band* or *bond.*

24. In 1871, the year after the Franco-Prussian War, Patmore visited Germany.

32. Patmore, it seems, accepted the view that as a result of the Ems Dispatch, Prussia went to war against France to protect her honor.

34–40. Here Patmore has written another indictment of "good politics," and a glorification of honest statesmanship. (Cf. *supra, Theme.*)

41. In *times past:* "The fool hath said in his heart: There is no God." (Psalm XIII, 1.) *But in his heart the fool now saith: etc.*

47. *a pious Pilot:* Queen Victoria.

55. *Yon bully:* this may possibly be Bismarck, who was a *bully* in the eyes of those pacifist Englishmen to whom this line is attributed.

56. *our friends:* Austria was an ancient friend and ally of Great Britain and after 1852 France, too, had been friendly.

69. Patmore likens England's settlement of the Alabama Claims, to *the old bargain of the Saxon with the Dane* when, in 991, Aethelred II levied a national tax upon the Saxons as a means of raising the tribute which was the price of the cessation of the ravages of the *Dane.* The Alabama Claims were claims brought against England for losses in American trade caused by ships fitted out in English ports under the direction of the Confederate government. The chief of these was "The Alabama." The international tribunal to which the question was referred awarded $15,500,000 in gold to the United States.

72–74. These lines recall an incident in the legend of St. Brandan. During the famous sea voyage of the saint and his companions they came to what appeared to be an island. "The monks landed and made a fire on which to dress their dinner, but when the fire became hot and the meat was almost cooked, the island began to move through the water. The monks fled in terror to their ship, leaving the fire and meat behind them, and marvelling much at the motion of the island. St. Brandan, who had remained in the vessel, comforted them and told them they had landed on the back of a great fish named Jasconye." (*Ireland and the Early Church,* J. M. Flood, pp. 42–43.)

72. *chine:* back.

75–80. "So the king took the two sons of Respha the daughter of Aia, whom she bore to Saul, . . . and the five sons of Michol the daughter of Saul . . . And gave them into the hands of the Gabaonites: and they crucified them on a hill before the Lord: and these seven died together in the first days of the harvest, when the barley began to be reaped. And Respha the daughter of Aia took haircloth, and spread it under her upon the rock from the beginning of the harvest, till water dropped upon them out of heaven: and suffered neither the birds to tear them by day, not the beasts by night." (2 Kings XXI, 8–10.)

83–85. This Patmorean irony had its inspiration in the Victorian echo of the Chosen People's cry to their prophets: "Behold not for us those things that are right: speak unto us pleasant things, see errors for us." (Isaias XXX, 10.)

86–96. Nothing so aroused Patmore's indignation as the spirit of *laissez faire.*

99–101. The power of this same spirit in poets is vividly expressed in Arthur O'Shaughnessy's great Ode:

"One man with a dream, at pleasure,
  Shall go forth and conquer a crown;
And three with a new song's measure
  Can trample a kingdom down."

But it is in the last lines of Padraic Pearse's play, "The Singer," that we find the most inspiring expression of this ideal in modern literature. On fire with an intensity of patriotism that borders upon religious ecstasy, the Singer cries: "One man can free a people as one Man redeemed the world. I will take no pike, I will go into the battle with bare hands. I will stand up before the Gall as Christ hung naked before men on the tree!" In the *Aeneid* (Bk. I, ll. 148–53) Virgil describes the power of a single man of honor to quell the violence of the rabble.

102–103. Silence such as Christ's in the presence of Herod, is a sign of the greatest fortitude. But silence such as Patmore excoriates here is sheer cowardice that too often masquerades as prudence. "Civil war can be waged by words as well as by swords; and in such conditions a man who refuses to take up the arms which are in fashion, should he be able to find or make an opportunity of wielding them with effect, is just as much a 'funk' as one who sits still and sees his house sacked and his family insulted while he has any hope of being able to defend them." (*Courage in Politics and Other Essays,* p. 19.)

104–105. We have known our own

dark hour
When phrases [were] *in power—*

"Make the world safe for democracy," for instance.

107. Nations as well as men are torn between the alternatives of life's inescapable dilemma expressed in this line and in these from Joseph Plunkett's "Heaven in Hell" (ll. 112–13):

"But I, alas! am torn between
The things unseen and the things seen."

113–14. These lines are quoted at the conclusion of Patmore's essay, "Minding One's Own Business." (Cf. *supra,* ll. 102–103.)

A FAREWELL

Publication: In *The Pall Mall Gazette,* Nov. 7, 1876, and included among Odes I–XXXI, 1877.

Theme: This is Patmore's valedictory to his dead wife's religious faith and to the former unity of belief he shared with her in life and with her spirit after her death, July 5, 1862. A devout and sincere Protestant, "she had been terrified from her cradle," wrote Patmore in his Autobiography, "with the hideous phantom which Puritanism conjures up when the Catholic religion is named . . . Only a few days before she died she said to me with tears, 'When I am gone, they (the Catholics) will get you; and then I shall see you no more.'" (Champneys II, p. 53.) When Patmore became a Catholic in 1864 he was conscious of having fulfilled the first part of his wife's prophecy: "When I am gone they (the Catholics) will get you." In this ode he expresses his fearful apprehensiveness of the fulfilment of the second part: "then I shall see you no more"—a prophecy that foretells a spiritual separation in eternity as well as in time. But Patmore's fear is tempered by the hope that in the revelation of eternity when vision succeeds faith, this eternal separation may be averted. (Cf. *infra,* ll. 18–25; "Beata" and "Toys," *Theme.*)

The full significance of this ode follows as a corollary to Patmore's constantly recurring theme that conjugal union, chiefly spiritual, is effected by an agreement of judgment and will. Even before he became a Catholic he thus expressed the necessity of a common religious faith as an essential of nuptial love:

"For, though we very seldom name
Religion, we now think the same!
Oh, what a bar is thus removed
To loving and to being loved!
For no agreement really is
In anything where none's in this."
(*Victories of Love,* Bk. II, Letter i, ll. 33–38.)

1. At times our hearts beat in union with our intellects and wills and lend vigor and ease to our good deeds. At other times virtue lies in unyielding fidelity to the clear dictates of conscience, when every affection of the heart pulls violently in the opposite direction. It is in the Dark Night of the Soul rather than in the ecstasy of Union that great mystics prove their spiritual greatness, and ordinary, plodding souls prove their fidelity to God in desolation rather than in consolation.

When we remember Patmore's intense love of his first wife, his profound reverence for her personal sanctity, his knowledge of her sincere and awful dread of the Catholic Church expressed almost with her last breath, we may imagine the passionate revulsion of his *heart,* at the clear dictates of his conscience and his *will* to follow it in becoming a Catholic. Here, indeed, is a separation more absolute and more poignant than that of "Departure" and "The Azalea." That parting was temporary and effected by God alone. This one was to be eternal and the result of his own deliberate choice in following the stern teaching of Christ: "If any man come to Me and hate not his father and mother and wife and children and brethren and sisters, yea and his own life also, he cannot be My disciple." (St. Luke XIV, 26.)

4. The *solace* of both lay in the realization that both had been faithful to the dictates of their respective consciences even though the conscience of one was through invincible ignorance erroneous.

8. *to persevere:* Great as is the sacrifice of setting out on an *opposed path,* fortitude in enduring the prolonged sacrifice of perseverance along that path is the ultimate test of fidelity. "He that shall persevere unto the end, he shall be saved." (St. Matthew X, 22.)

12–17. Cf. "Tired Memory," ll. 1–10.

18–25. This is no vain hope. It is founded on truth. There are Christians who after the manner of Walt Whitman, would substitute a sort of confraternity of good-natured rogues for the Communion of Saints. But the hope expressed here is built upon no such concept. It has as its sure foundation the stern truth that two souls, each faithful to his own conscience, may follow *opposed paths* in life and yet be faithful to God. (Cf. *supra,* l. 4.) Such souls will surely meet in Heaven, *amazed* at the revelation of Truth in Whom their differences, are, in a sense, reconciled, as they look upon Him and upon each other, *With tears of recognition never dry.* Here is no reconcilement of Truth and Error in a compromise effected through concessions on both sides, such as we find in Blake's "The Marriage of Heaven and Hell." This is the clear, unconditional triumph of Truth over Error when both are viewed, not in the dim light of human reason or of false religious faith founded upon invincible ignorance, but in the presence of the Beatific Vision whose light dispels error and reveals the unveiled vision of Truth which "We see now through a glass in a dark manner; but then face to face." (1 Corinthians XIII, 12.) In that moment, according to Catholic teaching, the soul that has been faithful to a conscience perfectly conformed to God's law, will glory in that unveiled vision of Truth. And the soul invincibly ignorant, that has been faithful to an erroneous conscience will glory no less in that same vision—simultaneously a revelation of Eternal Truth and of its own error. For, as St. Thomas writes: "Although the judgment of an erring reason is not derived from God, yet the erring reason puts forward its judgment as being true, and consequently as being derived from God, from Whom is all truth." (*Summa* II, i, q. 19, art. 5.) When the error of such souls is dispelled and the truth of others is confirmed in the revelation of Truth itself, souls spiritually separated in life, through error, will be spiritually united in eternity, through Truth.

"The spirit of man is like a kite which rises by means of those very forces which seem to oppose its rise; the tie that joins it to the earth, the opposing winds of temptation, and the weight of earth-born affections which it carries with it into the sky." (*Aurea Dicta,* XII.) And again: " 'To him that waits all things reveal themselves,' provided that he has the courage not to deny in the darkness what he has seen in the light." (*Ibid.* XLIX.)

1880–85

Publication: In *Odes* I–XLVI, 1879, under the title, "The Merry Murder," taking the place of "1877" which had been included in *Odes* I–XXXI, 1877.

Title: The most significant year of the five included in the title is 1884, the year of the Third Reform Bill whereby popular government became a fact in England.

Theme: Cf. "1867," *Theme.*

2. *Ye Wise:* the aristocrats to whom Patmore, an incurable Tory, attributed wisdom in all things.

by whom Heav'n rules: Cf. "1867," ll. 35–39.

3. *kingly hands:* English lords or aristocrats enjoy some of the prerogatives of kings and are entitled to wear coronets, lesser crowns.

hangman's tools: probably the executioner's axe or sword.

4. Cf. "1867," ll. 6–22.

5. *knaves and fools:* the liberal and popular elements in England, wicked or idiotic, according to Patmore, because they would change an aristocratic form of government into a democracy.

6. *For ages yet to come:* as long as the populace has the right to vote.

7. The political and social strife of England might well be symbolized as *smoke,* compared with the flame of revolution and political cataclysm that had enveloped *other Powers:* France had witnessed Revolutions in 1730, 1848, 1870 and 1889. In 1848, Germany, Austria, Italy and other nations had experienced the bloodshed and arson of insurrection.

9–10. The *tongues* of the common people had been loosed so recently that it was small wonder if their speech was inarticulate and unintelligible.

10. *'Wilder:* bewilder.

11. Patmore here expresses characteristic Tory contempt for the so-called remote and indefinite good for which the newly enfranchised people were striving.

13–14. These lines do Patmore small honor. The fate of English aristocrats is sealed and *tears are vain,* so let them *laugh* at the blundering idiocy of the unwise populace, as they attempt to use their newly acquired power. Let them laugh, *but not too loudly*—they may be overheard and vengeance may follow.

14. *brave:* here used with scornful irony.

15. The *Best:* οἱ ἄριστοι, the aristocrats. In the opening paragraph of Patmore's essay, "Courage in Politics," we read: "All men are born believers in aristocracy. Who is there—out of the House of Commons—who does not hold the fundamental dogma of politics, that the best should govern? Modern democracy means nothing but the possession of the elective power by ignorant aristocrats: by those who desire that the best should govern, but who have no sufficient means of discovering the best." (Cf. "1867," l. 23.)

Bigger Half. The British people of Patmore's day might well be divided into two classes or halves—one, composed of the upper and middle classes, had enjoyed a monopoly of power, wealth and opportunity until 1867; the other, numerically greater, the lower classes whose gradual rise to power so embittered the Tories. (Cf. "1867," *Title*.)

16. Henceforth the upper and middle classes will be as unable to make themselves heard as if they were actually dumb.

17. *dross:* slag, the refuse material which remains after ore has been smelted.

draff: refuse grain left after beer has been brewed or whiskey distilled.

21. *Tartarus:* Hell.

22. *their Leader:* Gladstone who sponsored the Reform Bill of 1884 and was for many years leader of the Liberals. In his essay, "Courage in Politics," Patmore describes him thus: "It is not the peculiar qualities of Mr. Gladstone, for example; not his profound humility; not his tender sympathies with his Fenian 'flesh and blood'; not his boundless humanity which remembers Mitchelstown, and sends a great army to vain graves, when to do so may improve his chance of helping humanity by securing his success at the next election; not his incomparable power of saying or implying the thing which is not. It is his courage: the courage which dared to make a total revolution in the constitution of the army by a stroke of his pen, in the face of the will of Parliament; which proposed and carried an Irish Coercion Bill that, among other decrees worthy of Louis XIV, revived the powers of *lettres de cachet* and of arbitrary imprisonment, supposed to have fallen forever with the Bastille; which did fifty other things that Lord Salisbury or Lord Hartington would have turned pale at the thought of; and which, now that he is down on his back, bites, kicks, spits and smiles, and will not own for a moment to being beaten: this it is which made him for so many years the supreme favorite of the people, and has been so nearly elevating him to the dignity of the Danton of an English revolution.

"The popularity of parties will henceforward be built upon the same foundation as that of individuals. The Conservatives must look to this. Courage is by no means the quality by which they have been most distinguished since the death of Lord Palmerston, the last man on their side who was 'brick' enough to oppose bullies and braggarts with bold justice instead of craven 'conciliation.'"

23. This is in many ways a very unjust characterization of Gladstone. He was a deeply religious man and enjoyed a high reputation for purity of life.

The *leprosy* here spoken of is the white leprosy of ancient times. In the Old Testament we read: "a leper as white as snow" (4 Kings V, 27)—an expression adopted by Father Tabb in his quatrain, "Father Damien."

24. Gladstone was an eloquent orator. He did not forgive Patmore for such allusions as this. After Tennyson's death when Patmore's name was suggested in connection with the vacant laureateship Gladstone answered that Patmore had died many years before.

25. *Puller at another's hay:* This may refer to Gladstone's doing in 1884 what his opponent Disraeli had done in 1867.

29–46. The sentiment of these lines is found in the passage from Sir Thomas Browne quoted in "L'Allegro," ll. 78–80.

35. Patmore, an extreme Tory, takes for granted that the life of the *Nation* necessarily depends upon the survival of the peculiar social and political inequalities consequent upon the old order.

36–45. In "Crest and Gulf" (ll. 29–32), Patmore declares that not all motion is forward motion. Here he goes a step further and says that not even all forward motion is *Progress*. The passage is an adaptation of the incident narrated in Our Savior's public life, "when He was come into the country of the Gerasens" [Gergesenes, in the King James Version]. After the exorcism of the two men possessed with devils, the evil spirit entered into a herd of swine, "and behold the whole herd ran violently down a steep place into the sea: and they perished in the waters." (St. Matthew VIII, 32.)

Mr. Shane Leslie suggests a comparison between these lines and "Tennyson's maudlin sonnet to Gladstone on the Redistribution Bill of 1886."

36. *Progress:* Apropos of this word so freely used and so little understood, Belloc has written: "When I went to the University of Oxford nearly thirty years ago, the teachers there regarded the existing political system of England as admirable. They never proposed anything more admirable. That was a very natural point of view in comfortable people concerned solely with this world and having pretty well all this world could give them. The then political constitution of England was part of that world only, but it was one of the formative causes of it, and therefore was regarded with final and conclusive affection. So far so good. But observe the effect on this very natural affection or mood when used independently as a basis of affirmation without reference to reason.

"These worthies presented the whole of English history to their pupils as one process of Progress, which was continuing. Now this attitude was a sheer negation of reason." (*Studies,* Dec. 1920.)

Passing, then, to a more philosophical consideration of Progress, Belloc continues: "There is not one superstition or religion of Progress (as applicable to temporal affairs), but two quite distinct ones.

"The first religion postulates the present as a realized ideal and therefore necessarily regards all steps of the past as a series of approaches to the best. For the past can never be like the perfect present, and being unlike the present must by definition be worse than the present. And since the past leads up to the present by successive steps, and since the present is a realized ideal, therefore there has been perpetual progression from the worse to the better.

"The second religion frames an ideal of temporal good. It recognizes that this ideal is not yet fulfilled. But it is more comfortable to believe that it will be fulfilled, because in that case the remainder of one's life will probably be led in happier circumstances, or at any rate one can contemplate a pleasanter future as a whole for one's fellow beings. Transmute this comfortable hope into a doctrine and you necessarily also have Progress, that is, advance from conditions which you regard as worse towards conditions which you regard as better." (*Ibid.*)

Obviously, Patmore regarded the conditions of the old aristocratic order as better than the conditions of the new democratic order to which the old order, in his day, was yielding.

The late G. K. Chesterton, whose views on democracy are so entirely opposed to Patmore's, agrees with his fundamental ideas. Indeed these ideas, the substance of the essay on Carlyle, subsequently became the theme of the romantic extravaganza, *The Napoleon of Notting Hill,* and finally were the underlying thesis of later volumes such as *Heretics* and *Orthodoxy.* Cecil Chesterton in his anonymous volume, *G. K. Chesterton, A Criticism* (pp. 145–46), gives the following simple summary of them: "Since in the hands of the philosophers ideas have thus become self-destructive, the common man abandons ideas altogether and puts his trust in phrases like 'progress' and 'efficiency.' Now, progress implies that you are going somewhere, and efficiency that you are doing something, and unless you know where you want to go and what you want to do, both words are useless and unmeaning."

41. *freedom which enslaves:* the freedom of unrestraint. (Cf. "Legem Tuam Dilexi," ll. 16–45.)

44–46. Whatever may be the faults of this prayer it does not err on the side of sentimentality or weakness. "A wise man learns by others' mistakes; an ordinary man, by his own; a fool, neither by his own nor by others'."

45. *Fool:* the common man. (Cf. l. 5 *supra.*)

46. *Wise:* the aristocrat. (Cf. l. 2 *supra.*)

52–61. Here Patmore applies to England the ancient parable of the state being a human body composed of different parts, some noble, some less noble but all working together not for themselves but for the common good of the whole body,

Equal in inequality.

Menenius Agrippa made use of this parable to induce the Plebs of Rome to return to the city, when, discontent with their unequal share in the government, they had deserted the Patricians and retired to the Mons Sacer.

St. Paul develops the parity between the human body and the Mystical Body of Christ. (Cf. I Corinthians XII.)

52. *strong and single:* This may refer to the policy of "splendid isolation" affected by British statesmen from the middle of the nineteenth century until its close.

60. *Equal in inequality:* In the Psyche Odes Patmore supernaturalizes the fact and necessity of inequality. (Cf. "De Nature Deorum," ll. 74–95; "Psyche's Discontent," ll. 7–8; "Eros and Psyche," *Theme* and ll. 77–84.) Here we have his apology for inequality in the natural, social order. The best commentary upon it is this: "The immense and unalterable inequalities in the knowing faculties of man are the source and in part the justification of that social inequality which roughly and very partially reflects them. Many otherwise amiable and conservative thinkers have, however, made the mistake of conceding that such inequality is, abstractedly considered, an evil, though a hopelessly incurable one. Conservative teaching would be much more effective than it is were it more frequently occupied with proving that such inequality is no evil, but a very great good for all parties." ("Thoughts on Knowledge, Opinion and Inequality.")

62–70. "'One can live in a house without being an architect,' and it is not at all necessary that the common people should understand the English constitution in order to feel that their lives are sweeter and nobler because they are members of its living organism. Not a ploughboy or a milkmaid but would feel, without in the least knowing why, that a light had passed from their lives with the disappearance of social inequalities and the consequent loss of their dignity as integral parts of a somewhat that was greater than themselves." (*Ibid.*)

In his essay, "A 'Pessimist Outlook,'" Patmore quotes these lines to illustrate the following passage: "The malaria of the universal marsh stupifies the brain and deadens the heart of the very ploughman who turns the sod, and he is hourly the worse for want of the healthy breeze and invigorating prospect of the ancient hills, which he himself was, perhaps, among the most eager to level. Though he knew it not, he was every day sensibly the better for being the member of a great nation . . .

"If he does not feel the loss of his corporate life, but is content to struggle, stink, and sting with the rest of the swarm into which the national body has been resolved by corruption, so much the worse for him. His insensibility is the perfection of his misery. To others, not so lost, there may be hope, though not in this stage of being. None who has ever lived through the final change, or who, being in the foul morass of resulting 'equality,' has been able to discern what national life means, can find in private fortune—wife, children, friends, money—any compensation for the great life of which his veins are empty."

69. *greet:* mourn.

71–78. The integrity of the whole British Empire was not seriously impaired, according to Patmore, by past concessions to excesses of aristocrats, and by unjust punishments such as the pillory meeted out to the common people!

79–80. When the *traitor,* Judas, met the *coward,* Pilate, *Heaven itself* could not withstand the combination! Thus it is with England, says Patmore.

81–82. *The Deluge* of *dross* and *draff* (l. 17) that engulfed England after the passing of the Third Reform Bill, would have been prevented by the stern *'No'* of the *Wise.* "Had the Conservatives, during the last twenty-five years, shown themselves above being frightened by a temporary loss of office, they would now, almost beyond doubt, have been in a strong and independent majority, with no necessity for adopting pillage as a principle. But when the pinch has come they have, of late years, always thrown over principle and shown themselves ready to purchase a continuance of place by measures in excess of the most revolutionary proposals of their adversaries. Almost all the Radical measures of this period have been passed directly by or through the connivance of frightened Conservatives: and there cannot be the least doubt that, had they never during this time been in office or had any chance of forming anything more than a fairly strong Opposition, the residue of Conservative feeling in the Liberal party—which has more than once been shocked by the Radical extravagances of the Tories—would have saved the country from a great deal of the 'progress' which has brought us to the pass we are now in." ("Courage in Politics.")

95. *Easter* and *Whitsuntide* are still favorite times for marrying and being given in marriage in England.

THE TWO DESERTS

Publication: One of the original nine Odes, April 1868, it afterwards appeared in *The Pall Mall Gazette,* Nov. 22, 1876.

Title: The two *deserts blank of small and great* (l. 31), are the deserts of the hidden, animate loveliness of the world revealed by the microscope, and the hidden inanimate ugliness of the heavens seen through a telescope.

Theme: An indictment of scientific inquisitiveness as a substitute for supernatural faith in viewing the commonplaces of life. (Cf. "Magna est Veritas," *Theme.*) It is a development of an incident narrated by Gosse (pp. 198–199) concerning a visit of Patmore to the Greenwich Observatory in company with Aubrey de Vere. "They were shown through the telescope a new comet and other fine things which filled them both with exultation, but De Vere unfortunately giving voice to his enthusiasm about the bigness of the starry heavens on the way home, Patmore suddenly 'dried up,' and maintained that the stars were only created *to make dirt cheap.*"

3. *five:* originally, "four."

4. *The best that's known:* originally, "The little that is known."

15. *Was all conceiv'd:* originally, "Devised was."

17. Cf. *supra, Theme.*

ll. 1–27. Gosse calls this: "A passage very characteristic of his captious and sarcastic indifferentism," and then adds: "Such speculations, macrocosmic or microcosmic, were equally unfitted to attract Patmore's serious thought. He lived in a contemplation of eternity, and he saw the whole of existence in relation to it. There were no softened outlines in his landscape; he perceived, as he thought, but two things, the radiance of truth, crystalline and eternal, and the putrescence of wilful and hopeless error" (p. 246). There was peculiar appositeness in these lines in Patmore's day, due to the advance in astronomy and the beginning of accurate knowledge of bacteria that marked the early nineteenth century. (Cf. "The Nineteenth Century," Thompson, ll. 75–98.) The underlying thought of these lines is interestingly though analogously expressed in Patmore's essay, "Real Apprehension." After making a clear distinction between comprehension and apprehension, he adds: "Men of vigorous apprehension look at the heavens of truth, as it were, through a powerful telescope, and see instantly as realities many living lights which are quite invisible to the common eye. But contemplation—a faculty rare at all times, but wellnigh unheard of in ours—is like the photographic plate which finds stars that no telescope can discover, by simply setting its passively expectant gaze in certain indicated directions so long and steadily that telescopically invisible bodies become apparent by accumulation of impression. Such men are prophets and apostles, whether canonical or not."

19–21. These lines do not appear in the version printed in the original Nine Odes.

27–36. "Exclusive study of material facts seems to lead to an absolute *hatred* of life. 'Écrasez l'infame' is the cry of modern science. Darwin admitted that 'fact-grinding' had destroyed his imagination, and made him 'nauseate Shakespeare.' Goethe thanked Heaven for saving him from the danger he was once in of being 'shut up in the charnelhouse of science.' Coleridge spoke gratefully of Boehme and some other poor mystics for helping to keep his heart from being withered by 'facts.' Profligacy and science (in its modern acceptation) bring about the same destruction of the higher faculties, and by essentially the same means, *i.e.* by dwelling continually on surfaces and ignoring substance." (*Knowledge and Science,* XXXI.) (Cf. "L'Allegro," ll. 81–83.)

30. *our:* originally, "Man's."

32–35. These lines are echoed in Thompson's "The Kingdom of God":

"The angels keep their ancient places;—
Turn but a stone, and start a wing!
'Tis ye, 'tis your estrangèd faces,
That miss the many-splendoured thing."

CREST AND GULF

Publication: In Odes I–XXXI, 1877.

Theme: Cf. "Magna est Veritas."

1–4. The personal element of man's spiritual life is a necessary corollary of the first commandment.

1–2. Man's *woe* is here attributed to his rejection of God. St. Thomas says: "God alone can satisfy the will of man, according to the words of Psalm CII, 5: *Who satisfieth thy desire with good things.* Therefore God alone constitutes man's happiness." (*Summa* II. i, q. 2, art. 8.) Here as well as hereafter: *In His will is our peace* (*Paradiso,* III). And peace is identical with perfect joy, according to St. Thomas. (Cf. "Winter," l. 6.)

10–12. The parable of the sower and the seed (St. Matthew XIII) refers to the seed sown and the harvest reaped in a man's own soul. Here the allusion is to the seed sown and the harvest reaped in the souls of others.

15. Our Lord bade us: "So let your light shine before men that they may see your good works and glorify your Father Who is in heaven." (St. Matthew V, 16.) But because of man's strong inclination to evil he more easily follows bad example and no amount of training can destroy his power to do so.

16–18. In Patmore's essay, "Love and Poetry," Patmore declares: "In the hands of the poet, mystery does not hide knowledge, but reveals it as by its proper medium." What that proper medium is he tells us in "Imagination": "The poet's eye glances from heaven to earth, from earth to heaven; and his faculty of discerning likeness in difference enables him to express the unknown in the terms of the known, so as to confer upon the former a *sensible* credibility, and to give the latter a truly sacramental dignity. The soul contains world upon world of the most real of realities of which it has no consciousness until it is awakened to their existence by some parable or metaphor, some strain of rhythm or music, some combination of form or color, some scene of beauty or sublimity, which suddenly expresses the inexpressible by a lower likeness." A more detailed commentary on these lines will be found in the essay, "Religio Poetae." (Cf. "Dead Language," ll. 2–8; "St. Valentine's Day," *Theme*.)

There is a close analogy between the function of the poet described in these lines and the function of the saint who would communicate to others the mystical vision granted to few. (Cf. "Winter," Theme.) The difference between profane and sacred literature in this matter is thus stated by St. Thomas in the *Summa* I, q. i, art. 9: "Poetry makes use of metaphors to produce a representation, for it is natural to man to be pleased with representations. But sacred doctrine makes use of metaphors as both necessary and useful.

"The ray of divine revelation is not extinguished by the sensible imagery wherewith it is veiled, as Dionysius says (*Coelest. Hierarch.* i); and its truth so far remains that it does not allow the minds of those to whom the revelation has been made, to rest in the metaphors but raises them to the knowledge of truths; and through those to whom the revelation has been made others also may receive instruction in these matters. Hence those things that are taught metaphorically in one part of Scripture, in other parts are taught more openly. The very hiding of truth in figures is useful for the exercise of thoughtful minds, and as a defence against the ridicule of the impious, according to the words: *Give not that which is holy to dogs.* (St. Matthew VII, 6.) (Cf. "Winter," *Theme*.)

18. *horny human eyes:* such as those of Wordworth's Peter Bell.

"At noon, when by the forest's edge
He lay beneath the branches high,
The soft blue sky did never melt
Into his heart: he never felt
The witchery of the soft blue sky."

("Peter Bell," Part I, ll. 71–75.)

19. One of the most ingenious blasphemers of the nineteenth century was Matthew Arnold. Chesterton in *Orthodoxy* considers the quiet reaches of Arnold's higher criticism: "more piercingly blasphemous than the shrieks of Schopenhauer."

20. *Capua:* An ancient city of Campania, Italy, was famous for its wealth and luxury.

20–24. The detailed expression of Patmore's aristocratic intolerance of the Many and his enthusiasm for the governing Few is given in the Political Odes—"1867," "Peace," and "1880–85." Here he succumbs to the subtlest of all temptations in attributing God's sanction to the political and social inequality of his day.

25–32. The idea here expressed, that not all motion is forward motion is further developed in "1880–85," ll. 36–46, where Patmore shows that not all forward motion is *Progress.* In *Rod, Root and Flower,* he ascribes linear motion to vulgar souls, and circular motion to the elect: "All life and joy is motion. That of time and vulgar souls is linear, and so not without change of place; and good to them is known only in the coming and the going. With souls of grace it is not so. They go about a centre, which planetary motion is their joy. They have also a self-revolving motion, which is their peace. Their own regularity enables them to perceive the order of the universe. Their ears with inmost delectation catch the sound of the revolving spheres. They live in fruition of the eternal novelty." (*Aphorisms and Extracts.*)

33–36. Patmore follows the precept of these lines in a more personal strain in "Magna est Veritas."

37–38. A *prophet* is primarily a seer who beholds the vision of truth, and a teacher who communicates that vision to others. He need not, necessarily, be one who foretells the future.

41–44. This is a very successful symbolic expression of one of Patmore's favorite themes—restraint in conformity to God's will as a necessary characteristic of the power that gives significance to life. (Cf. "Legem Tuam Dilexi.")

41. *fly wheel:* a heavy wheel whose weight resists sudden changes of speed, thus securing uniform motion.

42–44. God's *powerlessness to quell* man's violence and lust is a consequence of His free decree that man should possess freedom of will. God's unlimited power to lead man when his will is conformed to God's, is beautifully described by Dante in the last lines of the *Paradiso,* in the same figurative language as Patmore's:

> "the will roll'd onward, like a wheel
> In even motion, by the Love impell'd,
> That moves the sun in Heaven and all the stars."

'LET BE'

Date of Publication: In the *Pall Mall Gazette,* Nov. 3, 1876, and included in Odes I–XXXI, 1877.

Theme: Thus far the poet has dealt with nature as a parable of love (cf. "St. Valentine's Day," *Theme*); with human love as both parable and reality (cf. "Beata," *Theme*); with the inferences of both in civic life (cf. "1867," *Theme*) and in the life of the intellect (cf. "Magna est Veritas," *Theme*). Now he passes to the explicit development of his central theme, the relationship between man's soul and God. This he does in this ode and in the remaining odes of Book I, together with "Pain" and "Auras of Delight" in Book II. They portray Christian fortitude in physical pain and spiritual desolation, and describe the awful purification of the human will that is the necessary prelude of supernatural contemplation.

A facsimile of the original manuscript of this poem is printed in Champneys' *Life of Patmore* I, p. 250. It is interesting to see the obvious improvement effected by the changes that appear in the final draft.

1–2. "Either make the tree good and its fruit good: or make the tree evil and its fruit evil. For by the fruit the tree is known." (St. Matthew, XII, 33.) These words were spoken by Our Savior to the Pharisees when they had charged Him with casting out devils, "by Beelzebub the prince of devils." (*Ibid.* 24.) It is certain that normally, men of good will can distinguish between good and evil deeds. But there are instances in which this is extremely difficult—so difficult that with the coming of anti-Christ many will be deceived. This is not true of Our Savior, the "Lord, who knowest the hearts of all men." (Acts I, 24.) He was not deceived by the Pharisees' zeal for the law and their elaborate external profession of faith. Hence He could with justice and truth brand them, a "generation of vipers" (St. Matthew XII, 34). But, asks Patmore in these lines, *how* shall WE *tell these?* "Judge not, that you may not be judged." (St. Matthew VII, 1) If we may not excuse the deed which we see, at least we may excuse the intention which is hidden from us. As St. Bernard says: "Even if you discover some evil deed or other, do not judge your neighbor, but rather excuse him. Excuse the intention if you cannot excuse what is done. Attribute it to ignorance. Attribute it to a lack of deliberation. Attribute it to a mistake. But if the case is so clear that it cannot in any way be excused, persuade yourself, at least, to say: 'The temptation was a very violent one. What would it have done to me if it had taken possession of me with power so great?'" ("Sermons on the *Canticle of Canticles,* Sermon XL, § 5; Translation, p. 160.)

3–6. "God shall judge the secrets of men" (Romans II, 16). "Nor do I judge according to the look of man: for man seeth those things that appear, but the Lord beholdeth the heart." (1 Kings XVI, 7.)

8–9. In the spiritual life, height is measured by nearness of approach to God. Sweetness is really such if it savors of good. The ultimate measure of both is found in the first Commandment.

10. "There is nothing outwardly to distinguish a 'Saint' from common persons. A Bishop or an eminent Dissenter will, as a rule, be remarkable for his decorum or his obstreperous indecorum, and for some little insignia of piety, such as the display of a mild desire to promote the good of your soul, or an abstinence from wine and tobacco, jesting, and small-talk; but the Saint has no 'fads,' and you may live in the same house with him, and never find out that he is not a sinner like yourself, unless you rely on negative proofs, or obtrude lax ideas upon him, and so provoke him to silence. He may impress you, indeed, by his harmlessness and imperturbable good temper, and probably by some lack of appreciation of modern humour, and ignorance of some things which men are expected to know, and by never seeming to have much use for his time when it can be of any service to you; but, on the whole, he will give you an agreeable impression of general inferiority to yourself." (*Magna Moralia,* XIV.)

In *Victories of Love,* Bk. I, Letter xiv, ll. 71–74, we find a similar thought:

"oh,
How can we ever surely know
But that the very darkest place
May be the scene of saving grace!"

One very dramatic example of grace lurking where none could guess, was the repentant thief. (Cf. St. Luke XXIII, 40–43.) Another was St. Paul. (Cf. Acts IX, 1–18.)

14–16. Cf. *infra.* ll. 31–32.

17–19. Intense, impetuous natures such as St. Paul, St. Peter and St. Mary Magdalen are frequently the recipients of special graces. Slothful souls more often remain reprobate. (Cf. *infra,* ll. 20–30, and "Tristitia," *passim.*)

20–30. "The power of the Soul for good is in proportion to the strength of its passions. Sanctity is not the negation of passion but its order. . . . Hence great Saints have often been great sinners." (*Aurea Dicta,* CXXXII.) (Cf. "Victory in Defeat," ll. 7–8.)

20–25. The interior desire for *some high Virtue,* issues, through excess, in the opposite *besetting sin.* This indicates the willingness of *yon wretch* spiritually to die through despair of ever possessing the *favour sweet* of virtuous attainment.

23. *inmost contrary desire:* a hidden, intense, though as yet ineffectual desire to attain *some high Virtue* that is the very opposite of (*contrary* to) his manifest sin.

31–32. Patmore's daughter Emily, Sister Mary Christina, referred to these lines as: "one of those pieces of wisdom that see round the corner, like a looking-glass. What a comfort it is that God really knows every one; for we know very little of each other. I am more and more convinced." (*A Daughter of Coventry Patmore,* p. 142.)

"Many a man, who is pure and blameless in his own eyes, and in those of the world, is, in God's sight, as foul as the piebald hair of leprosy: and many another, the shame and scandal of himself and his neighbours, on account of falls like those of David, is, through his ardour to cast the scab of his corruption, a man after God's own heart, which only sees the end." (*Magna Moralia,* XXXI.)

34–40. These lines reflective of Patmore's spiritual wisdom are too clear, too chastening, and too profound for comment. They call, rather, for meditation. "Those who know how orphaned and widowed of truth even the best of us are, and how the destitution we may discover in ourselves is greater than that we can know of in any others, will discern, with the earlier and deeper interpreters of the words of our Lord and His Apostles, that there are two ways of reading their exhortations to help the poor." ("Christianity and 'Progress.'")

'FAINT YET PURSUING'

Publication: One of the original Nine Odes, 1868.

Title: "And Gideon came to Jordan, and passed over, he, and the three hundred that were with him, faint yet pursuing them" (Judges VIII, 4). Such is the King James Version. The Douay Version reads: "And when Gideon was come to the Jordan, he passed over it with the three hundred that were with him: who were so weary that they could not pursue after them that fled."

From a letter to his daughter Emily we learn that this was, at one time, Patmore's personal motto. "You ask what my motto is," he wrote. " 'Faint, yet pursuing' (from the Book of Judges). You will not think it a very pretty one, but you will like it better when you are older." (Chamneys II, p. 118.)

Theme: It is the mystery of divine grace—the several degrees of perfection in the souls of men. "Every one hath his proper gift from God; one after this manner, and another after that." (1 Corinthians VII, 7.) (Cf. *infra,* ll. 1–9.) By how hard and slow a road Patmore came to the balanced view expressed in this poem, we learn from the following passage in his Autobiography: "The sudden coming into me of faith in the Incarnation of God in Jesus Christ was accompanied with delight not less immense and far more abiding than the joy of that first glow of belief which had come upon me in childhood. I instantly recognized the obligations under which I had now come to lead a perfect life, and, so long as I could see any immediate possibility or hope of doing so, my happiness remained at an unspeakable height. But, as I was wholly unprepared by previous teaching for this 'conversion' of my intellect and feelings, and had no practical conception of the impossibility, which all religions recognize, of leading such a life in this world, I became, in a few weeks, fearfully discouraged by the discovery of my own inability to sustain my conduct, interior and exterior, at the elevation which seemed now to be absolutely demanded of me, on pain of separation from Christ. As long as I walked, or fancied that I walked perfectly, the vision of God with and in me, was, as before, clearer a thousand times than the sun of noonday; but the minutest fault—lying in bed a moment longer than the time appointed for getting up, a careless word, or the slightest indulgence in any of the somewhat undisciplined habits formed in me by the season of youth having been mainly spent at home—would cause a cloud, or at least a mist, to come between me and my glorious vision, and fill me with the horrors and regrets proper to mortal sin. A season of great despair ensued, with a subsequent season of recovery and violent renewal of effort; and, for years and years afterwards, my life was an alternation of periods of hope and despondency; the hope and despondency becoming, however, each time more and more subdued, until my frame of mind at last arrived at somewhat of that equable state of mingled hope and fear with which I ought to and should have begun had I had the means of seasonable instruction and direction." (Champneys II, p. 46.) (Cf. "Let Be": *Theme.*)

1–9. The best commentary on these lines is a paragraph from Patmore's remarks on Edmund Gosse's criticism of Juan Valera's novel, *Pepita Jiménez*. "*Pepita Jiménez* is essentially a 'religious novel'; none the less so because it represents the failure of a good young aspirant to the priesthood to attain a degree of sanctity to which he was not called, and depicts the working in his aspirations of a pride so subtle as to be very venial, though in some degree, disastrous. Mr. Gosse seems to me to mistake the *motif* of the novel entirely in regarding it as representing the *necessary* failure of a 'divine ardour brought face to face with an earthly love.' It represents nothing but the exceedingly common mistake of young and ardent minds in measuring their present capacity by their desires, and striving to take their station at the top of an alp, when they are only fit for the ascent of a very moderate hill. One of the many points in which Catholic philosophy shows itself superior to the philosophy of Protestant religionists in the knowledge of the human mind is its distinct recognition of the fact that there are as many degrees of human capacity for holiness as for any other kind of eminence, and that for most men a very moderate degree of spirituality is the utmost for which they are entitled to hope. An ardent Protestant, misinterpreting the words, 'Be ye perfect as I am perfect,' is apt to think that he is nothing if not a saint, whereas Juan Valera knew that to be a saint, as to be a poet is to be about one in twenty millions, and he has made a very amusing as well as a very useful book out of the vain strivings of his hero for—

Heroic good, target for which the young
Dream in their dreams that every bow is strung;

and the course of experience by which he is brought to conclude—*That less than highest is good, and may be high.*" ("A Spanish Novelette.")

Contrast these lines with "Eros and Psyche," l. 122.

10. This is the *via media* that lies between the heights of heroic sanctity and the depths of sin.

16–20. Were complete sinlessness granted me for a period followed by serious sin, yet would I not despair. I would still fight to regain my former state, even if I felt that it would be followed by *a like reverse*. "For the encouragement of the heart in the spiritual combat remember that no struggle, however faint or brief, is really unsuccessful. If we do not gain the victory, we at least diminish the future pain of defeat. Remember, also, that to rise and go on fighting after repeated disgrace and failure *is* victory over the three enemies of the soul, Sloth, Pride and Despair." (*Magna Moralia,* XVIII.)

21–22. Virtue has its reward, temporal and eternal. The evil result of sin *dies* with repentance.

23–24. "And because iniquity hath abounded, the charity of many shall grow cold. But he that shall persevere to the end, he shall be saved." (St. Matthew XXIV, 12–13.)

32. *should,* originally, "shall."

33. "For a just man shall fall seven times and shall rise again: but the wicked shall fall down into evil." (Proverbs XXIV, 16.)

34. "And the publican, standing afar off, would not so much as lift up his eyes towards heaven; but struck his breast, saying: O God, be merciful to me a sinner." (St. Luke XVIII, 13.)

39. In "Arbor Vitae" Patmore uses a tree as symbol of the Church and develops it in great detail.

VICTORY IN DEFEAT

Publication: In Odes I–XXXI, 1877.

Theme: A further development of the theme of 'Faint Yet Pursuing,' it expresses the fearful alternation of victory and defeat that marks the progress of a human soul along the Purgative Way of asceticism. (Cf. "Let Be," *Theme.*)

1–5. The figurative language of these lines was undoubtedly suggested by Our Savior's promise and exhortation to St. Peter and St. Andrew: "Come ye after Me, and I will make you to be fishers of men." (St. Matthew IV, 19.) This description of a soul's reaction to the desolation that so often follows spiritual consolation, has seldom been expressed with so happy a blend of lyrical expression and realistic fidelity to an awful theme. (Cf. 'Let Be,' ll. 17–19.)

6. Love, not fear, must be the motive of spiritual achievement. As Saint Bernard expresses it: "It is from loving, not from showing respect, that love takes its name. By all means, let him show honor who trembles and stands aghast with fear, who is filled with apprehension, who is struck with awe. But all these have no place in the case of one who loves." (Sermons on the *Canticle of Canticles;* Sermon LXXXIII, § 3; Translation, p. 229.)

7–8. "In vulgar minds the idea of passion is inseparable from that of disorder; in them the advances of love, or anger, or any other strong energy towards its end, is like the rush of a savage horde, with war-whoops, tom-toms, and confused tumult; and the great decorum of a passion, which keeps, and is immensely increased in force by, the discipline of God's order, looks to them like weakness and coldness. Hence the passions, which are the measure of man's capacity for virtues, are regarded by the pious vulgar as being of the nature of vice; and, indeed, in them they are so; for virtues are nothing but ordered passions, and vices nothing but passions in disorder." (*Magna Moralia,* II.) (Cf. "Let Be," ll. 20–30.)

9–10. "Life, unhindered by the internal obstruction of vice or the outward obscurations of pain, sorrow, and anxiety, is pure and simple joy; as we have most of us experienced during the few hours of our lives in which, the conscience being free, all bodily and external evils have been removed or are at least quiescent. And though these glimpses of perfect sunshine are short and far between, the joy of life will not be wholly obscured to us by any external evil, provided the breast is clear of remorse, envy, discontent, or any other habitually cherished sin." ("Cheerfulness in Life and Art.")

9. "Delight is pleasanter than pleasure; peace more delightful than delight." (*Aurea Dicta,* LI.)

11–12. There is a further development of these lines in "Pain." And in Thompson's poem, "Insentience," we find the same thought:

> "Weary, I no longer love,
> Weary, no more lack;
> O for a pang, that listless Loss
> Might wake, and, with a playmate's voice,
> Call the tired Love back!"

13–15. Patmore invariably views spiritual excesses with greater hope than spiritual sloth. (Cf. 'Let Be,' ll. 17–30.)

16–18. The spiritual delights of repentance and the spiritual greatness of penitents are among Patmore's favorite themes. (Cf. "Deliciae Sapientiae de Amore," ll. 125–30; "De Natura Deorum," ll. 51–52.)

19–25. God's mercy pursues even the impenitent who have grown weary of the ceaseless alternation of sin and repentance. "They that are in health need not a physician, but they that are ill. . . . For I am not come to call the just, but sinners." (St. Matthew IX, 12–13.)

27–31. A very subtle form of temptation suggests surrender to a life of sin and presumption upon God's mercy for a death-bed repentance. An analogous error in the early ages of the Church resulted in the practice of deferring baptism until the hour of death.

32–35. We find the same imagery differently applied in "The Hound of Heaven," ll. 111–14.

39–51. This portrayal of spiritual desolation is not unlike Thompson's in "The Hound of Heaven," ll. 111–42.

48. "How long, O Lord, shall I cry, and Thou wilt not hear?" (Habacuc I, 2.) "'If the Lord tarry wait for Him, and He will not tarry but come quickly.' The impatience of the Soul for vision is one of the last faults that can be cured. Only to those who watch and wait, with absolute indifference as to the season of revelation, do all things reveal themselves." (*Aurea Dicta,* CXL.)

49–51. "Man against Hell, without the help of God, is as a rabbit against the Russian empire." (*Aphorisms and Extracts.*) Cf. "De Natura Deorum," ll. 23–24. Compare with "The Hound of Heaven," ll. 178–79.

54–57. Cf. 'Faint Yet Pursuing,' ll. 23–24.

59–60. Concerning this miraculous happening recorded in the Old Testament (Josue VI, 20), St. Paul wrote: "By faith the walls of Jerico fell down." (Hebrews XI, 30.) (Cf. *infra.* ll. 61–63.)

61–63. "Eye hath not seen, nor ear heard, neither hath it entered into the heart of man, what things God hath prepared for them that love Him." (1 Corinthians II, 9.) In the following passage Patmore describes the nature of that spiritual peace that is attainable in this life, and the means by which it may be attained: "Joshua represents the power of God in the conquest and conversion of the natural man. All the 'nations' of the Wilderness fell, one by one, before his sword, but when he came to Jerico, the last of these nations, in the 'extreme West,' he was commanded not to fight, but persistently to surround it with the blasts of his trumpets, till the walls fell of themselves. This, being interpreted, means that the flesh or senses, the last power which is converted to God, does not fall through fighting; but, that when all the other faculties of Man have been brought into subjection, then the flesh is to be attacked by an incessant repetition of the blast of the amazing truth that God demands also the allegiance and praise of the Body, which, being outside the field of the 'spiritual combat,' and incapable of combating or of being combated by the forces which have subdued all else in Man, can only be overcome by the proclamation of an immediate and greater sensible good, than that which it is called upon to abandon. Persistent and incessant affirmation of this truth is the only way of rendering it credible to the senses that an immense increase of their *present* felicity is the reward of submission to spiritual order." (*Homo,* XXX.)

62. Cf. *supra,* l. 9.

REMEMBERED GRACE

Publication: In *Odes* I–XXXI, 1877.

Theme: This is the ode cited by Emily Patmore in a letter to her father in which she speaks of how easy and how dangerous it is to misinterpret such poetry: "St. Peter speaks of St. Paul's Epistles: 'in which are certain things hard to be understood, which the unlearned and the unstable wrest, as they do also the other scriptures, to their own destruction.' (*2 St. Peter III, 16.*) I think that might be said of the Odes, 'Remembered Grace,' for instance; but any one who would offend God on such a consideration could never have really known Him." (*Portrait of My Family,* Derek Patmore, p. 187.) (Cf. "Let Be," *Theme;* "The Body," *Theme.*)

1–4. Help needed and received is, even in the estimation of the least wise, a nobler thing than the false security of the fool.

1. *succour:* connotes the weakness which it would strengthen.

wise: Cf. Proverbs XXIII–XXX; Psalm XIII, *etc.* where will be found this same comparison between the security of the *wise* who put their trust in God's grace, and the false security of the *fool* who trusts in his own powers and material things.

2. *charge:* in the sense of a thing given into one's custody.

4. *a foolish soul's estate:* such as the rich man's who said: "I will pull down my barns and will build greater; and into them will I gather all things that are grown to me, and my goods . . . But God said to him: Thou fool, this night do they require thy soul of thee: and whose shall those things be which thou hast provided? So is he that layeth up treasure for himself and is not rich toward God." (St. Luke XII, 18–21.)

6. A fool's knowledge of such attributes of God as mercy and love will often make him presumptuous. In a wise man the appreciation of these same divine attributes leads to the loving dependence described in the rest of the ode.

7–8. "Yea I have loved thee with an everlasting love." (Jeremias XXXI, 3.)

10–17. We find the same idea in the parable of the sower and the seed. (Cf. St. Matthew XIII.)

12. *sin:* such as is largely the result of human frailty and followed by speedy repentance.

bitter shame: contrition for past offences, bitter in the remembrance of God's love.

14–15. In judging the relative heinousness of sin Patmore considers *envy, malice* and *pride* among the worst, because such sins are usually more deliberate than others. (Cf. "Tristitia," ll. 16–24.)

18–20. Nothing keeps a soul sinless more effectively than the remembrance of past graces, manifestations of God's love.

23. the *cleansing flame,* chiefly felt in the Purgative Way.

24–25. Deliberate mortal sin, alone, can cause a soul entirely to depart from the *small flock* of Christ.

25. "And when he (God) had removed him (Saul), he raised them up David to be king: to whom giving testimony, he said: *I have found David, the son of Jesse, a man according to my own heart, who shall do all my wills.*" (Acts XIII, 22.)

26. "All these things have I considered in my heart, that I might carefully understand them: there are just men and wise men, and their works are in the hand of God: and yet man knoweth not whether he be worthy of love, or hatred." (Ecclesiastes IX, 1.)

27–31. When among false Prophets *this or that new one* succeeds the *last high oracle,* the faith of those who look to such leaders changes according to the latest theory. But the faith of those who look to Christ and His Church for guidance, remains constant and begets in them confidence and peace of soul, while they heed the warning given in the Sermon on the Mount: "Beware of false prophets who come to you in the clothing of sheep, but inwardly they are ravening wolves . . . Many will say to Me in that day: Lord, Lord have not we prophesied in Thy name, and cast out devils in Thy name, and done many miracles in Thy name? And then will I profess unto them, I never knew you: depart from Me, you that work iniquity." (St. Matthew VII, 15, 22–23.)

32–42. Faith, as a virtue, implies an habitual state of soul. From the depths of the human soul of Our Model upon the cross went up a cry that revealed how complete may be the soul's darkness: "My God! My God! why hast Thou forsaken Me?" But subsequently came those other words: "Father, into Thy hands I commend My Spirit" (St. Luke XXIII, 46), and ultimately: "It is consummated." (St. John XIX, 30.) Like all solid virtues, faith must, with God's grace, withstand the temptations that assail it, the chief of which is doubt. While the soul resists, such doubt remains merely a temptation and faith grows deeper by the very act of resistance. However strong may be the doubt, however intense may be the darkness of soul induced by it, if the soul cooperates with God's grace, it will prevail. For: "God is faithful, who will not suffer you to be tempted above that which you are able: but will make also with temptation issue, that you may be able to bear it." (1 Corinthians X, 13.)

35–38. The imagery of these lines is a reminder of the time of affliction described in Ecclesiastes (XII, 1–2), when: "the sun, and the light, and the moon, and the stars be darkened, and the clouds return after the rain."

42. *Orion* and the *Bear:* constellations that are the chief guides of mariners.

VESICA PISCIS

Publication: In *Odes* I–XLVI, 1878.

Title: The literal meaning is difficult to know. To me it seems to be *the fish's bladder,* in which the coin was hidden as in a purse. (Cf. infra, ll. 12–13.) In Latin *vesica* means either *bladder* or a *purse made of bladder.*

Theme: It is a description of the perfection of a soul that has traveled far along the ways of purgation and illumination, and is now ready for union with God and destined for the heights of mystical attainment. The seeming suddenness with which this comes to pass beyond the soul's fondest hope, has a parallel in Patmore's experience as a poet. Among his *Aphorisms and Extracts* we read: "Dear Lord, for forty years I tried to raise in the wilderness a house for Thy abode. I painfully gathered bricks, and worked a bit of cornice here, and there a capital; but as I put it together all would suddenly fall, and still I gathered up material though the more I gathered the greater seemed the chaos; but one day, why none could tell, except perhaps that I felt more despair than ever I had done before, I heard a winnowing of unseen wings, and lo, the bricks and stones all took their place,

And a gay palace fine
Beyond my deepest dreamt design.
May He who built it all
Take care it does not fall."

This ode is an illustration of what Patmore has elsewhere written: "In the earlier half of the Soul's progress, human loves are the interpretation and motives of the divine; but, in the second, the divine love becomes the interpretation and motive of the human." (*Magna Moralia,* XXX.) (Cf. "Let Be," *Theme.*)

1. *strenuous hope:* Always in Patmore we find emphasis upon the active qualities of virtue that strives against temptation. One of the most notable examples is, *ardour virginal,* "Deliciae Sapientiae de Amore." l. 145.

4–6. "And Simon answering said to Him: Master, we have laboured all the night and have taken nothing: but at Thy word I will let down the net. And when they had done this, they enclosed a very great multitude of fishes." (St. Luke V, 5–6.)

6–11. Frequently material favors asked for in prayer are not granted. But invariably in such cases, greater spiritual graces are received. "Ask, and it shall be given you: seek, and you shall find: knock, and it shall be opened to you. For every one that asketh, receiveth: and he that seeketh, findeth: and to him that knocketh, it shall be opened. Or what man is there among you, of whom if his son shall ask bread, will he reach him a stone? Or if he shall ask him a fish, will he reach him a serpent? If you then being evil, know how to give good gifts to your children: how much more will your Father who is in heaven, give good things to them that ask Him?" (St. Matthew VII, 7–11.) "God usually answers our prayers according rather to the measure of His own magnificence than to that of our asking: so that we often do not know His boons to be those for which we besought Him." (*Aurea Dicta,* XLI.) Again: "I thank Thee for refusing so long my prayer, for when Thou delayest a gift it is always to give it more abundantly." (*Aphorisms and Extracts.*)

10. From this line we learn that the soul now attains God directly —not as before, indirectly, through creatures and external nature and human experiences.

12–13. At the conclusion of the discussion concerning the tribute Our Savior said to Simon: "Go to the sea and cast in a hook: and that fish which shall come up, take: and when thou hast opened its mouth, thou shalt find a stater: take that, and give it to them for Me and thee." (St. Matthew XVII, 26.)

14–15. There seems here to be a suggestion of the injunction which Christ gave to Peter, James and John after the transfiguration: "And as they came down from the mountain, he charged them not to tell any man what things they had seen, till the Son of man shall be risen again from the dead." (St. Mark IX, 8.) It is wise, usually, not to discuss with others the hidden graces we have received from God. " 'See that thou tell no man.' When our Lord gives vision to the Soul, He always speaks this command to the conscience." (*Aurea Dicta,* LXXXII.) But there are times when they should be revealed. The Apostles were not commanded never to reveal *what things they had seen.* Their silence was to endure only *till the Son of man shall be risen again from the dead.* The injunction laid upon the poet in these lines is disjunctive: *'Be dumb,*

Or speak of forgotten things to far-off times to come.

As is clear from the odes that follow, the poet chooses to speak to *far-off times* such as our own, and to speak *but of forgotten things* such as the ways of divine love revealed in the odes that comprise Book II. In "Dead Language" the poet expresses the belief that, judged by practical results, it was futile for him to address his own generation.

TO THE UNKNOWN EROS (Ode)

Publication: In *Odes* I–XXXI, 1877. But Patmore had been meditating on the theme as early as 1864, before he left the British Museum.

Title: Cf. notes on *Unknown Eros,* the sequence: *Title.*

Theme: This ode serves as a transition from the odes of Book I and an introduction to those that are to come, especially the Psyche Odes, which reveal the actual union of the soul with God. It describes the first mysterious stirrings of divine love in the soul that cannot as yet comprehend their significance. But even thus early the soul surmises that sacrifice is the essential condition of attaining to the perfect consummation of the mysterious love it feels. (Cf. "The Contract": *Theme.*) Hence the question asked in the concluding lines. (Cf. *Unknown Eros,* the sequence, *Theme.*)

1–10. Referring to this passage, Patmore's daughter, Sister Mary Christina, wrote: "For poetic beauty apart from the purely spiritual . . . it is wonderful and delicious." (*A Daughter of Coventry Patmore,* p. 141.)

1–3. Mr. Page (p. 120) calls attention to the fact that in 1866 Patmore wrote on the title-page of the fourth edition of the *Angel in the House,* this quotation from Shelley's translation of Plato's *Symposium:* "Is is not strange that there are innumerable hymns and poems composed for other gods, but not one of the many poets who spring up in the world has ever composed a verse in honour of Love, who is such a great god?"

3–10. "These lines are (it has never yet been said) Campbell's lines:

'Like angels' visits, few and far between,'

resurrected by him from *The Grave* of Blair:

visits
Like those of angels, short and far between':

restored to its archangelic brightness in Norris of Bemerton:

'How fading are the joys we doat upon!
Like apparitions seen and gone.
But those which soonest take their flight
Are the most exquisite and strong—
Like angels' visits, short and bright;
Mortality's too weak to bear them long';

and now glorified by Patmore." (Page, p. 121.)

The angels whose sudden wings fan the poet's face are the stirrings of divine love in the human heart, stirrings which are literally messengers from God to Man, making His love sensible, as it were. This first pulsing of the direct love of God is vague in its known origin (ll. 9-10), and is at first unrelated to any particular object (ll. 12–13).

27. *awful bliss:* a particularly Patmorean characterization of love. (Cf. *infra,* ll. 71–75.)

28–30. The first vague stirrings of divine love are a *portent,* a *Delphic word* enigmatically fortelling the love that is to come, just as the appearance of the snake in early Spring forebodes the coming of birds from which definite auguries may be deduced.

31–32. An awkward inversion for: "What eddies thus in me life's even flood?"—*i.e.* what is it that causes these eddies in my life's even flood?

34. *a perturbed moon of Uranus:* a satellite of the planet Uranus. The poet here imagines that such a celestial body moves the blood of the heart in a way analogous to the motion of the tides effected by the moon.

36–40. A sensible rapture stirs within the soul at the whispered command of the Unknown Eros—a sacramental sign prophetic of the bonds of divine love which is to come.

41–44. When first the human heart is stirred by the vague pulsings of divine love, it *longs* to be bound to a definite beloved by bonds both slight and strong—*gossamer* and *adamant*. The longing of a man's heart for the subjection which his love of a woman entails is thus expressed in the apology for the writings of Robert Waring found in Norris' translation of *Amoris Effigies,* p. xiii: "Writers must have remarked with Pleasure, this pretty Passage in the celebrated *Cato* of Mr. *Addison:*

The Strong, the Brave, the Virtuous, and the Wise
Sink in the soft Captivity together.

Amidst the Conflicts which this Passion excites in human Breasts, this soft Captivity is the agreeable and welcome portion of our Sex, and Victory is the glorious Share of the other."

41. *subject loyalty:* love.

45–47. It were difficult to match the lyric beauty of these lines as an expression of pure human love which, as it were, binds the lover between the *quivering wings* of his beloved whose flight is to *eternity.*

47. *hopeless:* because finite hopes will then be fulfilled.

53–54. It is Mr. Page's opinion that these lines are derived from the following passage in Norris' translation of Waring's *Amoris Effigies,* pp. 58–59: "Neither do I think any one can Envy at the Divinity of so mild a God, whose Anger may be appeas'd without Slaughter, who does not, like other Gods, require Beasts, but only cheerful Votaries for Sacrifice, and that he may not want Temples, Erects Flaming Altars in Human Breasts. . . . Then as to the Properties of the Ethereal Fire, it Burns and Refreshes, is Immortal without Fuel, Self-Sufficient, (for *Love* is content with itself, being its own Reward) it is Inviolable, not to be polluted by the Contagion of Filthiness, expiating and purging the Crimes, which it cannot admit, equalling the Virgin-excellency of the Vestal Flames."

53. *Amor:* Love.

55. *mooned Queen of maids:* Ashtaroth (Ashtoreth), an ancient moon-goddess to whom human sacrifice was offered. Thompson addresses her as the personification of pain: "Thou pale Ashtaroth who rul'st my life." ("Laus Amara Doloris," l. 22.) Here Patmore addresses her as a deity from whom *Bride and Bridegroom* may learn the nature of sacrifice, so essential to their love of each other and of God.

62–65. The centers of human and divine love coincide in a common point, sacrifice (*Nought*), not unlike the *compulsive focus* which is at once the center of the sun itself and of the motion of its satellites.

69. *the crown:* union of the soul with God.

71–75. Here we have the sacrifice required in Divine Love, of which sacrifices in human love are but parables. "The 'reconcilement of the highest with the lowest,' though an infinite felicity, is an infinite sacrifice. Hence the mysterious and apparently unreasonable pathos in the highest and most perfect satisfactions of Love. The Bride is always 'Amoris Victima.' The real and innermost sacrifice of the Cross was the consummation of the descent of Divinity into the flesh and its identification therewith; and the sigh which all creation heaved in that moment has its echo in that of mortal love in the like descent. That sigh is the inmost heart of all music." (*Magna Moralia* XLVIII.)

It is a paradox of divine love that only those who are willing to forego its consolations, if it be God's will, can ever know the fulness of its joy. "He who renounces goods, house, wife, *etc.* for God's sake, shall receive a hundredfold in this life, with life everlasting. But he who, having obtained this hundredfold return of all his natural delights transfigured, renounces this also, and acknowledges no consolation but his share in the agony of the Cross, shall shine forever in heaven as a sun among the stars. Yet even he cannot escape his temporal reward, but hyssop itself, in touching his lips, becomes honey." (*Magna Moralia* IX.) Again: "The true Temple has veil within veil, and one is rent for the ingress of God every time the soul dies upon the Cross, that is, resists interior temptations even to despair. 'Precious in the sight of the Lord is the death of His Saints;' and every soul which is destined for Sanctity dies many times in this terrible initiative caress of God." (*Ibid.* XXVI.)

Francis Thompson expresses the same thought thus:

"Lose, that the lost thou may'st receive;
Die, for none other way canst live."
("Mistress of Vision," ll. 136–37.)

Indeed this is the central theme of "The Hound of Heaven," and the essence of the fourth degree of love as St. Bernard describes it in his treatise *On the Love of God,* chapter X.

The natural parable of this divine truth revealed in nuptial love is expressed in "The Wedding Sermon," ll. 139–44. And in *Victories of Love* (Bk. I, Letter xii, ll. 86–87) we are told that the joy of love between human lovers springs from sacrifice:

"I'll love her! Yea, and love's joy comes
Ever from self-love's martyrdoms."

THE CONTRACT

Publication: Included among *Odes* I–XXXI, 1877.

Theme: It is an application of the general principle contained in the last lines of the preceding ode—sacrifice is an essential condition of divine love: "All men are led to Heaven by their own loves; but these must first be sacrificed." (*Aurea Dicta,* CVI.) The object of the particular sacrifice here described is the consummation of nuptial bliss voluntarily foresworn by Adam and Eve when, after their espousals, they freely impose upon themselves the restraints of prenuptial virginity. In this sacrifice, vividly but delicately described, Patmore typifies the virginity compatible with all pure nuptial love, virginity of mind. (Cf. "Deliciae Sapientiae" l. 23.) But there is a deeper significance in the sacrifice attributed to Adam and Eve when it is considered in relation to Patmore's ideas on virginity and marriage which he thus briefly expresses: "St. Augustine says of Our Lord: 'Joseph was not less the father because he knew not the Mother of our Lord; as though concupiscence and not conjugal affection constitutes the marriage-bond . . . What others desire to fulfil in the flesh, he, in a more excellent way, fulfilled in the spirit . . . Let us reckon, then, through Joseph . . . The Holy Spirit, reposing in the justice of them both, gave to both a Son.' Every true Lover has perceived, at least in a few moments of his life, that the fullest fruition of love is without the loss of virginity. Lover and Mistress become sensibly one flesh in the instant that they confess to one another a full and mutual complacency of intellect, will, affection, and sense, with the promise of inviolable faith. *That* is the moment of fruition, and all that follows is, as St. Thomas Aquinas says, 'an accidental perfection of marriage'; for such consent breeds indefinite and abiding increase of life between the lovers; which life is none the less real and substantial because it does not manifest itself in a separated entity." (*Magna Moralia,* V.)

An interesting figurative interpretation of the ode is given by Mr. Burdett (p. 138): "Adam, the lover, is used symbolically for the natural man whom God, that is Love, converts into the divine manhood, since the dogma of the Incarnation contains not only an historic statement but a mystery repeated in, and personally to be experienced by, every human being." This last statement is an echo of Patmore's: "Those who fear to call Mary the 'Mother of God' simply do not believe in the Incarnation at all; but we must go further, and believe His word when He rebuked the people for regarding her as exclusively His Mother, declaring that every soul who received Him with faith and love was also, in union with Her,

His Mother, the Bride of the Holy Spirit. We must not be afraid to believe that this Bride and Mother, with whom we are identified, is 'Regina Coeli' as well as 'Regina Mundi.' . . . 'It is not written that He has taken hold (or united Himself) with any of the angels'; but of the lowest of His spiritual creatures, who alone is also flesh, 'He has taken hold'; and the Highest has found His ultimate and crowning felicity in a marriage of the flesh as well as the Spirit; and in this infinite contrast and intimacy of height with depth and spirit with flesh He, who is very Love, finds, just as ordinary human love does, its final rest and the full fruition of its own life . . . Let Christians leave off thinking of the Incarnation as a thing past, or a figure of speech, and learn to know that it consists for them in their becoming the intimately and humanly beloved of a divine and yet human Lover; and His local paradise and heaven of heavens." (*Knowledge and Science,* VIII.)

2. *a heavenly Abyssinian vale:* "According to Josephus (*Ant. Jud.* I, i, 3) the Nile is one of the four great rivers of Paradise. (Cf. Genesis II, 10) This view, adopted by many commentators, is chiefly based on the connection described between Gehon, one of the yet unidentified rivers, and the land of Cush, which, at least in later times was identified with Ethiopia or modern Abyssinia." (Cf. Genesis II, 13.) (*Catholic Encyclopedia.*)

4. *Abora:* a mountain-range.

13. Cf. "Deliciae Sapientiae," l. 115.

30–33. Compare with "Deliciae Sapientiae," ll. 50–56.

35–36. Cf. *supra, Theme.*

52. Cf. "Pain," *passim.*

83. *virgin spousals:* Cf. *supra, Theme;* "The Wedding Sermon" ll. 107–108; "Deliciae Sapientiae" l. 23.

80–85. When Patmore makes the actual sin of Adam and Eve consist in their violation of self-imposed virginity, he is purely imaginative. There is nothing either in Holy Scripture or in Catholic tradition to justify this. According to St. Thomas the sin of our first parents was a sin of pride. "Man was so appointed in the state of innocence that there was no rebellion of the flesh against the spirit. Wherefore it was not possible for the first inordinateness in the human appetite to result from his coveting a sensible good, to which the concupiscence of the flesh tends against the order of reason. It remains therefore that the first inordinateness of the human appetite resulted from his coveting inordinately some spiritual good. Now he would not have coveted it inordinately, by desiring it according to his measure as established by the Divine rule. Hence it follows that man's first sin consisted in his coveting some spiritual good above his measure: and this pertains to pride. Therefore it is evident that man's first sin was pride." (*Summa Theologica,* II, ii, q. 163, art. 1.)

88–90. These lines are descriptive of Man's state subsequent to Adam's sin and previous to the Redemption.

91–99. Man was redeemed by the voluntary sacrifice of Him Who was born in virginal wedlock, *The Son of God and Man.* "Unless the Lord had come into the world and united the human with the divine, the perceptive faculty of good and truth would have been utterly lost to man." (*Aphorisms and Extracts.*) The effect of the Incarnation upon Patmore when, as a very young man, he first came to believe in it is given in his Autobiography. (Cf. "Faint Yet Pursuing," *Theme.*)

92. Cf. "The Child's Purchase," l. 106. "The Blessed Virgin is co-redemptrix with Christ. His visit converts the soul to acknowledge the truth and to obey it in intention, destroying the old Adam. Her visit converts the body, giving gentle disposition and affection, destroying the old Eve." (*Aphorisms and Extracts.*)

94. *like espousals:* such as the virginal espousals which the poet ascribes to Adam and Eve.

ARBOR VITAE

Publication: In *The Week,* January 5, 1878; later included in *Odes* I–XLVI, 1878.

Title: In adopting the Tree of Life to symbolize the Church, Patmore suggests the *tree of life in the midst of paradise* (Genesis II, 9) and *the tree of life, bearing twelve fruits,* mentioned in the Apocalypse XXII, 2.

Theme: After showing that the internal disposition essential for union with God is personal sacrifice that issues in complete detachment from material things and virginity of soul (Cf. "To the Unknown Eros" and "The Contract"), Patmore in this and the following ode presents the Catholic Church under different metaphors as the external guide indispensable to Man in his progress towards union with God, and his infallible norm in judging the authenticity of his intercourse with Him after that union has been accomplished.

1–10. This is a particularly well chosen symbol of the traditional wisdom of the Catholic Church and external growths that have attached themselves to it. There is here a blend of bitter and sweet—unlovely fungus-growths, deformities of untruth, closed scars, the *moss* of slothfulness, the over-growth of pagan lust and the croaking of false prophets.

7–8. After calling attention to this metaphor as descriptive of clusters of the Catholic clergy, Mrs. Meynell calls it "a most unjust image." (*Second Person Singular,* p. 103.)

11–16. The power of Truth to renew itself from within is greater than the power of man to stifle it from without. Through the medium of another symbol, the tides, Patmore express the same idea in "Magna Est Veritas," ll. 9–10.

17–25. The fruit of the tree rejected by the *forest-pigs* of Victorian England because of its unpromising rind, contains the meat and drink that bring savour to the heart and power to the mind.

26–29. Godless creatures despising tradition, wisdom and real culture, defer with a veneer of refinement to the popular vulgarities of their own day and hour. The result is thus described by Mrs. Meynell: "The decivilized have every grace as the antecedent of their vulgarities, every distinction as the precedent of their mediocrities."

28–29. The simile with which the poem closes can hardly be said to err on the side of weakness.

THE STANDARDS

Publication: In *The Pall Mall Gazette,* March 8, 1875, under the title, *"How It Seems to an English Catholic."* In 1877 it was included in the edition of *Odes* I–XXXI.

Title: It may have been suggested by one of the important meditations in St. Ignatius' *Spiritual Exercises* called, "A Meditation on Two Standards: the One of Christ Our Supreme Captain and Lord; the Other of Lucifer, the Mortal Enemy of Our Human Nature."

Theme: It is at once a justification of the Church's action in the Vatican Council, and a summons to all sincere Christians to uphold its teaching of truth. The necessity and difficulties of dogmatic pronouncements in the Church are clearly expressed in the following passage from Patmore's essay, "A People of a Stammering Tongue": "Dogmatic truth is the key and the soul of man is the lock; the proof of the key is in its opening of the lock; and, if it does that, all other evidence of its authenticity is superfluous . . . The key is not less the key because it will not open a lock of which the wards are filled with stones and rusted by disuse or destroyed by sin."

Occasion: The Vatican Council, the twentieth oecumenical council in the history of the Church and the last up to the present, convened December 8, 1869 and adjourned October 20, 1870. On July 18, 1870 it defined Papal Infallibility as "a divinely revealed dogma." This precipitated a storm of protest and opposition in England. One of the most violent objectors was Gladstone whose pamphlet against English Catholics was the immediate occasion of the ode. (Cf. *infra,* ll. 18–19.)

2. *Sion of the Seven Hills:* Rome.

3. *no uncertain blast:* The clear pronouncements of the Vatican Council, especially the Definition of Papal Infallibility. In this the Church followed St. Paul's prescription to the Corinthians (XIV, 6–9): "But now, brethren, if I come to you speaking with tongues, what shall I profit you, unless I speak to you either in revelation, or in knowledge, or in prophecy, or in doctrine? Even things without life that give sound, whether pipe or harp, except they give a distinction of sounds, how shall it be known what is piped or harped? For if the trumpet give an uncertain sound, who shall prepare himself to the battle? So likewise you, except you utter by the tongue plain speech, how shall it be known what is said? For you shall be speaking into the air."

4–6. An allusion to the many hostile reactions against the Decree of Infallibility.

7–11. In these lines Patmore alludes to those Christian sects against whom the *Powers of Hell* had prevailed, thus proving that they were not the churches of Christ. For, Christ had said: "And I say to thee: That thou are Peter; and upon this rock I will build my church, and the gates of hell shall not prevail against it." (St. Matthew XVI, 18.) Many of these sects had, since the Reformation, treated the Catholic Church with contempt. The activity of the Vatican Council provoked them to anger.

12. *our little English band:* English Catholics, especially the English Oratorians of St. Philip Neri, founded by Cardinal Newman.

16. *Edgbaston:* site of the Oratory.

18–19. In 1874, just after Gladstone had retired from his political leadership he launched his bitter attack upon the Vatican Council. He contended that since 1870 no one could become a convert to Catholicism without renouncing "his mental and moral freedom, and placing his civil loyalty and duty at the mercy of another." (Ward's *Life of Cardinal Newman,* vol. II, p. 401) In November 1874, he published a pamphlet entitled, "The Vatican Decrees in Their Bearing on Civil Allegiance." This was *the black flag of Hate.* The answering gleam of *Love irate* was Cardinal Newman's "Letter to the Duke of Norfolk," published in January 1875.

21–22. Simultaneously with these events in England was the Kulturkampf in Germany and the notorious "May Laws" (1873–75), legalizing the persecution of Catholics led by Bismark.

32. *the Flower of Sharon:* the bloom of faith in a particular country.

33. *the Stalk:* the parent Church.

42. *Egypt:* symbol of the idolatry and spiritual slavery of the Chosen People during the years of their exile in Egypt.

Canaan (Chanaan): symbol of true religion and spiritual emancipation. The Land of Chanaan, in Palestine, was given to Abram when the Lord appeared to him and said: "To thy seed will I give this land." (Genesis XII, 7.) From it the Chosen People went into exile in Egypt and to it they returned when their exile was over.

45. "For as lightning cometh out of the east, and appeareth even into the west: so shall also the coming of the Son of Man be." (St. Matthew XXIV, 27.) "The West in Scripture and all ancient mythologies symbolized the flesh, as the East the spirit. Hence, 'The coming of the Lord is as the shining light, which shineth from the East unto the West,' conversion beginning in the Spirit and ending in the flesh." (*Homo,* XXX.)

48–49. The *humility* of Christ as Man is still a stumbling block to some. To others His divinity is still a stumbling block.

50. *A stumbling:* "And he shall be a sanctification to you. But for a stone of stumbling . . . to the two houses of Israel." (Isaias VIII, 14.) "But we preach Christ crucified, unto the Jews indeed a stumbling block, and unto the Gentiles foolishness." (1 Corinthians I, 23.)

the first bid to the Feast: 1. The Jews to whom Christ came primarily. 2. The faithful, "that have borne the burden of the day and the heat." (St. Matthew XX, 12.)

53. *either gathering host:* enemies of the Church in England and Germany.

54. *false allegiance:* the allegiance given a false religious faith.

57. *our Flag:* the flag of the Church.

61–63. This would seem to be an allusion to Irishmen that does Patmore small honor.

68. *Borgia;* Alexander VI, type of false High-Priest of the New Law.

Caiphas: false High-Priest of the Old Law.

69–74. Here Patmore develops his favorite theme by contrast—the liberty of true faith in the Church of Christ, is opposed to the so-called liberty of faith in a man-made creed.

75–80. After describing the enemies of the Church as a majority that dislikes the *lesser host,* English Catholics, Patmore calls upon them to look to the Mount of Transfiguration and to eternity.

81–90. This is a summons to all Christians who believe in Christ as God.

83. *Yea:* In the King James Version we read: "For the Son of God, Jesus Christ, who was preached among you by us, . . . was not yea and nay, but in Him was yea. For all the promises of God in Him *are* yea, and in Him Amen, unto the glory of God by us." (2 Corinthians I, 19–20.)

86. *either:* any.

88. *order'd Angels:* the hierarchy of heavenly messengers from God to man as seen by Jacob. (Cf. Genesis XXVIII, 12.) They are suggestive of the hierarchical order in the Church. (Cf. "Wedding Sermon," ll. 387–93.)

91–107. After hailing unbelievers and summoning those *who adore in any way,* the poet now calls upon those souls bound by vows of obedience (ll. 91–94), poverty (ll. 95–101), and chastity (ll. 102–106). (Cf. "Legem Tuam Dilexi," ll. 62–102.)

94. *the Husband of all life:* Christ, the Spouse of the soul. "St. Augustine writes that 'Jesus Christ is the Bride as well as the Bridegroom; for He is the Body,' a saying confirmed by St. Paul's 'Nevertheless the man is not without the woman; but let God be all in all'; and by St. John of the Cross, who says that, at great heights of contemplation, it is possible to love the Son with the love of the Father—whose love is the love of a Bridegroom." (*Homo* VII.) (Cf. "Deliciae Sapientiae de Amore," l. 80.)

104. "And now there remain faith, hope and charity, these three; but the greatest of these is charity." (1 Corinthians, XIII, 13.)

109. This sanction is seldom understood and accepted. Yet it is the literal fulfilment of Christ's prophetic words at the Last Supper: "If the world hate you, know ye, that it hath hated Me before you. If you had been of the world, the world would love its own: but because you are not of the world, but I have chosen you out of the world, therefore the world hateth you. *Remember my word that I said to you: The servant is not greater than his master. If they have persecuted Me, they will also persecute you.*" (St. John XV, 18–20.)

115–16. In the King James Version of the Apocalypse (II, 17) we read: "He that hath an ear, let him hear what the Spirit saith unto the churches; To him that overcometh will I give to eat of the hidden manna, and will give him a white stone, and in the stone a new name written, which no man knoweth saving he that receiveth *it.*" The Vulgate uses *counter* instead of *stone.*

117–19. "And a mighty angel took up a stone, as it were a great millstone, and cast it into the sea, saying: with such violence as this shall Babylon, that great city be thrown down, and shall be found no more at all." (Apocalypse XVIII, 21.)

SPONSA DEI

Publication: In *Odes* I–XXXI, 1877.

Title: It was very probably suggested by the "Canticle of Canticles" and St. Bernard's sermons. This was the title, also, of Patmore's prose work which he destroyed. (Cf. Champneys I, pp. 315–19.) It may not be altogether irrelevant to remark here that according to the evidence at hand concerning this regrettable happening, it is far from certain that it was chiefly the result of a criticism made by Father Hopkins. (Cf. Champneys II, pp. 351–52.) Father Hopkins' comment, "That's telling secrets," was made in August 1885. Patmore, always impulsive and quick to act, did not destroy the work until Christmas 1887. When Father Hopkins wrote expressing his regret at Patmore's action, Patmore explained that he had consulted his confessor and had talked with Dr. Rouse and consequently felt free to do what Father Hopkins' condemnation of the little book inclined him to do. (Cf. *Portrait of My Family,* Derek Patmore, p. 220.)

Theme: Having shown the internal disposition of soul and the external directive force required for the personal approach of Man to God, the poet now abandons the parable as a medium of expression and directly reveals the nature of Man's personal relationship to God, a relationship that includes the body as well as the soul. Hence, in this ode, in "Legem Tuam Dilexi" and in "To the Body," Patmore reiterates his favorite theme that things of the flesh prefigure and are the foundation of those of the spirit.

As St. Bernard writes: "Because we are carnal (Romans VII, 14) and are born of the concupiscence of the flesh (1 St. John II, 16), it follows as a necessary consequence that our desire for personal gratification, or our love should have its source in the flesh. But if it is directed according to the right order of things, advancing by its several degrees under the guidance of grace, it will at last be consummated by the spirit because: *that was not first which is spiritual, but that which is natural; afterwards that which is spiritual."* (1 Corinthians XV, 46.) (*On the Love of God,* Chapter XV, § 1.)

Among many passages in Patmore's prose that throw light upon the theme of this ode is the following: "God has declared to us His mystic rapture in His Marriage with Humanity in twice saying, 'Hic est Filius meus dilectus in quo bene complacui.' He expressly and repeatedly calls this marriage, and pronounces the marriage of Man and Woman to be its symbol. *This is the burning heart of the Universe."* (*Aphorisms and Extracts.*)

Speaking of this ode as an expression of the very essence of Patmore's theme—the analogy between and in a very literal sense the identity of conjugal and divine love, Mr. Burdett writes: "It catches the theme at the highest point to which the Dean had carried it in 'The Wedding Sermon' . . . To Patmore, as we know, every mood of human love, however transient, was a symbol. Its immediate significance was explored in 'The Angel.' Its transcendental inference is the subject of 'Sponsa Dei.'" (p. 135.) The highest point to which the Dean carried the theme in "The Wedding Sermon" might well be ll. 55–106. The best and most complete expression of this theme in prose will be found in Patmore's essays, "The Precursor" and "Dieu et ma Dame."

Finally, this ode is the fulfilment of the poet's promise in *The Angel in the House,* Bk. I, Canto vi, Prelude ii:

"This little germ of nuptial love,
  Which springs so simply from the sod,
The root is, as my song shall prove,
  Of all our love to man and God."

1–7. This question is repeated in ll. 22–39. The answer is given in ll. 45–56.

3. *renew'd virginity:* this effect of human love is characteristic of Patmore's ideal.

4–6. It is a peculiarity of human love that its longings beget expectations of its consummating joys which, in the event, prove a disappointment. (Cf. *infra* ll. 45–56.)

7. "In love, the woman, who is 'the body,' desires to be utterly captive to the man's will, and he, in return, to be utterly captive to her body." ("Dieu et ma Dame.")

8–12. The element of infatuation in human love here described has its divine counter-part in the soul's love of God and God's love of the soul. "As with a mortal lover, there is . . . an appearance of infatuation in the love of God for the elect soul. Though just and beneficent to others, He has nothing but boundless indulgence to her." ("Dieu et ma Dame.")

13–17. The parity between this element of human love and divine is also described in the essay, "Dieu et ma Dame": "His soul lives in and is moved blissfully by every turn of her head and motion of her limbs. He already is carried hither and thither in all her movements, although he is not yet numerically one flesh with her; but this is much more so with the Divine Lover, who actually enjoys that distinctness in identity to which the mortal lover only and for ever in vain aspires, namely, to be 'man compassed by a woman,' as Isaiah says, speaking of that Incarnation which is effected more or less in each of the elect, as in Jesus Himself perfectly."

18. "Another phenomenon common to both kinds of love is the longing—almost the first that arises in every true lover's bosom—to die for the sake of the beloved. 'I have longed for this hour,' said Our Lord. But none, save God, can die and yet live for her." ("Dieu et ma Dame.")

19–21. "St. Theresa declares that more good is done by one minute of reciprocal contemplative communion of love with God than by the founding of fifty hospitals or of fifty churches. 'The elect soul,' says another great experimentalist, St. Francis of Sales, 'is a beautiful and beloved lady, of whom God demands not the indignity of service, but desires only her society and her person.'" ("Christianity and Progress.")

22–39. The question asked in ll. 1–7 is here repeated.

30–34. Cf. "The Child's Purchase" ll. 161–62.

30. *this only happy She:* Francis Thompson's love of ideal Woman, is reflected in the following record which he has left of his habits of prayer: "It was my practice from the time I left college to pray for the lady whom I was destined to love—the unknown She." (*Life,* p. 58.) (Cf. "Wind and Wave," ll. 7–13.)

35–36. Recall the Dean's words in "The Wedding Sermon," ll. 362–65.

36. *Earth's last lowlihead:* a human lover, whether man or woman.

37. *the Heaven high:* Christ, the Spouse of the soul. (Cf. "The Standards," l. 94.)

38. This line, descriptive of the eternal union of the soul with Christ is redolent of the imagery of the "Canticle of Canticles." "The love between God and the soul is constantly declared to be, in its highest perfection, the love that subsists between bride and Bridegroom ('thy Maker is thy Husband,' *etc.*), and our only means of understanding and attaining to these supernatural relations are meditations and contemplations of their types in nature. 'The unseen is known by that which is seen.'" ("The Precursor.") (Cf. "Deliciae Sapientiae," l. 80.)

39. Human love with its longings that no human being can satisfy, is *madness* if there be no satisfaction for it hereafter. But if in the soul's union with Christ it will know the fulness of satisfaction, its unrequited longings in this life, will prove a *prophecy* of what is to be.

"Every one who has loved and reflected on love for an instant, knows very well that what is vulgarly regarded as the end of that passion, is, as the Church steadfastly maintains, no more than its accident. The flower is not for the seed, but the seed for the flower. And yet what is that flower, if it be not the rising bud of another flower, flashed for a moment of eternal moment before our eyes, and at once withdrawn, lest we should misunderstand the prophecy and take it for our final good? If it be other than a symbol, that is, as Coleridge defines a symbol to be, a part taken to represent the whole, then love, which the heart of every lover knows to be the supreme sanity, must be condemned by the intellect as the supreme insanity; and its 'extravagances,' which, from the Church's point of view, are in the highest representative order, must be looked upon as those of a maniac who takes a green goose for a goddess and himself for a god. But all this becomes clear when the parties to love are regarded as priest and priestess to one another of the divine womanhood and the divine manhood which are inherent in original Deity. They are but ministers to each other of the 'great sacrament' of that glory 'which the Son had with the Father before the beginning of the world.'" ("The Precursor.")

The same sentiment concerning married lovers is found in the Encyclical *Casti Conubii:* "Therefore the sacred partnership of true marriage is constituted both by the will of God and the will of man. From God comes the very institution of marriage, the ends for which it was instituted, the laws that govern it, the blessings that flow from it; while man, through generous surrender of his own person made to another for the whole span of life, becomes, with the help and co-operation of God, the author of each particular marriage, with the duties and blessings annexed thereto from divine institution."

40–41. Apropos of these lines there is an interesting passage in Patmore's essay, "Religio Poetae": "Christ said, 'I have yet many things to say to you: but you cannot bear them now. But when He, the Spirit of truth is come, He will teach you all truth' (St. John XVI, 12–13). Under the first dispensation men were servants of God; under the second His sons: 'we are now the sons of God: and it hath not yet appeared what we shall be' (1 St. John III, 2). What if, under a third, 'the voice of the Bride and the Bridegroom shall be heard in our streets?'" (Cf. Jeremias VII, 34, and "Eros and Psyche," ll. 146–49.)

42–44. Cf. "Deliciae Sapientiae de Amore," ll. 135–45.

44. *One:* Christ.

45–56. In this answer to the question asked in ll. 1–7 and repeated in ll. 22–39, is the quintessence of the ode and of Patmore's message. In every case of the love between human lovers it promises more than it actually gives. In anticipation it appears to be able to satisfy the human heart. In actual attainment it proves incapable of fulfilling its high promise, unless it be referred to the reality of which it is a parable—the love of God.

"Woman is the sum and complex of all nature, and is the *visible* glory of God. The divine manhood, indeed, may be *discerned* in man through the cloud of that womanhood of which he is a participator, inasmuch as he also is the Body, which, as St. Augustine says, 'is the Bride.' The 'Word made Flesh' is the word made Woman, and therefore, as that Word constantly affirms, we can know or discern the First Person only through the Second; and, in the relations of Man and Woman and of Christ and the Soul, it is the common womanhood that is the ground and means of communion of the higher with the lower." (*Homo* X.) (Cf. "Beata," *Theme;* "Wind and Wave," ll. 7–13.)

45. "No writer, sacred or profane, ever uses the words 'he' or 'him' of the soul. It is always 'she' or 'her'; so universal is the intuitive knowledge that the soul, with regard to God who is her life, is feminine." (*Aurea Dicta,* XXI.)

48–50. Cf. "The Azalea," l. 25.

53–55. "Man and Woman are as the charcoal poles of the electric light, lifeless in themselves, but, in conjunction, the vehicles of and sharers in the fire and splendour which burst forth from the embrace of the original duality of Love, in the double-tongued flames of Pentecost. They are modes and means of God's fruition of Himself in Nature, and the more they confess and discern their own nullity, the greater will be their share in His power of felicity." (*Homo* XII.)

56. The poem ends with a stern reminder that purity in love is the condition of all that has been said of it as the source of human joy that is precursive of the divine. (Cf. *supra, Theme.*) This purity, moreover, cannot be lost unless it is deliberately forfeited, and the realization of this is the soul's surest source of consolation.

"So long as love in the soul is only in the initial state of light, or assent to and admiration of what is most excellent, the light may be quenched by other lights, less pure and bright, but nearer; when, again, the light descends into the will, this may not be able to bear the strain of a love that calls for continual fidelity of correspondence; but when it reaches the sensible affections and has been crowned in mutual and ineffable complacencies, there is no longer any practical danger of separation . . . His mercies are now 'the *sure* mercies of David,' and though she acknowledges that there is still a hypothetical possibility of divorce should she fall, as it is practically incredible that she now can, a possibility that causes her to 'rejoice with trembling,' yet, on the whole, she is '*sure* that neither death, nor life, nor angels, nor principalities, nor powers, nor things present, nor things to come, nor height, nor depth, nor any other creature,' shall be able to separate her from her Love." ("Dieu et ma Dame.")

LEGEM TUAM DILEXI

Publication: In *Odes* I–XXXI, 1877.

Title: It is Psalm CXVIII, 113 and is thus translated in the Vulgate: "I have loved thy law."

Theme: It is a development of the spiritual delight that results from man's joyous and free observance of the restraints of God's law. (Cf. "Sponsa Dei," *Theme.*) The central idea is expressed in *Aurea Dicta* III, and in the following passage from Patmore's essay, "Religio Poetae": "The Poet always treats spiritual realities as the concrete and very credible things they are. He has no slipshod notions about the immeasurable and 'infinite.' He knows, as Plato knew, that God Himself is most falsely described as infinite. God is the synthesis, as Proclus declares in his treatise on the Fables of Homer, of 'Infinite' and 'Boundary,' and is excellently intelligible, though forever unutterable by those who love Him." The development of this idea as we find it in this ode is foreshadowed in the last lines of "The Joyful Wisdom," descriptive of souls distinguished in God's service:

"Nay, continence and gratitude
So cleanse their lives from earth's alloy,
They taste, in Nature's common food,
Nothing but spiritual joy.
They shine like Moses in the face,
And teach our hearts, without the rod,
That God's grace is the only grace,
And all grace is the grace of God."

(*The Angel in the House,* Bk. I, Canto X, Prelude 1.)

Another foreshadowing of this theme is found in the following lines concerning which Patmore's daughter, Sister Christina, wrote: "To encourage myself in little trials I often repeat these lines. They make me so ashamed to complain of so little":

"Splendid privations, martyrdoms
To which no weak remission comes,
Perpetual passion for the good
Of them that feel no gratitude,
Far circlings, as of planets' fires,
Round never-to-be-reach'd desires,
Whatever rapturously sighs
That life is love, love sacrifice."

(*Victories of Love,* Bk. II, Letter X.)

Sister Christina wrote concerning 'Legem Tuam Dilexi': "It is delightful to me, and I do not know how people can object to it while God, of whom we name so many attributes, is defined to be 'A Simple Act' by the Christian Doctrine books." (*A Daughter of Coventry Patmore,* p. 142.)

1–3. The daring line with which the poem opens, at first reading seems blasphemous. To Patmore the idea of *Infinite,* in itself, with no beginning, no end, no limits, was *horrible* when viewed in the light of reason. But when considered in the light of Christ's revelation and its finite analogues of beauty, truth and love, the *Infinite* became the chief inspiration of his song and the chief delight of his soul. All finite *life, power, joy* and *love,* he tells us, is necessarily confined within limits and seeks satisfaction in a definite object. Hence, *at feud* with the *'Infinite.'*

"Nothing is so fatal to that 'real apprehension' which is the life of truth, as thinking about the 'infinite.' Truth must be intelligible to be influential. Our Lord's sufferings cease to impress us if we think of them as infinite, and the bliss of heaven itself requires the idea of limit to make it attractive. I was much helped, on reading the other day—I think in St. Thomas Aquinas—that some attain, in this life, to degrees of felicity beyond the felicity of some who are already in heaven. *Our* God is very Man, and we can know nothing of Him but in so far as He is mirrored in our own humanity. Hence the Church maintains that the supreme wisdom is to meditate continually on the Incarnation, which is limitation." (*Homo* III.)

4–6. "Paul standing in the midst of the Areopagus said: Ye men of Athens, I perceive that in all things you are too superstitious. For passing by, and seeing your idols, I found an altar also, on which was written: *To the unknown God.* What therefore you worship, without knowing it, that I preach to you." (Acts XVII, 22–23.)

7–8. *ere It was reveal'd:* Concerning the time of God's revelation of the mystery of the Trinity we read in the *Catholic Encyclopedia:* "Many of the early Fathers not merely believed that the Prophets had testified of it, they held that it had been made known even to the Patriarchs . . . But in others of the Fathers is found what would appear to be the sounder view, *viz.,* that no distinct intimation of the doctrine was given under the Old Covenant."

According to the central doctrine of the Christian religion signified by the term Trinity, in the unity of the *One* Godhead there are *Three* Persons, the Father, the Son and the Holy Spirit, these Three Persons being truly distinct one from another. "The Father, the Word, and the Holy Spirit are the three dimensions of God, and the apprehension of Him has no substance or reality without them." (*Aurea Dicta,* CLI.) In St. Bernard we read: "Nor let it seem absurd that I have said that even God lives by law, since I said by no other law save charity. What in that supreme and blessed Trinity preserves that supreme and unspeakable unity, save charity? It is law, then, and charity the law of the Lord which in a certain way holds the Trinity together in unity and binds it *in the bond of peace*." (Ephesians IV, 3.) (*On the love of God,* Chapt. XII, § 2.)

11–15. Despite the great perfection of Lucifer and the angels who revolted with him, they were still creatures, still finite. In the Prophecy of Isaias (XIV, 13–15) we read of Lucifer: "And thou saidst in thy heart: I will ascend into heaven, I will exalt my throne above the stars of God, I will sit in the mountain of the covenant, in the sides of the north. I will ascend above the height of the clouds, *I will be like the most High.* But yet thou shalt be brought down to hell, into the depth of the pit."

Patmore conceives God's punishment of the fallen angels as affording them some *relief* from their desire to be infinite. *In dashing of themselves against the shores of pain,* their very contact with finite reality, even though that reality be hell, is at once a relief and a frustration of their longing to be infinite.

16–30. The spirit of rebellion is found everywhere in nature. In minerals, in plants and in animals, the chaos that would follow upon the triumph of centrifugal over centripetal forces is prevented by the imposition upon every one, of an appropriate repressive force which gives them form and vigour—hardness to the stone, softness to plants and flowers, and pliancy to the worm.

18–20. In Patmore's essay, "Imagination," he tells the following remarkable incident about a child of nine who "lay stretched on a gravel path staring intently on the pebbles. 'They are alive,' he cried, in the writer's hearing: 'they are always wanting to burst, but something draws them in.' This infantine rediscovery of the doctrine of the coinherence of attraction and repulsion in matter seems to have been an effort of direct insight."

34–36. In the daily birth of new finite creatures God, *Buildeth new bulwarks 'gainst the Infinite;* and continues voluntarily to confine His Infinite Nature, as it were, within the bonds of finite beings. "The infinite circumscribed by the finite, the great by the small, is the insoluble paradox which teases human affection with inexhaustible delight, as it is the thought which kindles and keeps alive the devotion of the Saint." ("The Weaker Vessel.") The *just Man* imitates God, Patmore tells us, in voluntarily restraining his powers of body and soul in accordance with God's law and as a consequence shares God's *delight, freedom* and *right.* "To such a man the Incarnation becomes, not the central dogma of his faith, but the central fact of his experience; for it is going on perceptibly in himself." ("Christianity an Experimental Science.")

31–33. In St. Thomas we read: "In spiritual things there is a twofold servitude and a twofold freedom: for there is the servitude of sin and the servitude of justice; and there is likewise a twofold freedom, from sin, and from justice, as appears from the words of the Apostle (Romans VI, 20, 22): *When you were the servants of sin you were free men to justice; . . . but now being made free from sin, you are . . . become servants of God.*" (*Summa* II, ii, q. 183, art. 4.)

The *just Man* in affirming *God's limits* upon *himself* follows the example of Christ as St. Thomas describes it: "Christ conformed His conduct in all things to the precepts of the Law. In token of this He wished even to be circumcised; for the circumcision is a kind of protestation of a man's purpose of keeping the Law, according to Galatians V, 3: *I testify to every man circumcising himself, that he is a debtor to do the whole Law.*" (*Summa* III, q. 40, art. 4.)

The degrees of perfection in the observance of the law is thus briefly expressed by St. Bernard in commenting upon these words of the *Canticle of Canticles* (I, 1): *Let Him kiss me with the kiss of His mouth:* "If one is a servant he is in dread of his lord's face. If one is a hireling he hopes for pay from his lord's hand. If one is a disciple he gives ear to his teacher. If one is a son he honors his father. But the soul who begs a kiss, is in love. Among the gifts of nature this affection of love holds first place, especially when it makes haste to return to its Origin, which is God." ("Sermons on the *Canticle of Canticles,*" Sermon VII, § 2; Translation, p. 77.) This passage represents St. Bernard's adaptation of St. Paul's words to the Galatians, chapter IV, from which is taken the Epistle of the Sunday within the octave of Christmas.

37–46. By a divine paradox God's nature, infinite in itself and as it is in heaven, becomes finite (confined within bounds) in *His homestead in the human heart* and soul where He dwells through His love and grace. Thus God's infinite love seeks satisfaction in the finite, as it were, suing for man's love, using *His* infinite *art* to win man to repeat in his finite way, His infinite song of love. Patmore's own commentary on these lines is this: "If we must think of the Infinite, the most profitable way is to think of God as having made Himself infinitely small, a mere babe sucking a woman's breast, to suit Himself to the smallness of our capacities. Doubtless, the Beggar Maid, like other little Mistresses of great Lovers, did not love him for his greatness, but because he was not too great to kiss her, and to love to hear her sigh 'Darling!' as little maids do, in such circumstances, matching thus, by the greatness of their innocent audacity, the unguessed greatness of their spouses." (*Homo,* IV.)

Patmore's daughter, Sister Mary Christina, wrote to her father concerning these lines: "I must have the pleasure of telling you again how often your words come to my mind and answer my thoughts. I was wondering one day if it was pleasing to God to hear us say the same psalms over and over again, and I remembered what you say of the child wanting its mother to repeat her little song." (*A Daughter of Coventry Patmore,* p. 137.)

41–43. "God's strength, like man's, is perfected in weakness. When the Soul has entered upon her third and crowning stage of perfection and union, His divine weakness for her gives Him far more influence over her will than would be obtained by any display of His power and other attributes." ("Dieu et ma Dame.")

47. This is a reverent parody of the cry in Isaias (XXI, 11): "Watchman, what of the night?"

48–53. The physical elements that combine to form the beauty of the firmament take their significance from man for whom God created them and around whom His love moves as its centre.

53–56. The beauty and mystery of God's love for man could hardly be expressed more tenderly or in symbols more beautiful and clear. In view of man's freedom of will, God literally *woos* but does not force him. Again, from God's infinite love and Man's finite capacity to love arises the divine paradox here so tenderly expressed in Patmore's concept that the essence of God's love is distilled, as it were, into a drop, man's span when compared with God's infinity. Of these lines Mr. Page writes (p. 20): "This is the sensitive life of the soul, at least; and in effect it is the 'unitive life.' "

57–58. Select souls find the requirements of God's law insufficient to prove their love for Him. Consequently, they impose upon themselves added bonds, religious vows, as a further proof of their love for Him. "Between lovers, things which, under ordinary relationships, are only 'counsels of perfection,' become obligatory duties." ("Dieu et ma Dame.")

62. *the threefold golden chain:* the religious vows of Poverty, Chastity and Obedience.

63–66. By the vow of Poverty a Religious surrenders the right to possess material things as his own. But the necessary material things of life are given him *without care or thought.* This is a part of the hundredfold: "And every one that hath left house, or brethren, or sisters, or father, or mother, or wife, or children, or lands for my name's sake, shall receive an hundredfold, and shall possess life everlasting." (St. Matthew XIX, 29.)

67–76. By the voluntary submission of one's will in the vow of Obedience, a Religious finds more complete freedom than others. (Cf. *supra,* ll. 31–33.)

77–81. By the vow of Chastity a religious sacrifices the *dear bliss* of family life but attains a loftier bliss of the spirit.

79–81. There are many striking expressions of this same thought in Patmore's prose, such as the paragraph from "Cheerfulness in Life and Art," quoted in the notes on "Victory in Defeat" (ll. 9–10), and this from "Peace in Life and Art": "The peace which is 'identical with perfect joy' in life and its expression in art, is also identical with purity, which is so far from being, as is commonly supposed, a negative quality, that it is the unimpeded ardour of ordered life in all its degrees, and is as necessary to the full delight of the senses as it is to the highest felicity of the spirit." And in St. Paul (Romans VII, 22–23) we read: "For I am delighted with the law of God, according to the inward man. But I see another law in my members, fighting against the law of my mind, and captivating me in the law of sin that is in my members."

82–95. The *self-dissipating* wave of *natural sense* confined within the *artful dykes* of restraint exacted by the vow of Chastity, quickens the whole being with love and drives it back to its source, God, instead of allowing it to dissipate itself in natural love. Just so, the waters of a river restrained by dykes flow backward to their source and irrigate the soil, bestowing upon it a fecundity far beyond that which it otherwise would have had.

In St. Bernard we read: "Love is a great thing if only it returns to its First Principle, if it has been restored to its Source, if having flowed back to its Fountain-head, it draws from thence the power to flow on forever." ("Sermons on the *Canticle of Canticles,*" Sermon LXXXIII, §4; translation, p. 230.) (Cf. "The Wedding Sermon," ll. 17–20.)

It is interesting to contrast the intensity of these lines with the cold restraint of Patmore's earlier ideas on chastity and virginity. (Cf. "Deliciae Sapientiae," *Theme.*)

96–101. The *intense life* of vowed Chastity may be entirely missed by those who are not Religious. Seen at too great a distance it may appear *ludicrous,* as do physical objects when not viewed in proper perspective.

104. *the Wild Ass's bray:* the cry raised against the religious life in post-Reformation England when the monasteries were despoiled.

105–107. Signs of the violence in the spoliation and devastation of English monasteries are still preserved in their melancholy ruins. (Cf. *The Ruined Abbeys of Great Britain,* Ralph Adams Cram.)

TO THE BODY

Publication: First included in the sequence of the *Unknown Eros,* as one of *Odes* I–XLVI, 1878.

Theme: Together with "Legem Tuam Dilexi" and "Pain," this ode completes the foundation upon which rests the significance of the best that Patmore has written. In many of the other odes we enjoy the *rod* and *flower* of human love. Here we have its *root* and its soil, the human body. To Patmore the body was literally the temple of the Holy Ghost, and it was more. It was such a body as had been made the special dwelling-place of God when the Second Person of the Blessed Trinity became Man. Hence, for Patmore, the body derived its ultimate significance from the Incarnation in which a human body gave form, as it were, to God Himself and was thus sanctified beyond our powers of comprehension.

"The boldest confession of the doctrine of the Incarnation, with all its corollaries, has been the father of that splendid virtue which was but dimly foreshown in pre-Christian ideas of purity. Where-ever this doctrine has been denied or hesitatingly taught, it is a fact of simple experience that chastity has suffered with it. For what considerations can ordinary morals or the widest suggestions of worldly expediency substitute for those with which the New Testament abounds? *Glorify and bear God in your bodies* (1 Corinthians VI, 20); *Shall I take the members of Christ and make them the members of a harlot?* (*Ibid.* 15); and, *the body is . . . for the Lord, and the Lord for the body.* (*Ibid.* 13.) ("Ancient and Modern Ideas of Purity.")

In his essay, "Christianity an Experimental Science," Patmore speaks of, "that first kiss of God, that baptism of fire which is the tacit knowledge of the Incarnation—for is it not God made one with his body?"

This ode is the lyrical result of Patmore's literal acceptance of St. Paul's bidding: "Glorify and bear God in your body." (1 Corinthians VI, 20.) In his prose we find the same idea expressed on nearly every page as in the following passages: "The Catholic Church, which alone of all Churches teaches the Incarnation as a present reality, attaches the first importance to the preservation of the sanctity and purity of the body, as actually the 'House of God.'" (*Homo,* II.) And again: "'Your bodies are the Temple of God,' and they who go out of their bodies, *i.e.* their higher senses and powers of real apprehension, to seek Him, burn their powder in a dish instead of a gun-barrel, and the result is much flame but little force." (*Homo* XXXIII.)

Technique: Here we find Patmore's technique at its best. Maurice Francis Egan says of the sweeping phrase with which the ode opens: "It is like the full tide of the first movement of a symphony; it gives the time and the scope of the piece." (*Studies in Literature,* p. 103.)

1–12. Of these lines Maurice Francis Egan has written: "This is dignified; this is solemn; it is pitched in the highest plane of aspiration; it will bear any analysis based on Patmore's theory of catalexis." (*Ibid.* p. 104.)

1–2. "Spirit craves conjunction with and eternal captivity to that which is not spirit; and the higher the spirit the greater the craving. God desires depths of humiliation and contrast of which man has no idea; so that the stony callousness and ignorance which we bemoan in ourselves may not impossibly be an additional cause in Him of desire for us." (*Homo* XXVII.)

1. "And He said: Let us make man to Our image and likeness: and let him have dominion over the fishes of the sea, and the fowls of the air, and the beasts, and the whole earth, and every creeping creature that moveth upon the earth." (*Genesis* I, 26.)

2. The living, human body is chief of the finite analogues that make the word *Infinite* less horrible. (Cf. "Legem Tuam Dilexi, l. 1.) It hems in, as it were, and is the literal incarnation of God's infinite attributes thus made visible to man. "You may see the disc of Divinity quite clearly through the smoked glass of humanity, but no otherwise." (*Aurea Dicta* CL.) The rhyme of *infinitude* with *good* is certainly no technical excellence.

3. This is a figurative reiteration of l. 1.

4–5. The decree of creation was from all eternity and God *long'd for* its execution, as it were, until it became effective on the last day of creation. (Cf. Genesis I, 31.) As Patmore expresses it: "The Incarnation was an act done in eternity as well as time. The Lamb, the 'I am before Abraham was,' was 'slain from the beginning'; and if we look from the point of view of eternity, we may see that effects of that act, apparently retrospective, were not really so." ("The Bow Set in the Cloud.")

The complete satisfaction of divine longing, however, was not attained in the mere creation of the human body. "In His union and conjunction with Body, God finds His final perfection and felicity. 'It is not written that He has taken hold of any of the angels; but of us He has taken hold.' 'Deliciae meae esse cum filiis *hominum.*' The great prophecy, 'Man shall be compassed by a woman,' was fulfilled when Jesus Christ made the body which He had taken from Mary, actually divine by the subdual of its last recalcitrance upon the Cross. The celestial marriage in which, thenceforward, every soul that chose could participate, was then consummated." (*Knowledge and Science,* I.)

5. The rhyme of *eternity* with *sky* is hardly an example of rhyme that should, according to Patmore, appeal primarily to the ear.

7–8. Cf. *infra,* ll. 13–22. The sense of these lines would seem to be improved by the following changes in punctuation—the deletion of the comma after *dome* and the insertion of a comma after *music.*

8–10. A further development of l. 2.

11–12. Here Patmore parts company with the false doctrines of Puritans and Manicheans concerning the body and its pleasures. There can be no sin in bodily pleasures so long as the soul remains the *Spouse* of Christ. Such pleasures are as compatible with spiritual joy, as illegitimate pleasures are opposed to it. (Cf. "Pain," ll. 44–60.)

Patmore was convinced that Swinburne had borrowed these lines in a volume of his poetry that appeared just before the publication of this ode. Hence the explanatory note which Patmore wrote: "The proofs of the additional sixteen Odes were in print and in the hands of many of my friends, Lord Houghton, Mr. Monteith, A. de Vere, Woolner, *etc.,* about twelve months before their publication in the second edition of *Eros.* Just before their publication a volume of Mr. Swinburne appeared with these lines in it:—

'God's little pleasure house
For him and for his spouse.' "

20–22. "God's Law is the 'ten-stringed harp' of David, and all the music of life resides in the various and measured vibration with which it responds to the touch of the passions. Sin snaps the strings in its ignorant and brutal preference of noise to music." (*Aurea Dicta* C.)

Again: "The glorified body, which some, for instance St. Theresa, have seen in this life, is the ten-stringed harp of David, each of its members constituting a distinct note, corresponding to one of the ten spheres; and its tones and combinations of tones are

Sweet as stops
Of planetary music heard in trance.

In the brief, virginal vision of natural love this fact is sufficiently apparent to take away all excuse for irreverent regard for the Soul's blissful and immortal companion, the Body, and to supply the most *sensible* motive for whatever self-denial may be necessary to the attainment of that vision in perpetuity." (*Homo* XXXII.)

22. The harmony *of the spheres,* as a reverberation of the harmony of God and a symbol of the nuptial dance of the angels, is described by Milton. (Cf. *Paradise Lost,* Bk. V, ll. 620–27.)

23–24. One of the chief functions of the human body is procreation. This function with its pleasures as well as its pains Christ raised to the dignity of a sacrament, Matrimony. This is a fact but *darkly* named by false *prophets* who cry *"Shame"* upon that which Christ has blessed.

There is, undoubtedly, in these lines an inference of that higher destiny of the human body joined with the human soul in a union in which, as it were, God becomes again incarnate in Man through the indwelling of the Holy Ghost. "There is one secret, the greatest of all—a secret which no previous religion dared, even in enigma, to allege fully—which is stated with the utmost distinctness by Our Lord and the Church; though this very distinctness seems to act as a thick veil, hiding the disc of the revelation as that of the Sun is hidden by its rays, and causing the eyes of men to avert themselves habitually from that one centre of all seeing. I mean the doctrine of the Incarnation, regarded not as an historical event which occurred 2000 years ago, but as an event which is renewed in the body of every one who is in the way to the fulfilment of his original destiny." (*Homo* XIX.) (Cf. *infra,* ll. 4–5.)

24. "The foul, puritanical leaven of the Reformation has infected the whole of Christianity, and it is now almost impossible to speak with any freedom and effect on the doctrine of the Incarnation without shocking the sensibilities of those who, like the angels who fell, insist on being purer than God, and refusing worship to 'the fullness of the Godhead manifested bodily.'" (*Homo* XXXIV.)

25–26. These lines declare the power of the human body over the human soul. In this fight Manicheans would give the palm to *Hell.* In the teaching of the Church concerning matrimony, for instance, Heaven triumphs.

"Perfect, easy and abiding control over the senses is the fundamental condition of perceptive knowledge of God, and this control consists, not in the destruction of the senses, and in the denial of their testimonies, but in the conversion of them from smoky torches into electric lights. 'He who leaves all for my sake shall receive a hundredfold *in this life'* of the same felicities—which we can only obtain by abandoning the pursuit of them." (*Homo* XXIV.)

Again: "'The human form divine.' It is *actually* divine; for the Body is the house of God, and an image of Him, though the devil may be its present tenant." (*Aurea Dicta* LXXXVI.)

29–37. The Jebusites, relentless enemies of *the Chosen People,* could never be entirely conquered nor could they be driven beyond the walls of *Jerusalem.* Consequently a *formal truce* was made with them allowing them to live high up in the hills and mountains of the city: "But the children of Juda could not destroy the Jebusite that dwelt in Jerusalem; and the Jebusite dwelt with the children of Juda in Jerusalem until this present day." (*Josue* XV, 63.)

The parity between *the Jebusite* and the abiding effects of original sin in man, as developed in these lines, bears a close resemblance to the following passage from St. Bernard: "Evil tendencies which are cut down shoot up again; those which have been driven away return; the fires which have been extinguished are, in a while, rekindled; and those desires which seemed fast asleep awake again. It is of little avail therefore, to have pruned once; we must prune frequently, nay, if it were possible, always; because if you are honest with yourself, you will always find something within requiring to be sternly repressed. Whether you are willing or unwilling, the Jebusite dwells within your borders. (Cf. *Judges* I, 21.) He may be subjugated, but he cannot be exterminated. *I know,* says the Apostle, *that in me dwelleth no good thing.* But that is little in comparison with the confession which he goes on to make—that evil dwells in him. He adds: *For I do not that good which I will, but the evil which I hate, that I do. If then I do that which I will not, I consent to the law, that it is good. Now then it is no more I that do it, but sin that dwelleth in me."* (*Romans* VII, 15–17.) ("Sermons on the *Canticle of Canticles,"* LVIII, §10.)

38–40. In God's ordinary providence, His grace does not destroy such effects of original sin as physical death and the conflict between the spiritual aspirations of the soul and the concupiscence of the body. But the death of the body—a direct consequence of original sin (cf. Genesis III, 19)—will be followed by the resurrection of the body on the Last Day. According to the Fourth Lateran Council, all men, whether elect or reprobate: "will rise again with their own bodies which they will bear about with them." (Cap. *Fortiter.*)

41–43. During the interim between the death of the body and its resurrection, the soul, theologically speaking, is said to be in a *violent state,* desiring to reenter *its old abode,* the body. In the *Paradiso* (Canto XIV), Solomon thus describes this condition: "When the glorified and hallowed flesh shall be resumed, our person shall be more blessed through being all and whole. Wherefore shall be increased that which the Supreme Good gives us of light freely given, light that conditions us for seeing Him; whence the vision needs must grow, the fervour grow that is enkindled by it, the radiance grow that cometh from that fervour. But even as coal that gives forth flame, and by its living brightness doth surpass it, so that its own appearance is maintained, so this glowing, that already swathes us round, shall be exceeded in aspect by the flesh, which for this while the earth doth cover." In this translation by Edmund Gardner, the rendition of *fulgor* as *glowing,* suggests not only the thought but the expression in l. 42.

Chapter XI of St. Bernard's treatise *On the Love of God* should be read in its entirety as the best commentary upon these lines. Here we must be content with the following excerpt from §1: "Without their bodies the souls of the blessed have neither the desire nor the power to attain their ultimate consummation. And so, before the restoration of their bodies there will not be that complete absorption of souls in God which is their perfect and highest state; nor would the spirit now seek again for the fellowship of the flesh if it could attain to its perfect consummation without it. In truth, not without progress for the soul is the body laid down or taken up again. *Precious,* indeed, *in the sight of the Lord is the death of His saints* (*Psalm* CXIV, 15). But if death is precious, what is life, and *that* life? Nor is it any wonder if the body, now glorified, seems to confer something upon the spirit, since even when weak and mortal it is manifest that it was of no little help to it. O how truly did he speak who said: *to them that love God, all things work together unto good.* (*Romans* VIII, 28.) To the soul that loves God the body avails in its weakness, it avails in its death, it avails in its restoration. In the first instance, for the fruit of penitence; in the second, for rest; in the last, for consummation. Rightly she does not wish to be made perfect without that which she feels helps her to what is good for her in every state." St. Thomas' discussion of the quality of glorified bodies will be found in *Contra Gentiles* Bk. IV, ch. LXXXVI, and his reconcilement of the soul's beatitude with its yearning for its body before its resurrection will be found in the *Summa* II. ii, q. 18, art. 2, ad 4. Both of these passages are quoted in *Saint Bernard on the Love of God,* translation, pp. 245–246.

The function of the body in cooperating with the soul is thus briefly stated in the *Summa* (III, q. 79, art. 2, ad 3): "Although the body is not the immediate subject of grace, still the effect of grace flows into the body while in the present life we present *our* (Vulgate, *your*) *members as instruments of justice unto God* (Romans VI, 13), and in the life to come our body will share in the incorruption and the glory of the soul."

45. *Enoch* (cf. *Ecclesiasticus* XLIV, 16), *Elijah* (cf. 4 *Kings,* II, 1), *and the Lady* (the Blessed Virgin) were translated into heaven, body and soul.

46. According to an ancient tradition, after the Blessed Virgin in the mystery of her Assumption had been assumed into heaven, body and soul, roses were found in her tomb. Shortly before the publica-

tion of the *Unknown Eros,* the following line appeared in a volume of Tennyson's poetry: "With snow in lieu of lilies." Patmore, evidently, did not consider it a coincidence, and he wrote: "my 'who left the lilies in her body's lieu' was in print and circulation many months before." The line as Patmore quotes it is the earlier version. (Cf. "The Child's Purchase," ll. 148–51.)

47–53. If *I,* a sinner, have known in the legitimate pleasures of the body, *my poor faith's poor first-fruits,* what will be the *bliss* eternal of him who has never lost his baptismal innocence?

The legitimate pleasures of the body "have been praised most intimately by Patmore, who is the purest of poets because the frankest, in that, though the word hardly occurs in his entire works, *sex* is the substance and the tissue of his poetry. According to his philosophy, its [the soul's] divine birthright is the hereditary honour of the soul, to which, for its proving, original sin is, by comparison, but the bad fairy god-mother. For this reason, in a Puritan world, the only poet whose poetry is really steeped in sex . . . has been regarded as a prude! For he alone can accept it in simplicity. The world has now gone mad on the subject of sex, for sex must drive anyone mad who approaches it as a Puritan. The Pagans built their myths upon it, the very savage his superstitions. It has been left to the Puritan to accuse the Creator of indecency." (Burdett, pp. 140–41.)

50. *his:* rhyming with *kiss!*

51. *birth-time's consecrating dew:* waters of Baptism.

52. *death's sweet chrism:* the holy oil used in anointing the bodily senses in the sacrament of Extreme Unction.

'SING US ONE OF THE SONGS OF SION'

Publication: First included in the *Unknown Eros* sequence, among *Odes* I–XLI, 1878.

Title: It is the King James Version of Psalm CXXXVII, 4. In the Vulgate, as Psalm CXXXVI, it reads as quoted below. (Cf. *Theme.*)

Theme: It is a development of the analogy between the status of the Chosen People during the Babylonian captivity, and the English in Patmore's day when Christian and aristocratic traditions of the past were yielding. The text upon which the analogy is founded is this: "Upon the rivers of Babylon, there we sat and wept: when we remembered Sion: On the willows in the midst thereof we hung up our instruments. For there they that let us into captivity required of us the words of song. And they that carried us away, said: *Sing ye to us a hymn of the songs of Sion.* How shall we sing the song of the Lord in a strange land?" (Psalm CXXXVI, 1–4.) Patmore himself reflects a similar state of soul in this sentence from a letter to Mrs. Jackson written March 6, 1891: "The utter uselessness of such writing as I can write in face of the 'great mud deluge' which is sweeping away all that is worth living for, weighs continually on my heart and paralyses my pen." (Champneys II, p. 217.)

1. *so strange a Land:* how strange it was to Patmore he tells us in such odes as "1867," "Peace," "1880–85," "The Standards," and the *Proem,* ll. 39–52.

5. *Sacred River:* literally, the Nile; figuratively, the Thames.

7–9. This description of the new Liberal Parliament is particularly Patmorean.

7. *cats:* frequently symbolic of laziness and undeserved ease.
apes: often a symbol of malignant activity.

8. *the poor trick of earth and star:* possibly, the relationship between Man and God, earth and heaven.

10–11. Francis Thompson expresses the same idea in these lines:

> "The stars still write their golden purposes
> On heaven's high palimpsest, and no man sees."
> ("From the Night of Forebeing," ll. 352–53.)

In Patmore's essay, "Religio Poetae," we read: "'Where there is no vision the People perish; and of thought without vision it may be truly said, 'dust shalt thou eat all the days of thy life,' and 'dust thou art and to dust shalt thou return.' All realities will sing, but nothing else will. Judge then how much reality there is in the modern teaching of religion, by the songs of its prophets!" (Cf. "L'Allegro," ll. 81–83.)

10. *Prophets:* In the Old Law, prophets were not only given a supernatural power of foretelling the future; they were especially enlightened to see the will of God so that they might communicate it to Israel.

Among the false prophets of Patmore's day were Materialists and Agnostics such as Herbert Spencer; Economists such as John Stuart Mill; Positivists such as Frederick Harrison; and Broad Churchmen such as Mark Patterson and the Arnolds.

"To live holily," wrote Patmore, "and to believe nothing is the way of that 'broad Church' which leadeth to destruction; for really so to live is worse than to live in harmony with its no-belief; since the conjunction of good in externals with evil in internals is as destructive a profanation as that of the opposite kind of conjunction, a real faith and an evil life." (*Magna Moralia,* I.)

Again: "I believe Christianity primarily, because it gives me, in still greater abundance and perfection, what I want and must have. If Mr. Huxley will offer me something yet more substantial, I will accept that; but, in the meantime, it is no use to set me down to a Barmecide's Feast, which is not even bran, and to tell me that I do not know how I came by my bread and butter." (*Knowledge and Science* XXXV.)

12–15. God sent ten plagues upon the Egyptians to force them to allow the Chosen People to return to Jerusalem. When the first plague, the corrupting of the waters, failed in its purpose (Exodus VII, 14–25), the land was visited with a plague of frogs. Then, "the magicians also by their enchantments did in like manner, and they brought forth frogs upon the land of Egypt." (*Ibid.* VIII, 7.) When Pharao still remained obdurate God sent a third plague of gnats. "And the magicians with their enchantments practised in like manner to bring forth sciniphs, and they could not." (*Ibid.* 18.) Previously, the magicians had imitated the miracle by which Aaron had changed his rod into a serpent. (Cf. *ibid.* VII, 8–11.)

There are those, says Patmore, who pay no attention to miracles that prove the existence of God and the power of His providence. Like the Pharisees they ignore the great fundamental relationship between themselves and God, and give themselves over to purely speculative questions and intellectual subtilties such as this: "How is it that the magicians who imitated the miracle of the toads and outdid, as it were, the miracle of the serpent, were unable to imitate the miracle of the gnats?"

The practical result of all this is summed up by Patmore in such passages as this: "The knowledge which can be made common to all, is a foundation upon which a certain increasing school, finding popular 'opinion' too sandy, is endeavoring to build up a new state of things, religious, moral, political and social. This kind of 'positivism,' which claims for its sanction the common, that is to say, the lowest experience of mankind, is and always has been the religion of the vulgar, to whatever class they belong. The growth of an unconscious and undogmatic positivism among the people at large is perhaps the most notable fact of the time. It shows itself not only in an increasing impatience of the notion that there is any reality which cannot be seen and felt, but in an intolerance even of any experience which is not, or cannot immediately be made, the experience of all . . .

"Incommunicable knowledge, or knowledge which can be communicated at present only to a portion—perhaps a small portion—of mankind, is already affirmed to be no knowledge at all . . .

"The religion of universal experience must of course begin, as the dogmatic positivist insists, in the denial of God, or, what is exactly equivalent, in the assertion that, if God exists, He is altogether unknowable and removed from the practical interests of life." ("Thoughts on Knowledge, Opinion and Inequality.")

16–18. The *lie* in England's *right hand* included rationalistic philosophy, undogmatic religion, and the democracy that was supplanting the old aristocratic tradition so dear to Patmore. (Cf. "1867," "1880–85," *passim.*)

19–21. Cf. "1867," "1880–85," *passim.* "And the magicians said to Pharao: This is the finger of God. And Pharao's heart was *hardened,* and he hearkened not unto them, as the Lord had commanded." (Exodus VIII, 19.)

22. Cf. *Theme, supra.*

30–35. In his essay, "Distinction," Patmore quotes these lines to illustrate how completely his feelings were "in unison with the mild amenity of Dr. Newman," to whom allusion is made in these lines and in those that follow.

40–41. Newman's *Apologia pro Vita Sua,* written in 1864 in reply to Charles Kingsley who accused Newman of insincerity, illustrates how *foolish* the *foes* of *fair Sion* could be, and what final *blows* could be dealt in gentleness and sweetness.

DELICIAE SAPIENTIAE DE AMORE

Publication: One of the original *Nine Odes,* 1868.

Theme: This impassioned song in praise of virginity is Patmore's best expression of his favorite theme at the highest point of its development. It is interesting to contrast its intense ardor in praise of consecrated virginity with the view so coldly expressed in "The Pearl," one of the Accompaniments in Idyl VI of *The Espousals,* the early edition of the *Angel in the House,* Bk. II. These lines are omitted in later editions:

"Say, Muse, who warblest at mine ear
That Prothalamium jubilant
Which I, in weakness and in fear,
Repeat, and of its glory scant,

Say, what of those who are not wives,
   Nor have them; till what fate they prove
Who keep the pearl which happier lives
   Cast in the costly cup of Love?
I answer, (for the sacred Muse
   Is dumb,) 'Ill chance is not for aye;
'But who with erring preference choose
   'The sad and solitary way,
'And think peculiar praise to get
   'In heaven, where error is not known,
'They have the separate coronet
   'They sought, but miss a worthier crown.
'Virgins are they, before the Lord,
   'Whose hearts are pure: the vestal fire
'Is not, as some misread the Word,
   'By marriage quench'd but burns the higher.' "

Thus early we find insistence upon virginity as an essential of pure conjugal love, the central theme of "The Contract." But the view of virginity expressed in "The Pearl" is far different from the view we find in the ode we are now considering. Here we have the glorious flowering of Patmore's conception of virginity as it grew and developed under the influence of his Catholic faith. In "The Pearl" we have the unpromising seed of all this—virginity that might well be symbolized by a snow-capped mountain-peak—cold, bare and inaccessible for all but a few. Similarly, in *Victories of Love* Bk. II, Letter xi, virginal love is compared with conjugal love, much to the disadvantage of virginity. (Cf. "Eros and Psyche," ll. 72–73.)

The theme is briefly expressed in the ode itself: the *half-remember'd dreams* of worthy lovers. In its development the purifying effects of love are described with rare lyrical felicity.

Title: It is an abbreviated form of the text which Patmore placed at the beginning of the *Unknown Eros* sequence: *"Deliciae meae esse cum filiis hominum*—my delights were to be with the children of men." (Proverbs VIII, 31.) It may be freely translated, "Wisdom's Love-Delights." (Cf. "To The Body," ll. 4–5.)

Technique: Here is Patmore's technique at its best, although the ode was written, he said, in two hours. His daughter, Sister Mary Christina, spoke of it as "too beautiful to praise."

1–5. This notably beautiful prayer inspired by the poet's humility, begs the grace worthily to sing the delights of love that is inspired by divine wisdom.

8–19. First, the poet warns off from his song those unworthy to hear it—those who have never known the delights of pure love (ll. 9–10), those who once knew such delights but have now deliberately forgotten them (l. 11), and those who have called lust by the fair name of love. (ll. 12–19.)

20–27. Worthy lovers whether betrothed or wed are now invited to attend the poet's song. "Chastity is a necessary virtue: for it is written that nothing defiled shall enter into the Kingdom of Heaven (cf. *Apocalypse* XXI, 27); and without chastity it is impossible not to defile both body and soul.

"Chastity is a virtue that befits all sorts of persons: it befits all ages, man as well as woman, the aged as well as the child, the rich as well as the poor, the ignorant as well as the learned, virgins as well as the married, the most illustrious and most powerful monarch as well as the lowest of his subjects." (*Writings of Marie Lataste,* vol. II, p. 350.)

23. The purity of thought peculiar to those who are married is thus described in the Encylical on Christian Marriage issued by His Holiness Pius XI December 31, 1930: "Nor did Christ our Lord wish only to condemn any form of polygamy or polyandry, as they are called, whether successive or simultaneous, and every other external dishonorable act, but, in order that the sacred bonds of marriage may be guarded absolutely inviolate, He forbade also even wilful thoughts and desires of such like things: *But I say to you that whosoever shall look on a woman to lust after her, hath already committed adultery with her in his heart* (St. Matthew V, 28). Which words of Christ Our Lord cannot be annulled even by the consent of one of the partners of marriage, for they express a law of God and of nature which no will of man can break or bend." (§ 21.)

28–31. The insensible attraction of *the magnet* for *the steel* is a symbol of sheer physical attraction in love that, without the spiritual element of which it is the corollary, kills true love, whereas it should quicken it.

32–33. The passing kiss of *the clouds of summer,* with their violent accompaniment of lightning and rain is a symbol of passionate, unworthy love that knows no permanence, and quickly surfeits the human heart.

34–40. The symbol of pure love is the sun, the perpetual fire of the heavens, perpetual and inexhaustible.

43–48. When, for the first time, a man ceases to be in love with love immortal, only, and falls in love with a particular human being, he must doff the crown he has been wearing and humbly put on the crown of mortal human love, with its limitations.

49–71. At that moment a man envies the distant, insentient, hopeless love of one star for another, because such love, unlike his own, is eternal. As two planets follow their respective elliptical paths, once a year they come as near to each other as their paths will allow. In this position one planet is kissed by the doubled light of the other that *whispers of its source,* the sun. Then they move on again in *that ellipse*

Wherein all citizens of ether move,

rejoicing, as they look forward to their next annual proximity to each other. (Cf. "Wedding Sermon," ll. 118–27.)

50–56. In "The Contract" (ll. 30–33) Patmore makes a different application of the symbolism of stars.

71. "He hath set His tabernacle in the sun: and He, as a Bridegroom coming out of His bride-chamber, hath rejoiced as a giant to run the way." (Psalm XVIII, 6.)

76. In the *Marriage-Feast* of the soul's union with Christ, it will be *unsated,* but completely and perfectly satisfied. "Let us be glad and rejoice and give glory to Him; for the marriage of the Lamb is come and His wife hath prepared herself." (Apocalypse XIX, 7.)

79. "*Cor meum et caro mea exultaverunt in Deum vivum*—My heart and my flesh have rejoiced in the living God" (Psalm LXXXIII, 3). "God said to Moses: *I am who am.*" (Exodus III, 14.)

80. *The Husband of the Heavens:* In the King James Version of Isaias LIV, 5, we read: "Thy Maker is thine husband." The Douay Version reads: "He that made thee shall rule over thee." From the context, according to the interpretation of accepted commentators it is evident that the expression, "shall rule over thee," means *shall rule over thee as a husband rules over his wife.* In this chapter the Prophet is speaking of the restored nation of Israel as the spouse of God, a spouse who in her youth had proved unfaithful, chiefly through the sin of idolatry. As a punishment God had sent her into exile, the days of her mourning, and now through her delivery from the Babylonian exile (539 B.C.), a delivery typical of man's redemption, she is to be restored to God's favor. Thus she will be brought once more under the dominance of God as her Husband. Obviously the passage in its literal sense refers to the restoration of Israel as the spouse of God, typical of the Church, spouse of Christ. Patmore very aptly extends the meaning to apply to the soul as the spouse of Christ. (Cf. "Sponsa Dei," l. 38.) In this he follows St. Bernard in such passages as this: "The Church confidently and securely calls herself the Spouse of Christ . . . But although no one of us would dare presume to such a degree that he would make bold to call his soul the Spouse of the Lord, nevertheless, because we are mem-

bers of the Church which rightly glories in this title and in this reality, not unjustly we appropriate to ourselves a share in this glory. For, what we all together possess fully and wholly, that, as individuals, we must share. Thanks to Thee, Lord Jesus, Who have deigned to add us to the flock of your beloved Church, not only that we might be among the Faithful, but that after the manner of a spouse we might be joined to you in embraces joyous, chaste and eternal, when, in the revelation of Your Countenance we are admitted into the contemplation of Your glory, which You have equally and in common with the Father and the Holy Ghost forever." ("Sermons on the *Canticle of Canticles*"; Sermon XII, § 11: Translation, p. 106.)

The Lamb: "And they sung as it were a new canticle before the throne, . . . and no man could say the canticle, but those hundred forty-four thousand who were purchased from the earth. These are they who were not defiled with women: for they are virgins. These follow *the Lamb* withersoever He goeth." (Apocalypse XIV, 3–4.)

81–84. Penitence, love and effort restore purity of heart when it has been lost by impurity. Hence Patmore places repentant sinners very close to those souls who have never lost their baptismal innocence. (Cf. *infra,* ll. 125–130.)

86. *five-strung:* possibly an allusion to the five bodily senses. (Cf. "The Wedding Sermon," l. 517.)

87. *Spirits,* in Nine Odes, "spirits."

89. Cf. "To the Unknown Eros" and "The Contract," *Theme.*
Choirs, in Nine Odes, "choirs."

92–93. Between these lines in the Nine Odes was inserted the following line: "The new and ever new to us and them."

93. *The,* in Nine Odes, "And."

95. Cf. *infra,* ll. 99–100.

96–98. Read St. Luke I, 26–38, where the Evangelist describes the coming of the angel Gabriel to Mary, in Nazareth, with the tidings of her great destiny and its miraculous accomplishment.

98. *Nazareth,* in Nine Odes, "Bethlehem."

99–100. Our Lady's great prerogatives as Virgin and Spouse of the Holy Ghost are here beautifully but analogously applied to Religious.

99. *brides,* in Nine Odes, "Brides."

101–104. It were difficult to find a more beautiful expression of the love of God in the heart of one grown old in God's special service.

105–24. This is a more explicit development of the invitation given in ll. 20–23.

106–12. Apropos of those who are wed and are *virginal of thought* (l. 23), there are some interesting passages in the writings of Marie Lataste: "The act contrary to virginity is a sin only when there is an abuse in the doing of it, and in circumstances and in cases in which it is not permissible. But this act, in the marriage state, when the laws fixed by God are observed, becomes a religious act." (Vol. II, p. 362.) The same idea is found in St. Thomas: "The marriage act is always either sinful or meritorious in one who is in a state of grace. For if the motive for the marriage act be a virtue, whether of justice that they may render the debt, or of religion, that they may beget children for the worship of God, it is meritorious." (*Summa:* Supplement, Pt. III, q. xli, art. 4.)

Again we find in the writings of Marie Lataste, these words attributed to Our Lord Himself: "All that passes in the inferior part of the soul and in the body, whether it be thoughts or movements, or impure delectations, is not sin if the superior will does not give its consent." (Vol. II, p. 363.)

109. *The lily sacrificed:* virginal love, which must be sacrificed in the attainment of the flower of nuptial love. It is here especially that Patmore, as Mrs. Meynell expresses it: "Darkly sings the triumph of virginity and its sacrifice at once." (*Second Person Singular,* p. 102.) In Patmore's prose we find this daring expression of the same thought: "Theologians say that the essential of the Sacrifice of the Altar is the infinite humiliation suffered by the Second Person of the Holy Trinity in becoming flesh in the moment of transubstantiation; and has not this humiliation its analogue in the case of the Virgin when she allows her love and beauty, hitherto nothing but spiritual splendour and ethereal freedom, to become the ally and thrall of the body?" ("Dieu et ma Dame.")

114. *Lover,* in Nine Odes, "lover."
Maid, in Nine Odes, "maid."

115–17. In the enjoyment of the Beatific Vision the soul's love of God will heighten but will not destroy nor lessen the pure delights of earthly love. This is the subject of Patmore's essay, "The Precursor," in which St. John the Baptist is spoken of "as the 'Precursor' of Christ, as Natural Love is the Precursor of the Divine." Francis Thompson expresses the same thought thus: "Love in this world is a pilgrim and a wanderer, journeying to the New Jerusalem: not here is the consummation of his yearnings, in that mere knocking at the gates of union which we christen marriage, but beyond the pillars of death and the corridors of the grave, in the union of spirit to spirit within the containing spirit of God." ("Paganism Old and New.")

A very brief expression of the same thought is found in Patmore's essay, "Love and Poetry": "Nuptial love bears the clearest marks of being nothing other than the rehearsal of a communion of a higher nature."

122. In Nine Odes: "And each to the ***kindling*** other, well content."

126. For a complete and beautiful lyrical expression of repentant love as it is known in heaven this is a notable line. The same thought is thus expressed in *Aurea Dicta* CLVI: "The Soul's shame at its own unworthiness of the embraces of God is the blush upon the rose of love, which is the deeper the more angelic her intelligence and consequent discernment of God's purity."

127–30. By a bold stroke Patmore places Mary Magdalene next in glory to Our Lady. The following is an interesting prose commentary on these lines: "Past corruptions that are really past and no longer active are so far from hindering love that they act as manure in which the seed of Divine Love and the seed almost divine of a pure and fervid mortal affection flourish wonderfully, many a Magdalen, the just envy of many who were always pure, having been formed into a spouse, 'more innocent than any maid,' by the inveterate and purifying ardour of either love." ("Dieu et ma Dame.") (Cf. "De Natura Deorum," ll. 51–52.)

138. *mediate:* chiefly through the medium of conjugal love.
direct: as in the case of Religious.

140. Cf. *supra,* l. 80.

141–45. Cf. 'Faint Yet Pursuing,' ll. 1–9.

145. *ardour virginal:* this is a particularly happy expression of one of Patmore's most essential doctrines—the positive, active nature of purity. In his essay, "Ancient and Modern Ideas of Purity," he writes: "The ancient idea of positive purity, as a sacred fire which consumes and turns into its own substance all that is adverse to it, is now replaced by the conception that it is of the nature of stored snow, which must be kept artificially dark and cool, lest it disappear forever." (Cf. *supra, Theme.*)

THE CRY AT MIDNIGHT

Publication: First included in the *Unknown Eros* sequence, among *Odes* I–XLVI, 1878.

Theme: It is an indictment of the false philosophy in which man, not God, is made the measure and centre of all things. "Rationalism begins at the wrong end. Religion rationalizes from the primary and substantial Reason, and explains all things. Rationalists take zero for their datum, and, do what they may they can make nothing of it." (*Aurea Dicta* CII.) Again:

"Who search for truth and do not start from God
For a long journey should be shod."
(*Aphorisms and Extracts.*)

3. *Sirius' ball:* The most brilliant star in the whole sky is Sirius. It is a million times as distant as the sun and has about twenty-six times the candle-power and light-radiating power of the sun.

8. *St. Michael:* Chief of the angelic host.

11–12. The wonder is not, as homocentric philosophy teaches, that God who created man, also created St. Michael. Rather, as theocentric philosophy suggests, the wonder is that God who could create a being so exalted as St. Michael, should be pleased to create so lowly a being as man.

13–14. God, not Man, is the measure of all things. It was the neglect of this fundamental principle that lead nineteenth century Rationalists to substitute reason for faith, and humanitarianism for charity.

15–16. In philosophy, as in life, "Pride goeth before destruction: and the spirit is lifted up before a fall." (Proverbs XV, 18.)

17–18. "Idiots take the prologue for the piece,
And think that all is ended just when it begins."
(*Aphorisms and Extracts.*)

20. *brummagem:* cheap, bogus.

23. For the Parable of the Wise and Foolish Virgins, cf. St. Matthew XXV, 1–13.

25. When Christ before Caiphas admitted His divinity, "the high priest rent his garments, saying: He hath blasphemed." (St. Matthew XXVI, 65.)

AURAS OF DELIGHT

Publication: First included in the *Unknown Eros* sequence, in *Odes* I–XLVI, 1878.

Theme: Cf. "Let Be": *Theme.*

2–5. This description of the difficulties and sacrifices necessary for attaining the *realm of Love,* reminds us of "the splendid spears" that threaten blindness to unheroic souls that weakly seek the vision of "Truth's naked beauty," in Joseph Plunkett's poem, "Seals of Thunder."

10–25. In his presentation of perverted love under the symbol of the unnatural union of a serpent and a dove in *frightful nuptials,* Patmore makes a right use of realism. The *tortured knot* is made a symbol of the awful disillusionment and confusion consequent upon a union in which the object of nuptial love is sheer bodily satisfaction. The result is disordered and unsatisfied passion without peace and without rest. (Cf. "Winter," l. 6.) Such love is in awful contrast with that great passion when the balance is kept between the wisdom of the serpent and the simplicity of the dove as described in the *Angel in the House,* Bk. I, Canto x, Prelude ii:

> "Love, kiss'd by Wisdom, wakes twice Love,
> And Wisdom is, thro' loving, wise.
> Let Dove and Snake, and Snake and Dove,
> This Wisdom's be, that Love's device,"

Here Patmore follows the recommendation of Our Savior to His apostles: "Be ye therefore wise as serpents and simple as doves." (St. Matthew X, 16.)

15–17. These lines will remind the reader of Patmore's description of Platonic love described in the *Angel in the House,* Canto I, Prelude ii, where a kite is made its symbol:

> "all sail
> It heav'nward rush'd till scarce descried,
> Then pitch'd and dropp'd, for want of tail."

26–30. Such passion fills the *golden Cup* of love with the *fornications foul of Babylon,* and disquiet of soul accompanies the realization that such love in its attainment betrays its promise. In the unhappiness of disillusionment that follows, such souls suffer the spiritual unrest of those who know what is right but deliberately refuse to do it.

31–38. God cannot restore the lost vision of the innocence of childhood, nor can He quicken the soul of an unrepentant sinner, but He who created man out of dust can restore a repentant sinner to the state of grace,

> *can make live again,*
> *The dust.*

39–53. But is the vision of love, visible only to the eyes of innocence, altogether dead? No. Through God's grace the remembrance of that vision is no more, lest, having it, I might be false to it and, as it were, *refuse God to His face.* But the mere remembrance of the fact that once I had that vision, is enough for me, *in straits which else for me were ill.*

53. The river Jordan issues from the *thymy* slope of Mount Hermon.

PSYCHE ODES, IN GENERAL

Publication: The three Psyche Odes—"Eros and Psyche," "De Natura Deorum," and "Psyche's Discontent"—first appeared among the poems of the *Unknown Eros* sequence, in *Odes* I–XLVI, 1878. They were not then arranged in sequence as they now are. This idea was first introduced in *Collected Poems,* undated, but probably edited in 1879.

Form: They are written as dialogues. In "Eros and Psyche" and "Psyche's Discontent," the dialogues are between Eros and Psyche; in "De Natura Deorum," between Psyche and the Pythoness.

Pagan Myths, Precursive Types of Christian Truth: This, one of Patmore's favorite beliefs, was analogous to his conviction that the pagan concept of pure love was precursive of the Christian ideal. (Cf. "The Precursor," and Thompson's "Sister Songs," Part II, ll. 310–16.) In *Knowledge and Science* XXVII, we read: "The Pagan who simply believed in the myth of Jupiter, Alcmena, and Hercules, much more he who had been initiated into the unspeakable names of Bacchus and Persephone, knew more of living Christian doctrine than any 'Christian' who refuses to call Mary the 'Mother of God.'" We find this same thought expressed by a contemporary writer, E. I. Watkin. Speaking of certain rites, he says: "Such ceremonial, which after took the form of a sacred marriage, ἱερὸς γάμος, between the mother-goddess of earth's fertility and a vegetation- or sky-god, points to its anti-type, the wedlock between nature, represented by the human microcosm, and God." (*The Bow Set in the Clouds,* p. 131.)

Francis Thompson, making bold but reverent use of a familiar pagan myth as precursive of the Incarnation, attributes these words to Our Lady:

> 'Cloud down-raining the Just One (I) am,
> Danaae of the Shower of Gold.'
>
> ("Assumpta Maria," ll. 33–34.)

As early as 1856, Patmore's fondness for the myth of Eros and Psyche is reflected in his description of a tapestry that hangs in the nuptial chamber of the *Angel in the House* (Bk. II, Canto v), whereon:

> "translated Psyche fed
> Her gaze on Love, not disallowed."

When Patmore passed through Paris on his way to Rome in 1864, he saw Gérard's "Cupid and Psyche" in the Louvre and wrote: "Certainly love has never been expressed with more force, delicacy, and spiritual science . . . As I mean to have [but he did not have] a vignette of this picture for the title-page of the next edition of the *Angel of the House* I will say no more about it." (*Patmore, a Study in Poetry,* Page, pp. 122–23.)

Theme: Here we have the climax of Patmore's message, the apotheosis of human love. The general dogmatic truth of the odes is: "God is love." (1 St. John IV, 8.) But Patmore was never content with generalities, and in these odes he particularizes his favorite theme in a way:

tender-soft as seem
The embraces of a dead Love in a dream.
("Dead Language," ll. 7–8.)

His method was a shock to many of his contemporaries, particularly to his friend Aubrey de Vere. (Cf. Champneys II, pp. 341–42.) Today there is less danger of such a reaction but it may be said of these odes that they should not be read until the reader has first grasped the germ of Patmore's thought in such poems as, "Legem Tuam Dilexi," "To the Body," "Pain" and "Deliciae Sapientiae de Amore." For these poems, as St. Bernard says concerning the "Canticle of Canticles": "are not to be listened to except by ears and hearts which are chastened and wise. For, unless the flesh has been mastered by discipline and subjected to the spirit [as outlined in *Ecclesiastes*]; unless the burdensome pomp of the world has been despised and cast away as insupportable [as recommended in the *Book of Proverbs*], the heart is impure and unworthy to peruse the sacred Song. Just as the pure light is poured vainly and to no purpose upon blind eyes, or upon eyes that are closed, so 'the natural man receiveth not the things of the spirit of God.'" (1 Corinthians II, 14.) (Cf. "Sermons on the *Canticle of Canticles*" Sermon I, § 3.)

It is clear from the intensity and poignancy of these odes that they were inspired by Patmore's personal spiritual experiences. "Once, then, we realize that his Psyche Odes are the relation of no abstract desire, but a confession of personal intimacy, we can accept them simply for what they are, namely, the story of a love affair as real and personal as any other, though God is the hero and the Soul the betrothed heroine of its adventures." (Burdett, p. 152.)

As we should expect from what has already been said concerning the theme of these odes, in their development there is the clarity of a seer, not the vagueness of a visionary. Mr. Page (p. 125) has said: "Calderon would have encouraged their gaiety and St. John of the Cross their sensuousness." (Cf. Champneys I, pp. 317–18.)

It might be well here to recall the warning St. Bernard gave his monks when he was discussing with them the "Canticle of Canticles." "Take heed," he said, "that you bring chaste ears to this discourse of love, and when you think of those two lovers, remember always that not a man and a woman are to be thought of, but the Word of God and the soul." ("Sermons on the *Canticle of Canticles,*" Sermon LXI, § 2.)

Sequence: Passing from the consideration of the *root* of divine love in man's physical nature, and its noblest *rod,* virginity, Patmore comes now to a consideration of the full-blown *flower* of human love when purified by suffering and illuminated by grace the soul becomes God's spouse. In these three odes Patmore describes the nature and consequences of this divine union. "Eros and Psyche" deals with the marriage between the soul and God, as an actual experience. In "De Natura Deorum" the soul seeks to know the nature of the Bridegroom and of the bond by which she is united to Him. "Psyche's Discontent" is an expression of the soul's realization that pain and suffering and a will perfectly conformed to the will of God is the essence of the Christian ideal of love.

EROS AND PSYCHE

Publication: First included in the *Unknown Eros* sequence, in *Odes* I–XLVI, 1878.

Title: Eros: Cf. notes on the *Unknown Eros* sequence. *Psyche:* In Greek mythology it is the personification of the human soul, beloved by Eros (Amor).

Legend of Eros and Psyche: "Eros caused Psyche . . . to be carried off by Zephyrus to a secluded spot, where he visited her at night alone, without being seen or recognized by her. Persuaded by her sisters, she transgressed his command and wished to see him, when the God immediately vanished. Amid innumerable troubles and appalling trials she sought her lover till at length, purified by the sufferings she had endured, she found him again and was united to him forever." (*Dictionary of Classical Antiquities.*)

Patmore has made some very interesting observations concerning this legend and its significance: "That this exquisite novelette is in the main a parable is obvious; but none of the tasks imposed by Venus upon her poor little rival and victim were more seemingly hopeless than is that of explaining this parable fully, though the light of its obscure significance flashes from almost every sentence. It seems to us very doubtlful whether Apuleius himself had always a perfectly clear intelligence of what he was about.

"He seems to have taken the fable as it stood in its older and simpler forms and to have decked and obscured it with ideas of his own. Notwithstanding this and other deductions from its literary merits that might be alleged, this story must be reckoned among the best of books by those who adopt the lively but sound saying that 'a good book is a book which does one good.' It is impossible for any but a very dull person to remain a merely passive recipient of the ideas and images of this tale. It excites the reader to a sort of active co-operation with the writer.

"We seem constantly to be on the point of discerning some happy secret of the soul, and are constantly but only partially disappointed. 'I know not how it is,' writes St. Bernard, 'but the more the realities of heaven are clothed in obscurity the more they delight and attract; and nothing so heightens longing as such tender refusal.'" (Champneys II, p. 91.)

As is evident, there are many analogous details between the myths that centre about Eros and Psyche, and the revealed story of God's love for man which centres about the Incarnation. But the chief analogy lies in the fact that in the myth the love-union between Eros and Psyche was a union between a god and a human being, and in the Incarnation, perpetuated in the life-story of every individual soul, there is a union between the human and the divine.

Theme: It is thus briefly expressed in one of Patmore's *Aphorisms and Extracts:* "The soul becomes mystically united with God and impregnated by Him the instant she perfectly submits and says, 'Behold the handmaid of the Lord: be it done to me according to Thy word.'" (Champneys II, p. 70.) A more detailed statement of this theme will be found in Patmore's essay, "Christianity, an Experimental Science." It should be read in its entirety.

The same idea is found in the writings of Marie Lataste who attributes the following words to Our Lord: "God desired not only that I should dwell in Mary, He desired also that I should dwell in the children of men; He desired that from among the children of men I should choose a people, a privileged people, whose mind should be elevated above earth and the senses, and, in a flesh subject to corruption and a captive to the senses, should meditate upon the mystery of the incorruptible union between God and man; that this people should be continually asking itself: 'How, in my weakness, in my misery, in my unworthiness, shall I succeed in uniting God to my flesh?' and, like Mary, should rely on the words of the angel: 'The Holy Ghost shall come upon thee; the power of the Most High shall overshadow thee; and that which shall be born of thee is Holy, and shall be called the Son of the Most High.' " (Vol. I, p. 168.) (Cf. *supra,* notes on the PSYCHE ODES in general, and read *The Idea of Coventry Patmore,* Burdett, pp. 153–4.)

1–9. Psyche here confesses how futile her efforts of the past have been to lure Love into her arms. "Perception," writes Patmore, "is hindered by nothing so much as by impatience and anxiety to attain it, and by trying to recall and dwell upon it when attained. 'If the Lord tarry wait for Him,' and then, 'He will not tarry but come quickly.' [Cf. Hebrews X, 35–37.] To them that wait in quietness, attention, and silence of their own thought, all things reveal themselves." (*Magna Moralia* XIII.) Here Patmore is speaking of "That higher order of *perception* which is usually the ultimate reward of so 'doing God's commandments' that we may 'know of the doctrine.' " ("Christianity an Experimental Science.") In this higher state there is a clearly *passive* element such as is described in the lines now being discussed. But this is not a *completely passive state*. It is, rather, as Father Poulain suggests, a *passivo-actif* state, because the soul's activity takes a part in the reception of the grace bestowed upon it. "In a strictly passive state the soul would receive without doing anything at all." (*Graces of Interior Prayer,* Poulain, p. 4.) As is clear from ll. 10–13, the soul, by a deliberate act of will prepares itself for the reception of the grace to come and deliberately assents to it. (Cf. *infra,* ll. 64–65.)

10–17. Wearied by the failures of the past when she trusted too much to her own efforts, Psyche is startled to find that Eros has come to her now that she has abandoned her too active search and is content deliberately to await his coming. " 'If the Lord tarry wait for Him, and He will not tarry but come quickly.' The impatience of the Soul for vision is one of the last faults that can be cured. Only to those who watch and wait, with absolute indifference as to the season of revelation, do all things reveal themselves." (*Aurea Dicta* CXL.) This same idea will be found in St. Bernard's "Sermons on the *Canticle of Canticles,*" Sermon XXXII, §2; Translation, p. 141.

15. This may be one of the lines alluded to by Father Gerard Hopkins, S. J. when, in a letter to Patmore concerning the Psyche Odes he wrote: "What I feel least at my ease about is a certain jesting humor, which does not seem to me quite to hit the mark in this profoundly delicate matter . . . A single touch in such a matter may be 'by much too much.' " (Champneys II, p. 347.)

18–25. "You have not chosen Me: but I have chosen you." (St. John XV, 16.)

24–25. It is true of man's soul, as well as of his body, that it is:

"So rich with wealth conceal'd
That Heaven and Hell fight chiefly for this field."
("To The Body," ll. 25–26.)

26–40. Some critics have found this development of the human analogy of divine love, too vivid. But the lines should be read in the spirit that inspired them, a spirit that had actually known the delights of being *Wife and Virgin too,* of God, the *Husband of the Heavens.* (Cf. "Deliciae Sapientiae," l. 140.) As Patmore reminds us: "There are infinite degrees of this experimental knowledge, from that first sensible 'touch' of God's love, which usually accompanies the first sincere intention of perfection for His sake, to that of the Saints who have united themselves to God by a series of agonizing initiations of self-sacrifice, and by years of actual and habitual perfection of obedience in the smallest as well as the greatest things; and, further still, to the knowledge of the angels, whose purification and consequent capacity goes on increasing for ever." ("Christianity an Experimental Science.") In the highest reaches of man's union with God, Patmore goes on to say: "he finally becomes, not so much an adorer as an actual participator in the nature and felicity of that Divinity which alone 'has fruition in Himself,' and 'who became man that men might become gods.'" (*Ibid.*) In ll. 36–37 and 39–40 we have the same idea expressed with rare lyrical felicity.

41–49. Here are the misgivings of a soul to which divine Wisdom has revealed: "Satan himself transformeth himself into an angel of light." (2 Corinthians XI, 14.) (Read St. Bernard's "Sermons on the *Canticle of Canticles,*" Sermon XXXIII; Translation, pp. 146–149.)

44. Seeking *a sign* is in itself indifferent. The Pharisees asked a sign of Our Savior, *tempting Him,* and He answered: "Amen, I say to you a sign shall not be given to this generation." (St. Mark VIII, 12.) Moses asked a sign in the same spirit as the soul in this line and it was granted him. (Cf. Exodus XXXIII, XXXIV.) In his essay, "Dieu et ma Dame," Patmore writes: "The Divine Lover like a wise mortal lover, knows well that, however favourably the Soul may be disposed to Him, by His greatness, power, wealth, goodness, and abundant benevolence to her, He must *desire* her and give her some sensible proof by smile, touch, or caress, which shall say to her heart, as the God of David says to the chosen, *Rex concupiscet decorem tuum.*"

45: *in the pitchy night:* "If the realities of love were not in themselves dark to the understanding, it would be necessary to darken them—not only lest they should be profaned, but also because, as St. Bernard says, 'The more the realities of heaven are clothed with obscurity, the more they delight and attract, and nothing so much heightens longing as tender refusal.' 'Night,' says the inspirer of St. Bernard, 'is the light of my pleasures.' " ("Love and Poetry.") (Cf. "De Natura Deorum," l. 11.)

50–58. "The soul becomes nuptially united with God and impregnated by Him the instant she perfectly submits and says, 'Behold the handmaid of the Lord: be it done to me according to Thy word' " (*Aphorisms and Extracts*). It is as true of the interior motions of the soul as it is of prophets: "By their fruits you shall know them." (St. Matthew VII, 16.)

54. *sweet pain:* Cf. "Pain," *passim.*

57–58. "I live, now not I: but Christ liveth in me." (Galatians II, 20.)

60–62. "My yoke is sweet and My burden light." (St. Matthew XI, 30.) Cf. "Legem Tuam Dilexi," *passim.*

64–65. Father Poulain uses a slightly different comparison to illustrate the spiritual truth expressed in these lines: "Ordinary prayer may be compared to the atmosphere that surrounds our globe. The birds move about in it *at will.* Thanks to its aid, they can rise above the earth, and they mount higher in proportion to the strength of their wing-beats.

"But this atmosphere has its limits. Above, lie those vast expanses that stretch away to the stars and beyond. Try as they may they cannot penetrate thither, *even by redoubling their efforts.* The eagle is as powerless as the rest. God alone can transport them to this region; were He to do so, they would lie passive in His hand, there would be no further need to use their wings. . . . This upper region where the wing no longer has any power, is a figure of the mystic state." (*Graces of Interior Prayer,* p. 2.)

66–68. "A thing harder, to those who love, than actual sacrifice is to submit to the greatness of God's beneficence towards us. His promises so far exceed our power of desiring, that we cling to limitations, not discerning that, whatever form the unknown felicity of His Chosen may take, and however far beyond our present capacity it may be, it must include all the felicity and fidelity of limitation to which we now cleave." (*Aurea Dicta* LXXIV.)

72–73. In these later odes white heat seemed a more appropriate symbol of pure love than *the sudden moon* or

the permeating fires
That smoulder in the opal's veins,
(*Angel in the House,* Bk. II, Canto iii, ll. 83–84)

or of the ice and snow of Patmore's earlier work such as the line: *Her beauties were like sunlit snows.* (*Ibid.* Canto ii, l. 77.) (Cf. "Deliciae Sapientiae": *Theme* and l. 145.) St. Bernard makes use of the same symbol in speaking of God's love: "Moses says, 'The Lord thy God is a consuming fire' (Deuteronomy IV, 24) . . . In truth the fire which is God consumes, to be sure, but it does not destroy. It burns sweetly. It leaves one desolate unto bliss. It is truly a desolating burning, but one which directs the flame of fire against sin in such a way that it has the effect of unction upon the soul." ("Sermons on the *Canticle of Canticles,*" Sermon LVII, §7; Translation, p. 196.)

76. *kingdoms three:* There are three kingdoms alluded to in the first and greatest commandment: "Thou shalt love the Lord thy God with thy whole *heart* and with thy whole *soul* and with thy whole *strength.*" (Deuteronomy VI, 5.) Mr. Burdett interprets *kingdoms three* as: "the body not less than the soul, and the soul not less than the spirit." (p. 153.) To me they seem to be the intellect, the will and the senses.

77–84. This is an adaptation of the words of Our Lady's Magnificat: "He that is mighty hath done great things in me; and holy is His name." (St. Luke I, 49.) A familiar theme with Patmore is inequality as an essential of love, whether human or divine. "In the infinite distance between God and man, theologians find the secret of the infinite felicity of divine love; and the incomparable happiness of love between the sexes is similarly founded upon their inequality." ("The Weaker Vessel.") Again: "Nothingness is capacity, and night the opportunity of light." (*Aphorisms and Extracts.*) (Cf. "Psyche's Discontent," ll. 7–8; "De Natura Deorum," ll. 74–75; "1880–85," ll. 60–70, and *supra, Theme.*)

86–87. "Happy the soul which reclines upon the breast of Christ and takes its rest within the arms of the Word." (St. Bernard, "Sermons on the *Canticle of Canticles,*" Sermon LI, §5; Translation, p. 186.) And in the "Dark Night" of St. John of the Cross we read:

"Upon my flowery breast, kept wholly for himself alone,
There he stayed sleeping, and I caressed him."

88–89. Cophetua, a legendary king of Africa, had great riches and despised all women until he fell in love with a beggar-maid, Penelophon. Shakespeare's development of the legend in *Love's Labour Lost* (Act IV, scene i) is very similar to Patmore's. But Patmore's application of it is entirely different. His chief interest in the legend is its similarity to the story of God's love for Man in the Incarnation. "The myth of King Cophetua and the Beggar-Maid," he writes, "is representative of the most perfect nuptial relationship." ("The Weaker Vessel.") In "King Cophetua the First," included in the appendix, Patmore develops this myth in detail.

94–95. The king selects the beggar-maid because he divines in her the power *of growing king-like* in answer to his love—a power lacking in many of the ladies of his court. Similarly Christ selects as objects of His special love, those souls in whom He sees the power of growing Christ-like in correspondence with His love. The perfection of this human correspondence with the divine plan is the inspiration of St. Paul's cry: "I live, now not I: but Christ liveth in me." (Galatians II, 20.) (Cf. "De Natura Deorum," ll. 62–64.)

108. In his "Sermons on the *Canticle of Canticles,*" Sermon LII, §§2–3, (Translation, p. 189) St. Bernard, commenting upon *Canticle* II, 7, writes: "The Heavenly Bridegroom is clearly represented as most zealous for the repose of a certain bride of His, anxious to hold her in His own arms while she is sleeping . . . For there is, in truth, a sleep which does not, however, steep the senses in forgetfulness but transports them. It is also a death. This I may say without hesitation, since the Apostle by way of commendation speaks thus to some still living in the flesh: 'You are dead: and your life is hid with Christ in God.'" (Colossians III, 3.)

111–117. There are times when the consciousness of our nothingness by virtue of our origin and our sins tempts us to cry out with St. Peter: "Depart from me, for I am a sinful man, O Lord." (St. Luke V, 8.) Then, to the gentle rebuke of Our Saviour's question, "Will you also go away?" we are forced to reply in those other words of the same Apostle: "Lord, to whom shall we go? Thou hast the words of eternal life." (St. John VI, 69.)

118–20. There is just such a soul-cry as this, in Thompson's "Any Saint," ll. 29–32:

"Rebate Thy tender suit,
Lest to herself impute
Some worth
Thy bride of earth."

(Cf. "Psyche's Discontent," ll. 1–2.)

121–122. This is the cry of a great soul that has accepted in its literal sense the exhortation of Our Saviour: "Be you therefore perfect, as also your heavenly Father is perfect." (St. Matthew V, 48.) It is an interesting contrast with "Faint Yet Pursuing," ll. 1–9. Among Patmore's *Aphorisms and Extracts* we read: "If you wish to be commonly good, the easiest, indeed the only way, is to be heroically so."

129–32. This is a soul-cry for *pain, the exceeding keen edge of bliss.* (Cf. "De Natura Deorum," ll. 59–60; "Pain," *Theme;* and *infra,* ll. 152–66.)

129. The imagery of this line is taken from the "Canticle of Canticles" I, 12: "A bundle of myrrh is my Beloved to me, He shall abide between my breasts." One of the most beautiful among St. Bernard's "Sermons on the *Canticle of Canticles*" is Sermon XLIII in which he develops this, one of his favorite texts. (Cf. Translation, pp. 168–70 and notes, pp. 253–54.)

138–39. The ultimate explanation of these lines is found in the mystery of the Incarnation. (Cf. "To the Body," "Legem Tuam Dilexi," *etc.*) Patmore quotes these two lines to illustrate a passage in his essay, "Dieu et ma Dame"—a passage which is cited in the notes on "Sponsa Dei," ll. 7; 13–17. He also uses them to illustrate his meaning in the following observation: "Woman desires the infinite, man the finite. She is the continent of the infinite, making it conscious and powerful by limitation." (*Aurea Dicta* CLIII.)

140. Cf. *supra,* ll. 86–87.

140–49. Here, as in the original myth, Psyche's ecstasy of love ends with the dawn. "One of the many paradoxes common to both loves [human and divine] is that they can see best in the dark. 'Night is the light of my pleasures.'" ("Dieu et ma Dame.") But: "It is one thing to be blind, and another to be in darkness." (*Aurea Dicta* XLVI.)

146–49. In his commentary upon stanza III of the *Living Flame of Love* (§§23–24), St. John of the Cross thus distinguishes spiritual *espousals* from spiritual *nuptials.* "It is well to note clearly," writes the Saint, "the difference that exists between the possession of God through grace in itself alone and the possession of Him through union; for the one is a question of mutual love and the other is one of communication. There is as great a difference between these states as there is between betrothal and marriage. For in betrothal there is only a consent by agreement, and a unity of will between the two parties . . . But in marriage there is likewise communication between the persons, and union. During the betrothal, although from time to time the bridegroom sees the bride, . . . there is no union between them, for this comes at the end of the betrothal. Even so, when the soul has attained to such purity in itself and in its faculties that the will is well purged of other strange tastes and desires, according to its lower and higher parts, and when it has given its consent to God with respect to all this, and the will of God and of the soul are as one in a consent that is ready and free, then it has attained to the possession of God through grace of will, in so far as can be by means of will and grace; and this signifies that God has given it, through its own consent, His true and entire consent, which comes through His grace.

"And this is the lofty state of spiritual betrothal of the soul with the Word, wherein the Spouse grants the soul great favors, and visits it most lovingly and frequently, wherein the soul receives great favors and delights. But these have nothing to do with those of marriage, for they are all preparations for the union of marriage; and, though it is true that they come to the soul when it is completely purged from all creature affection (for spiritual betrothal cannot take place until this happens), nevertheless the soul has need of other and positive preparations on the part of God, of His visits and gifts whereby He purifies the soul ever more completely and beautifies and refines it so that it may be fitly prepared for such lofty union. For some souls more time is necessary than for others, for God works here according to the manner of the soul."

But, however intimate may be the spiritual relationship between God and the soul in this life, it is not the perfect and complete consummation of its love. In Heaven alone can it be said: "The marriage of the Lamb is come, and His wife hath prepared herself." (Apocalypse XIX, 7.) (Cf. "Sponsa Dei," ll. 40–41; and St. Bernard's "Sermons on the *Canticle of Canticles,*" Sermon XXXII, §2; Translation, p. 141.)

149. "Eye hath not seen nor ear heard; neither hath it entered into the heart of man, what things God hath prepared for them that love Him." (1 Corinthians II, 9.) Again: "We see now through a glass in a dark manner; but then face to face." (*Ibid.* XIII, 12.)

150–51. "If you love Me, keep My commandments." (St. John XIV, 15.)

152–66. "O sane madness, which can find, in the sharpest austerities and troubles a present heaven: O mad sanity, which, in all the pleasures of earth, can find no testimony that there is any heaven at all!" (*Aurea Dicta* CXLV.)

157–66. "But in all these things we overcome, because of Him that hath loved us. For I am sure that neither death, nor life, nor angels, nor principalities, nor powers, nor things present, nor things to come, nor might, nor height, nor depth, nor any other creature shall be able to separate us from the love of God, which is in Christ Jesus our Lord." (Romans VIII, 37–39.)

In one of Crashaw's poems inspired by St. Teresa we find the same thought expressed in imagery very similar to Patmore's:

"Love's passives are his activ'st part:
The wounded is the wounding heart.
O heart! equal poise of Love's both parts,
Big alike with wound and darts.

. . . . .

Live here great heart; and love, and die, and kill;
And bleed, and wound; and yield and conquer still.
Let this immortal life where'er it comes
Walk in a crowd of loves and martyrdoms.
Let mystic deaths wait on't; and wise souls be
The love-slain witnesses of this life of thee.
O sweet incendiary! show here thy art,
Upon this carcass of a hard cold heart;
Let all thy scattered shafts of light that play
Among the leaves of thy large books of day,
Combined against this breast at once break in
And take away from me myself and sin."
("The Flaming Heart," ll. 73–76; 79–90.)

169. Not infrequently we live to pray deliverance from a trial we have desired in order to prove our fidelity.

170–71. The allusion here is to that spiritual desolation analogous to the Dark Night of the Soul described by such mystics as St. Teresa and St. John of the Cross. But even in this hour of relative darkness, the soul's light is not entirely extinguished although it may be *like to the moon at dawn,* in comparison with the full light of the sun.

173. When night returns, the soul's darkness will be dispersed by the return of her Lover. (Cf. *supra,* ll. 140–149.)

175–77. A sinless soul filled with grace is, in a sense, *part and parcel* of divinity. But the grace given to a particular soul is measured by its capacity and need. As St. Thomas says (III, q. vii, art. 10): "The Blessed Virgin is said to be full of grace . . . inasmuch as she had sufficient grace for the state to which God had chosen her, *i.e.* to be the mother of His Only-begotten. So, too, Stephen is said to be full of grace, since he had sufficient grace to be a fit minister and witness of God, to which office he had been called. And the same may be said of others." And again: "The grace of any man, however, is compared to the grace of Christ as a particular to a universal power; hence as the force of fire, no matter how much it increases, can never equal the sun's strength, so the grace of a man, no matter how much it increases, can never equal the grace of Christ." (*Ibid.* art. 11, ad 3.)

185. Cf. "Deliciae Sapientiae," l. 80.

187. *Rainbow:* Patmore makes a different use of this symbol in his essay, "The Bow Set in the Cloud."

190–91. Cf. *supra* ll. 138–39.

192–93. Though *the whole of life is womanhood* to God, His ways are different with every individual. (Cf. *supra* ll. 146–49.)

196–97. St. Bernard speaking of the *Canticle of Canticles* II, 5, interprets "faith as a flower and good works as fruit." (Cf. Translation, p. 184.) But the Saint would be the first to concede to others different applications of the same symbols, according to his own principle of exegesis. (Cf. Translation p. 186.) In one of his descriptions of the soul during the absence of its lover St. Bernard writes: "When what is loved is present, love grows strong. When it is absent, love languishes. This is nothing else than a kind of exhaustion brought on by the impatient longing with which the mind of one who loves intensely must of necessity be affected when he whom she loves is absent. And while he is the only object for which she waits, she considers speed howsoever great, as slow. And hence the bride entreats that she may heap up for herself the fruits of good works with the sweet odor of faith, wherein she may find refreshment while the Bridegroom tarries." ("Sermons on the *Canticle of Canticles,*" Sermon LI, §3; Translation pp. 184–85.)

205. Professor Robinson is of the opinion that the first use of sweetness and bitterness combined in literature, is found in Sappho's fragment "To Atthis" where love is spoken of as "that creature bitter-sweet"—γλυκύπικρον. (Cf. *Sappho and Her Influence,* p. 57.) The idea is, of course, a commonplace of Christian literature. (Cf. "Pain," *passim.*)

206–207. The most awful example of truth deliberately concealed to save it from profanation is found in Christ's use of parables when addressing his followers in the presence of those who had rejected Him: "Therefore do I speak to them in parables: because seeing they see not, and hearing they hear not, neither do they understand. And the prophecy of Isaias is fulfilled in them, who saith: By hearing you shall hear, and shall not understand: and seeing you shall see, and shall not perceive. For the heart of this people is grown gross, and with their ears they have been dull of hearing, and their eyes they have shut: lest at any time they should see with their eyes, and hear with their ears, and understand with their heart, and be converted, and I should heal them." (St. Matthew XIII, 13–15.) (Cf. "Dead Language," l. 18.)

"The Psyche Odes have fulfilled this warning, for though a few timid spirits have been repelled at the identity here expressed between the human and the divine relation, the truth is that their intimacy has prevented them from seeming credible to normal men. But it was just this identity that Patmore lived and wrote to emphasize. He that hath ears let him listen. The word here spoken he will not easily hear anywhere else." (*The Idea of Coventry Patmore,* Burdett, pp. 155–56.) (Cf. "Dead Language.")

DE NATURA DEORUM

Publication: It was first included in the *Unknown Eros* sequence, in Odes I–XLVI, 1878.

Title: "Concerning the Nature of the Gods." It is the same as the title of Cicero's famous dialogue in which he presents and appraises the philosophies of his day on a question which as he says: "is incomparable for acquiring knowledge concerning the nature of the soul, and indispensable for the regulation of religion—*et ad cognitionem animi pulcherrima est et ad moderandam religionem necessaria.*" (Bk. I, §1.) *Religio* among the Romans, as we know, meant the exact fulfilment of the rites of cult, many of which had lost their religious significance and had become purely civil functions. Nevertheless there is much in Cicero's work that with very little adaptation may be applied to the truths of Christianity which Patmore treats in this ode.

Theme: It is really a fulfilment of the promise given in the *Angel in the House:*

> "This little germ of nuptial love,
> Which springs so simply from the sod,
> The root is, as my song shall prove,
> Of all our love to man and God."
>
> (Bk. I, Canto vi, Prelude ii.)

The soul's fear that she may lose her Divine Lover is banished by the revelation she receives as she grows in the knowledge of the nature of God and the supernatural life of grace. Her Beloved will never depart from her, she learns, unless she deliberately rejects Him. In answer to her fearful questionings that spring from the remembrance of her past infidelities, comes the voice of her Divine Lover reassuring her that her present love is the sweeter because He has something dreadful to forgive: From the soul's realization of her own nothingness and her Beloved's greatness, comes the revelation that this is the very source of God's love for her, the fulfilment of "the reciprocal desire of the great for the small and the small for the great." The severity of her Lover which at first bewildered the soul, is finally revealed as the strength of His justice that so perfectly balances the tenderness of His mercy.

Mr. Page is of the opinion that the transcripts from Marie Lataste's writings found among Patmore's notes used in the writing of the Odes, indicate that she was Psyche and that the Pythoness was her confessor. (Cf. notes on PSYCHE ODES in general.)

Metre: In this ode and in "Psyche's Discontent" the appropriateness of the metre for dialogue is notable.

1. Psyche: Cf. "Eros and Psyche": *Title.*

2–7. Here Patmore describes the external manifestation of the two-fold transfiguration of life by love that is divine. "What love does in transfiguring life, that religion does in transfiguring love." ("Love and Poetry.")

8–9. Recall Patmore's symbolic expression of the opposite state of a soul that is at peace and all its powers directed to one end when, *all the heaving ocean heaves one way.* ("Wind and Wave" l. 23.)

10. *Pythoness:* Pythia, prophetess of the Delphic Oracle. In the early days of the oracle she was a young girl but in a later age she was a woman of over fifty. (Cf. l. 6.) She is a type of that divine revelation that is necessary in order that the human soul may know the *nature of the gods.* A passage in Patmore's essay, "The Precursor," is the best exposition of this idea: "John, though naturally nearer to Jesus than any other man 'born of woman' (nature) 'knew Him not' but by the coming of the Holy Spirit, *i.e.* divine inspiration. So natural love though so pure an image of the divine, knows not the divine until this is supernaturally revealed to it."

11. *in the dark:* The mystics speak frequently of the night of contemplation. St. John of the Cross tells us: "In order that the soul may be divinely prepared and tempered with its faculties for the Divine union of love, it would be well for it to be first of all absorbed, with all its faculties, in this Divine and dark spiritual light of contemplation and thus to be withdrawn from all the affections and apprehensions of the creatures, which condition ordinarily continues in proportion to its intensity. And thus, the simpler and purer is this Divine light in its assault upon the soul, the more it darkens it, voids it and annihilates it according to its particular apprehensions and affections, with regard both to things above and to things below; and similarly, the less simple and pure is it in this assault, the less deprivation it causes it and the less dark it is. Now this is a thing that seems incredible, to say that the brighter and purer is supernatural and Divine light, the more it darkens the soul, and that the less bright and pure it is, the less dark it is to the soul. Yet this may well be understood if we consider what has been proved above by the dictum of the philosopher—namely, that the brighter and the more manifest in themselves are supernatural things the darker are they to our understanding." (*Dark Night of the Soul,* Bk. II, chapt. viii, §2.)

St. John makes the Soul describe the spiritual night of contemplation in these stanzas from his poem, "Dark Night":

3. "In the happy night, In secret, when none saw me,
Nor I beheld aught, Without light or guide, save
that which burned in my heart.
4. "This light guided me More surely than the light
of noonday
To the place where he (well I knew who!) was
awaiting me—
A place where none appeared.
5. "Oh, night that guided me, Oh, night more lovely
than the dawn,
Oh, night that joined Beloved with lover,
Lover transformed in the Beloved!"

(From the translation by E. Allison Peers.)

The Saint's commentary upon stanza 4 is given in Bk. II, chapt. xxv. (Cf. "Eros and Psyche," ll. 45; 140–149.)

14–17. "He comes and goes according to His good pleasure, as if visiting the soul *early in the morning* and *proving* her *suddenly* (Job VII, 18). His going away is in some way or other entirely under His control. His return is a matter of His free will. And both are entirely a matter of His judgment. The reason for them is known only to Himself." (St. Bernard, "Sermons on the *Canticle of Canticles,* Sermon LXXIV, §3: Translation, p. 217.)

19. This line suggests Thompson's lines in the "Orient Ode" (ll. 100–104):

"even the kisses of the just
Go down not unrewarded to the dust.
Yea, not a kiss which I have given,
But shall triumph upon my lips in heaven,
Or cling a shameful fungus there in hell."

25–26. Psyche's fear that she may prove unfaithful during the absence of her Lover springs from the inspired warning: "Wherefore he that thinketh himself to stand, let him take heed lest he fall." (1 Corinthians X, 12.) And in St. Bernard we read: "Even in this body of ours the joy of the Bridegroom's presence is frequently felt, but not the fulness of it, for although His visitation gladdens the heart, the alternation of His absence makes it sad." ("Sermons on the *Canticle of Canticles;* Sermon XXXII, §2; Translation, p. 141.) (Cf. "Psyche's Discontent," ll. 42–58.) The reasons for God's seeming withdrawal from the soul are given by Marie Lataste in her writings, vol. I, pp. 316; 320–22.

27. Cf. *supra,* ll. 14–17.

28–29. Cf. *supra,* ll. 34–35.

30–33. It is by a perverse and deliberate act of will, only, that the soul can lose God's love. Similarly, it is by conformity of the human will to the divine that man becomes the object of God's love. Temptations, whether they spring from the lower passions or from the higher faculties of the soul merely test the strength of one's will and prove one's virtue.

34–35. Even in the Dark Night of the Soul, God does not really withdraw from the soul although, to the soul, He seems to do so. The faint light of dawn is darkness compared to the full light of midday, but yet it is sufficient to guide our footsteps. And the light of a candle or a star may be sufficient to guide our steps until that feeble light is absorbed in the light of the sun. (Cf. St. John of the Cross, *The Spiritual Canticle,* Stanza XXVII, §2.)

36–41. "The Babe sucking its mother's breast, and the Lover returning after twenty years' separation to his home and food in the same bosom, are the types and princes of Mystics." (*Aurea Dicta* CXXVIII.)

43. *O, hateful light:* Cf. *supra,* l. 11; *infra,* l. 45; "Eros and Psyche," ll. 140–49.

45. "The clearer and more manifest are Divine things in themselves, the darker and more hidden are they to the soul naturally; just as, the clearer is the light, the more it blinds and darkens the pupil of the owl, and, the more directly we look at the sun, the greater is the darkness which it causes in our visual faculty, overcoming and overwhelming it through its own weakness. In the same way, when this Divine light of contemplation assails the soul which is not yet wholly enlightened, it causes spiritual darkness in it; for not only does it overcome it, but likewise it overwhelms it and darkens the act of its natural intelligence. For this reason S. Dionysius and other mystical theologians call this infused contemplation a ray of darkness—that is to say, for the soul that is not enlightened and purged—for the natural strength of the intellect is transcended and overwhelmed by its great supernatural light." (*The Night of the Soul,* Bk. II, chapt. v, §3.)

Thompson expresses a similar thought in "The Mistress of Vision," ll. 138–45:

'When earth and heaven lay down their veil,
And that apocalypse turns thee pale;
When their seeing blindeth thee
To what thy fellow-mortals see;
When their sight to thee is sightless;
Their living, death; their light, most lightless;
Search no more—
Pass the gates of Luthany, tread the region Elenore.'

46–49. Spiritual writers make use of various comparisons to illustrate the fact that man is God's image. Here Patmore uses a rather obvious symbol, a mirror. Another frequent comparison makes silver the symbol of the soul and God the Refiner who watches it in the fire of suffering, as it grows purer and purer until finally, undimmed by any alloy, it clearly reflects Him.

47. In the beginning of the Pre-Raphaelite Movement, Patmore, who was then very friendly with the Brethren, suggested this line as a motto for their paper, *The Germ—Thoughts towards Nature in Poetry, Literature and Art.* (Cf. "Pain," l. 29.)

51–52. It is a favorite theme with Patmore that past infidelity is no barrier to pure love so long as the infidelity is past. But Puritanism, as Cardinal Manning expressed it: "expects to see Mary Magdalen *skulking* among the saints." Patmore with his sure Catholic sense redolent of the spirit of Christ, places her next to the Mother of God, in glory. (Cf. "Deliciae Sapientiae de Amore," ll. 125–30; "Victory in Defeat," ll. 16–18.)

57–58. Such are the tears of repentance that flow from *living Love* which *yet blushes for dead shame.* (Cf. "Deliciae Sapientiae de Amore," l. 126.) There is here a reverberation of St. Augustine's cry: "Late have I loved You, O Beauty so ancient and so new! Late have I loved You!" (*Confessions,* Bk. X, chapt. xxvii.)

59–60. Cf. "Pain," *Theme:* "Eros and Psyche," ll. 129–32.

61. "The mutations of things spiritual and celestial. Life without such changes would be uniform, consequently *nothing;* nor would goodness and truth be known or distinguished, much less perceived." (*Aphorisms and Extracts.*)

62–64. "Favors and honours, when they become exceedingly great, become very manifestly what they are, and are far less dangerous to humility than lesser graces. The Beggar Maid was not nearly so likely to be made proud by her marriage with King Cophetua as the highest of his Court-Ladies would have been. Hence the subtlest and most successful device of the enemy is to persuade the soul that she cannot *please* God, much less excite His desire for her, and to represent as extravagant figures of speech His assurances to the contrary, such as 'The King shall greatly desire thy beauty' (*Concupiscet Rex decorem tuum*), 'I have longed for her,' *etc.* True, she knows that none but a Goddess can be the desire of a God, but she is taught daily by His withdrawals that the divine beauty in her which He loves is His own reflection, and that, without it, she is at best but a flower in the dark." (*Magna Moralia* III.) (Cf. "Eros and Psyche," ll. 94–95; "King Cophetua the First.")

65–68. "Heaven becomes very intelligible and attractive when it is discerned to be—Woman." (*Aurea Dicta* LXXII.)

69–70. For the necessity of sacrifice in love, cf. "Pain": *Theme.*

71–72. Cf. "Eros and Psyche," ll. 77–84, *etc.*

74–75. According to Apuleius, the daughter of Psyche (Depth) and Eros (Height) is Voluptas (Delight). "Dr. Johnson, who sometimes let fall, in off-hand talk, sayings of such depth, simplicity and significance that we must go back to the philosophers of antiquity to find the like of them, once remarked that 'inequality is the source of all delight.' This saying, which must seem surprising to most modern ears, is absolutely true, even demonstrable.

"All delight—not all pleasure, which is quite a different thing—will be found, when thoroughly examined, to consist in the rendering and receiving of love and the services of love. Hence the great and fortunately inextinguishable fountains of delight in the relationships of man and woman and of parents and children." ("Thoughts on Knowledge, Opinion, and Inequality.") (Cf. *infra,* ll. 123–24; "1880–85," ll. 60–70; "The Child's Purchase," ll. 58–59, *etc.*)

76–77. In these lines we have the above principle applied to divine love, of which human love is a parable. " 'My soul hath rejoiced in God my Saviour because He has regarded the lowliness of His handmaiden.' All joy is in the conjunction of opposites, height with depth, spirit with sense, honour with humility, above all, the Infinite with the finite. Hence an appearance of infatuation in all love. The highest Angel prostrates himself before a village-maiden. She says, 'Behold the bondmaiden of the Lord,' to Him who asks her to be His Bride and Mother. God lies swathed and swaddled in her flesh, 'reconciling the highest with the lowest.' Only lovers can think of these things; and they can think of nothing else." (*Magna Moralia* XXXVIII.) (Cf. "Eros and Psyche," ll. 77–84; "Psyche's Discontent," ll. 7–8.)

78–84. In Patmore's day as in our own, the popular notion of God was of a rather *pompous but good-natured Jove.* God as He is known through the truth of revelation is Wisdom, in whom the gentleness of love and the sternness of justice are perfectly balanced. It is His love that is the inspiration of God's warning to the people of Israel when they had sinned: "Therefore will I visit upon you all your iniquities." (Amos III, 2.)

85–86. "She loves intensely who is so intoxicated with her own love that she does not think upon the majesty of Him whom she loves. What! *He looketh upon the earth and maketh it tremble* (Psalm CIII, 32) . . . But what can be plainer than that *perfect charity casteth out fear."* (1 St. John IV, 18.) (Cf. St. Bernard, "Sermons on the *Canticle of Canticles,"* Sermon VII, §3.)

87–99. The blend of tenderness and strength characteristic of the genuine love of God or man, distinguishes it from sadism on one hand, and on the other, from sheer sentimentality. The purifying effect produced in man's soul by God's punishment is described in "Pain," ll. 12–29. (Cf. "Eros and Psyche," ll. 152–66.)

97–101. The motive and end of bodily penances are discussed in detail in "Pain." Here it will be enough to say that when the infliction of pain is an end in itself, it is a form of sadism. When it aims at the suppression of concupiscence so that the great powers of the soul and body may enjoy freer scope according to God's law, it is an act of the virtue of penance. As St. Paul reminded the Romans (VIII, 13): "If you live according to the flesh, you shall die: but if by the Spirit you mortify the deeds of the flesh, you shall live." (Cf. "Eros and Psyche," ll. 152–66.)

102–104. The excellence of divine Wisdom and the beauty of its effects upon the soul, contrasted with the results of worldly wisdom will be found in the first chapters of the Book of Wisdom. The abode of divine Wisdom is beautifully described in Job XXVIII, 12–18.

106. "Let us therefore love God, because God first hath loved us." (1 St. John IV, 19.)

107. "If you love Me keep My commandments." (St. John XIV, 15.) *"Thou shalt love the Lord thy God with thy whole heart, and with thy whole soul, and with thy whole mind.* This is the greatest and the first commandment. And the second is like to this: *Thou shalt love thy neighbor as thyself.* On these two commandments dependeth the whole law and the prophets." (St. Matthew XXII, 37–40.)

109–111. "But for myself I will glory nothing, but in my infirmities." (2 Corinthians XII, 5.)

112–15. Cf. "The Azalea," ll. 24–25.

118–19. There is here undoubtedly a contrast between God as He was known in the Old Testament, and as He revealed Himself in the New, when *the Word was made Flesh and dwelt among us* (St. John I, 14).

123–24.

"When the soul owns herself sincerely to be nought
The whole of heaven flows in as freely as a thought."

(*Aphorisms and Extracts.*)

"An ordinary man requires in his mistress abilities corresponding to his own, and he who cannot love much commonly demands from her a greater power of love for him. A great man has a wilful and somewhat amused delight ('Olli subridens') in binding himself in wedlock to one who, indeed, implicitly believes in his greatness, but who is really nothing but a little, ignorant Love, who gives all her mite and understands only caresses. To a great man and a God a little love is a great thing. As the greatest of souls is infinitely little to God, it follows that this peculiar source of felicity in extremes is, in the divine marriage, unfathomable and inexhaustible." ("Dieu et ma Dame.") (Cf. *supra,* ll. 74–78.)

124–25. Cf. "Sponsa Dei," l. 18.

130–31. Cf. "Eros and Psyche," ll. 88–89; 94–95.

130. "If any one perseveres in the path of perfection, points of likeness between Divine and human love will become *res cognita et visa;* and he will see that the phenomena of the human relationship of love are such because they are the realities of the Divine. For all properly human instincts are no other than the lineaments of God; and man (*homo*) is an image and likeness of God, most especially in those mysteries which—let all remark well—are quite as inscrutable in their secondary or human, as in their primary manifestation." ("Dieu et ma Dame.")

137. This line is quoted in Patmore's essay, "Thoughts on Knowledge, Opinion and Inequality," in a passage cited in "Psyche's Discontent," ll. 7–8.

138. *darkness:* Cf. *supra,* l. 11.

141–50. In his earlier work Patmore frequently mentions the necessity of reverence and awe in love, whether human or divine. For instance:

> "intimacy in love is nought
> Without pure reverence."
> (*Victories of Love,* Bk. II, Letter xii.)

And:

> "What were love should reverence cease."
> (*Angel in the House,* Bk. II, Canto ii, Prelude i.)

Here Patmore blames excessive reverence that degenerates into sheer formality and destroys rather than controls the ardor of love. In Protestant sects such as Puritanism, this results in a false idea of God in which His awful attributes inspire servile fear and reverence while attributes that are more attractive to human nature and lead to familiar love and joyousness are forgotten. In his essay, "Dieu et ma Dame," Patmore, after developing the analogy between human and divine love, concludes: "Should any believing reader object that such thoughts as I have suggested to him imply an irreverent idea of the intimacies of God with His elect, I beg him to remember that in receiving the Blessed Sacrament with the faith which the Church demands, he affirms and *acts* a familiarity which is greater than any other that can be conceived."

"There should be courtesy, courtliness, high breeding, in our converse with the King of Kings," wrote one of Patmore's contemporaries, "but anything is better than a pompous frigidity, a conventional stiffness, in presence of the royal and eternal love." (*Post Liminium Essays,* Lionel Johnson, p. 114.) And Francis Thompson in his essay on Crashaw speaks of "the human and lover-like tenderness which informs Crashaw's sacred poems, differentiating them from the conventional style of English sacred poetry, with its solemn aloofness from celestial things."

145–50. These lines would be more convincing were they expressed with a touch of dignity and gentleness.

151–56. "They understand little of love who do not see how great a part is played in it by mirth and paradox." ("The Weaker Vessel.") " 'Rejoice always: and again I say, Rejoice,' says one of the highest authorities; and a poet who is scarcely less infallible in psychological science writes—

'A cheerful heart is what the Muses love.'

Dante shows Melancholy dismally punished in Purgatory; though his own interior gaiety—of which a word by and by—is so interior, and its outward aspect often so grim, that he is vulgarly considered to have himself been a sinner of this sort. Good art is nothing but a representation of life; and that the good are gay is a commonplace, and one which, strange to say, is as generally disbelieved as it is, when rightly understood, undeniably true." ("Cheerfulness in Art.")

158–61. When, like Psyche, we doubt if God is pleased with the pure delights of love and the innocent pleasures of life, we would do well to gaze steadily upon *yon starless deep.* There we shall see no *Titan forging thunderbolts,* but *three fair butterflies at lovesome play.* As Mr. Burdett suggests (p. 159), it is God's delight "to be with the *children* of men."

We may say of the human soul what Thompson has said of Poetry: "Suffer her to wanton, suffer her to play, so she play round the foot of the cross." ("Shelley.")

166-67. Truth is sometimes mysterious though clear. (Cf. "Wedding Sermon," ll. 1–2.) At other times it is mysterious but obscure because of the nature of the subject. Such obscurity is genuine and far removed from that deliberate obscurity that is the result of incoherence of thought and vagueness of expression. (Cf. "Obscurity and Poetry," Joseph Plunkett.)

168–70. The deafness of men to spiritual truth is the theme of "Dead Language."

PSYCHE'S DISCONTENT

Publication: Included in the *Unknown Eros* sequence for the first time in *Odes* I–XLVI, 1878.

Theme: The soul seeks a respite from the love with which God overwhelms her. But her Divine Lover bids her be prudent in what she asks, lest, through excess of love He grant *her beseeched harm.* The soul then fervently pleads to be allowed to labor and suffer, and thus to prove her love. But God bids her:

Accept the sweet, and say 'tis sacrifice!

It is the lyrical expression of the Fourth Degree of Love described by St. Bernard. (Cf. notes to PSYCHE ODES, in general.)

1–2. This recoil from God's embrace in a soul where love has grown seemingly too intense for endurance, is common in the writings of the saints. (Cf. "Eros and Psyche," ll. 118–20.)

1. *"Love* is feign'd to be a Boy." (*Amoris Effigies,* translation, p. 63.)

2–3. In the delights of God's love all lesser loves lose their savour.

" 'Tis to have drunk too well
The drink that is divine,
Maketh the kind earth waste,
And breath intolerable."
("The Dread of Height," Thompson, ll. 8–11.)

5–8. Mr. Shane Leslie cites this quatrain as a perfect expression of, "the relations of Soul and Lover, Virgin and God." (*Studies in Sublime Failure,* p. 155.) (Cf. "De Natura Deorum," ll. 123–24; *infra,* ll. 7–8.)

5. *clay-conceived birth:* The human soul was, in a sense, conceived in clay: "And the Lord God formed man of the slime of the earth: and breathed into his face the breath of life, and man became a living soul." (Genesis II, 7.) Similarly, according to Catholic teaching, every individual soul is created by God and infused into the body prepared for it by the parents. (Cf. "Eros and Psyche," ll. 118–20.)

7–8. "The doctrines of liberty, fraternity, and equality are known instinctively only by very bad children; and most women when once they have been in love, repudiate such teaching indignantly, under whatever polity they may have been born.

Between unequals sweet is equal love;

and the fact is that there is no love, and therefore no sweetness, which is not thus conditioned; and the greater the inequality the greater the sweetness. Hence the doctrine that infinite felicity can arise only from the mutual love of beings infinitely unequal—that is, of the creator and creature. Inequality, far from implying any dishonour on either side of the mutual compact of love, is a source of honour to both. Hooker, writing of marriage says: 'It is no small honour to a man that a creature so like himself should be subjected to him'; and we all know that the honour to woman which the chivalry of the Middle Ages made an abiding constituent of civilization, was founded upon Catholic views of her subjection, and the obligation to give special honour, as of right, to the weaker vessel." ("Thoughts on Knowledge, Opinion, and Inequality.") (Cf. "Eros and Psyche," ll. 77–84; "De Natura Deorum," ll. 74–75; "1880–85," ll. 60, 62–70; "The Child's Purchase," ll. 58–59.)

9–12. Cf. "De Natura Deorum," ll. 151–56; 158–61.

13–17. Cf. *supra,* ll. 1–2.

18–22. Stars are favorite symbols in Patmore to illustrate the intensification of love caused by separation. (Cf. "The Contract," ll. 30–33; "Deliciae Sapientiae," ll. 50–56.)

24. This is a timely warning for the Soul praying that God depart from her. Will she be able to sustain the pain of separation?

25. "Love not only levels but subjects." (*Aphorisms and Extracts.*)

26–27. "Blessed is the soul that loves," says St. John of the Cross, "for it has made a captive of God Who obeys its good pleasure. Such is the nature of love that it makes those who love do what is asked of them." ("A Spiritual Canticle of the Soul," translation by Lewis, pp. 244–45.)

29. *to do:* to be done.

30–31. There is here an implicit complaint not unlike the protest of the opening lines. It springs from the difficulty of meeting the obligations of the active life, while the soul, in contemplation, is ravished with love.

32–36. "I must work the works of Him that sent Me, whilst it is day: the night cometh when no man can work." (St. John IX, 4.) Patmore seems in these lines to apply this text to the Night of the Soul.

37–41. "Who is there who can enjoy the light of contemplation—while he still remains in the body? But as often as he falls from the contemplative way, he devotes himself to the active, whence, as from a neighboring retreat he will be able to return better acquainted, to his former state. For these two ways of life are companions one to the other and they live under the same roof on terms of equality. Martha, surely, is Mary's sister. And although she falls from the light of contemplation, she does not stumble into the darkness of sin or into the sloth of inactivity, but keeps herself in the light of doing good. And that you may know that good works are a light, *let your light shine,* says Our Lord, *before men* (St. Matthew V, 16). And there is no doubt that this was said concerning good works which men could see." (St. Bernard, "Sermons on the *Canticle of Canticles,* Sermon LI, §2; Translation, p. 184.) (Cf. "The Wedding Sermon," ll. 36–48.)

42–58. Here, the Soul grown strong pleads that God may withdraw from her for a while, that in separation she may prove her fidelity. In "De Natura Deorum," anticipating such a separation, the soul feared for her constancy.

43. *Goddess-like:* Cf. "Eros and Psyche," ll. 94–95.

44–50. Cf. "Eros and Psyche," ll. 170–71.

51–54. Cf. "Eros and Psyche," ll. 152–66.

59–65. Here is a sudden fulfilment of the hope expressed in ll. 55–58.

65. The great mystics have frequently used homely similes such as this to express the completeness with which God possessed their souls.

67. *more than mortal chaste:* chaste in temptations that must have proved fatal to man's *mortal* powers unassisted by grace.

69. *this fond indignity, delight:* consolation and *delight* are a manifestation of God's love. But to a strong soul they may seem an *indignity* by comparison with desolation and pain which give her a greater opportunity to prove her love.

72–73. The disparity between the Soul and God makes the Soul's reverence, in itself, ridiculous. It is only God's gracious condescension that gives it meaning. Hence, the priest's words at Mass just before he repeats the Our Father: "Instructed by Thy saving precepts and following Thy divine example, we dare to say: *Our Father Who art in heaven, etc.*

Patmore's own commentary upon these lines is this: "If we may credit certain hints contained in the lives of the Saints, love raises the spirit above the sphere of reverence and worship into one of laughter and dalliance; a sphere in which the Soul says:

> *Shall I, the gnat, which dances in Thy ray,*
> *Dare to be reverent?"*
>
> (*Aurea Dicta* XXXIX.)

74. "Eye hath not seen, nor ear heard, neither hath it entered into the heart of man, what things God hath prepared for them that love Him." (1 Corinthians II, 9.)

75–76. It is more difficult to distinguish good from evil in the delights of love, than in suffering and pain. (Cf. 'Let Be,' ll. 8–9.)

83. "Again, as with a mortal lover, God . . . complains, as He did to Martha, of all attempts to please Him otherwise than by giving Him her society and her person in contemplation." ("Dieu et ma Dame.")

86. *thy proud cup:* The chalice of life must be drunk by a soul who glories in God's grace. This symbol was used by our Blessed Saviour himself in speaking of His passion and death, as Man: "The chalice which My Father hath given Me, shall I not drink it?" (St. John XVIII, 11.)

pearl of price: "The kingdom of heaven is like to a merchant seeking good pearls. Who when he had found one pearl of great price, went his way and sold all that he had and bought it." (St. Matthew XIII, 45–46.)

88. " 'God leads us by our own desires,' after we have once offered the sacrifice of them with full sincerity. The 'ruling love,' the best-beloved good, which we offer to slay, as Abraham did Isaac, that very good is given back to us glorified and made indeed the thing which we desired. We have, with the 'Wise Man,' to leave our own people and our father's house, before we can see 'Jesus with His Mother,' but, after that, God bids us 'go back *another way into our own country.*' " (*Magna Moralia* XLV.)

89–92. "When God has arduously wrought the six degrees of the Soul's new creation, and she is pronounced *'very good,'* He rests from His labour, and bids her also to rest in the Sabbath of contemplation of His love and of His beauty as mirrored in herself. She 'wakes up after His likeness and is satisfied with it'; and greater wonders are wrought in her in one minute of mutual felicity than would be worked by a day of martyrdom, or a year of heroic action." (*Magna Moralia* VIII.)

89. The figure of the sleeping centre which communicates love to life's circumference, is an echo of the same figure so effectively used in the "Wedding Sermon," ll. 311–16.

PAIN

Publication: This was one of the original Nine Odes published in 1868.

Title: It refers chiefly to bodily pain.

Theme: It was first expressed in a couplet in "De Natura Deorum," ll. 59–60:

> "Sadness is beauty's savour and pain is
> The exceeding keen edge of bliss."

In the marriage of Pain and Pleasure, is begotten their climax, Joy, such joy as is compatible with pain and sorrow. (Cf. "Victory in Defeat," ll. 9–10: "Legem Tuam Dilexi," ll. 79–81, *etc.*) It is an indictment, alike, of Hedonism and Sadism and a corollary of the teachings and example of Jesus Christ in His passion, death and resurrection. (Cf. "Let Be," *Theme.*)

"A self-indulgent age like ours," wrote Aubrey de Vere, "will be little disposed to such a strain. It might, notwithstanding, find its capacities for joy indefinitely increased if it adopted that philosophy, even to the extent of not hunting its pleasures to death, and not shrinking from what slight endurance is implied in the most obviously necessary sacrifice." (*Essays Literary and Ethical,* pp. 142–43.)

As much as anything Patmore has left us, this ode illustrates the profound truth expressed in the motto he selected for *Rod, Root and Flower:* "There shall come forth a rod out of the root of Jesse, and a flower shall rise up out of the root." (Isaias XI, 1.) "My covenant shall be in your flesh" (Cf. Ecclesiasticus XLIV, 21.)

1–29. These lines are a challenge to the Hedonism of the nineteenth century that culminated in the 1890's. (Cf. "De Natura Deorum," ll. 59–60.)

1. *Pain* is a *mystery* which man will accept only when the motive of his faith is love.

2–3. The nearness of *joy* and *delight* to *pain* accepted in the spirit of Christ is one of Patmore's most abiding themes. In his essay, "Cheerfulness in Life and Art" he writes: "In the whole range of art, joy is nowhere expressed so often and with such piercing sweetness as in the *Paradiso;* and it flashes occasionally through the dun atmosphere of the other parts of the poem. The *Inferno* is pervaded by the vigorous joy of the poet beholding thoroughly bad people getting their deserts; and the penances of Purgatory are contemplated by him with the grave pleasure which is often felt by the saner sort of persons, even in this world, under sufferings they acknowledge to be the appropriate punishment of and purification from the sins they have fallen into." (Cf. "De Natura Deorum," ll. 151–56; "Winter," l. 6; "Eros and Psyche," l. 51; *etc.*)

Again: "God is the only reality, and we are real only so far as we are in His order, and He is in us. Hell or Hades, was truly regarded by the ancients as the realm of shades, or phantoms and frightful dreams . . . All evils are phantoms, even physical pain, which a perfectly courageous heart converts by simply confronting it, into present and sensible joy of purgation and victory. 'Savages' will laugh and sing under excruciating tortures, and many a Saint has been forbidden by his director to inflict on himself corporeal pain, because it has become a luxury." (*Magna Moralia* XXII.)

4. "Hate pleasure, if only because this is the only means of obtaining it. Reject the foul smoke, and it will be forced back on you as pure flame. But this you cannot believe until you shall have rejected it without thought of reward." (*Aurea Dicta* XV.)

5–6. In the *Writings of Marie Lataste* (vol. I, p. 56) we read: "God lays His hand heavily on the just and on sinners: on the just, in order to facilitate their acquisition of greater merits; on sinners, to chastise them in their bodies and thus to save their souls by a sincere repentance."

5. Those who have attained to a high degree of sanctity prefer pain and suffering after the manner of their Divine Model. As St. Paul says: "And therefore we also having so great a cloud of witnesses over our head, laying aside every weight and sin which surrounds us, let us run by patience to the fight proposed to us: Looking on Jesus, the Author and Finisher of faith, Who having joy set before Him, endured the cross, despising the shame, and now sitteth on the right hand of the throne of God." (Hebrews XII, 1–2.)

6. *Pain* as *medicine of sin* is the theme of St. Paul's Epistle to the Hebrews (XII, 3–7): "For think diligently upon Him that endured such opposition from sinners against Himself; that you be not wearied, fainting in your minds. For you have not yet resisted unto blood, striving against sin: And you have forgotten the consolation which speaketh to you as unto children, saying: *My son neglect not the discipline of the Lord; neither be thou wearied whilst thou art rebuked by Him. For whom the Lord loveth, He chastiseth; and He scourgeth every son whom He receiveth. Persevere under discipline.*" (Cf. *infra,* l. 32.)

"It must be observed," writes St. Thomas, "that a medicine never removes a greater good in order to promote a lesser; thus the medicine of the body never blinds the eye in order to repair the heel: yet sometimes it is harmful in lesser things that it may be helpful in things of greater consequence. And since spiritual goods are of the greatest consequence, while temporal goods are least important, sometimes a person is punished in his temporal goods without any fault of his own. Such are many of the punishments inflicted by God in this present life for our humiliation and pain." (*Summa,* II, ii, q. 108, art. 4.)

7–10. There is no avoiding pain in this life. There is only question of how we accept it—as medicinal or retributive. As St. Thomas says: "The punishments of this life are medicinal rather than retributive. For retribution is reserved to the Divine judgment which is pronounced against sinners *according to truth.*" (Romans II, 2.) (*Summa* II, ii, q. 66, art. 6.)

Again: "Even the punishment that is inflicted according to human laws is not always intended as a medicine for the one who is punished, but sometimes only for others: thus when a thief is hanged, this is not for his own amendment, but for the sake of others, that at least they may be deterred from crime through fear of punishment, according to Proverbs XIX, 25: *The wicked man being scourged, the fool shall be wiser*. Accordingly the eternal punishments inflicted by God on the reprobate, are medicinal punishments for those who refrain from sin through the thought of those punishments, according to Psalm LIX, 6: *Thou hast given a warning to them that fear Thee, that they may flee from before the bow, that Thy beloved may be delivered*." (*Summa* II, i, q. 87, art. 3.)

Even impenitent sinners who reject pain as *food of sanctity* or *medicine of sin* must accept it as a retributive punishment to satisfy God's justice, since His mercy has been deliberately rejected.

11. This is an adaptation of the prayer said by the priest at Mass just before he reads the Gospel: "Cleanse my heart and my lips, O Almighty God, who didst cleanse the lips of the prophet Isaias with a burning coal: and vouchsafe, through Thy gracious mercy, so to purify me, that I may worthily proclaim Thy holy Gospel." (Cf. Isaias VI, 6–7.)

12–29. Though pain sears the flesh it brings peace to the mind (ll. 12–13) and clarifies man's spiritual vision (l. 14). It burns away spiritual sloth and the corruption of sin; begets real spiritual joy (ll. 19–27) and makes man a clear, bright mirror reflecting God's love (ll. 28–29).

12–13. He who would attain the spiritual peace of the Unitive Way must first tread the Way of Purgation through bodily penance. And he who would enjoy the rapture of mystical union must endure the Night of the Soul. (Cf. "Legem Tuam Dilexi, ll. 79–81.)

13. *arduous peace:* Such peace is far removed from the passive peace of Quietism.

14. *bright'nest my dull view:* By purging man of sin and its spiritual consequences. (Cf. *infra,* ll. 23–24.)

19–27. A notably successful lyrical expression of the spiritual purgation effected by pain as the *medicine of sin.*

29. Cf. "De Natura Deorum," ll. 46–49.

32–43. When a little respite from pain is granted man, through sloth he is inclined to forget it, his greater spiritual good.

32. "Persevere under discipline. God dealing with you as with His sons; for what son is there whom the father doth not correct? But if you be without chastisement, whereof all are made partakers, then are you bastards, and not sons." (Hebrews XII, 7–8.) (Cf. *supra,* ll. 5–10.)

44–60. In view of the spiritual good that accrues to the soul from bodily pain, man should not wait for Pain to *woo* him, nor should he fear its *fierce kiss* when first it becomes the aggressive lover. Above all he should not turn to dally with *Pleasure,* when Pain has withdrawn from him.

In his essay, "Emotional Art," Patmore thus differentiates *Pleasure,* Pain's *pale enemy,* from the spiritual joy begotten of her: "Pleasure is an itch of the cold and corrupt flesh, and must end with corruption; joy is the life of the natural and innocent breast, prophesying peace, but too full of desire to obtain it yet; peace is the indwelling of God and the habitual possession of all our desires, and it is too grave and quiet even for a smile."

61–66. This prayer against spiritual sloth and spiritual cowardice which is sometimes called prudence, clearly distinguishes presumption from confidence. It were presumptuous (*unlawful*) for any but those who *love so well,* deliberately to seek pain. They would not be able to bear it.

PROPHETS WHO CANNOT SING

Publication: First published as one of the Nine Odes, 1868. Later it appeared in the *Pall Mall Gazette,* December 20, 1876.

Theme: It is an indictment of religious poetry that takes as its theme the highest reaches of spiritual experience. The completest explanation of the ode and its best commentary is the following passage from Patmore's prose: "Thoughts and feelings may be too high as well as too low to 'move harmonious numbers.' The inner life of the saint, which is well called the 'hidden life,' has no adequate expression. The most delicate and glowing poetic imagery in the hands of the most inspired and accomplished poet scarcely suffices to shadow forth the affections of ordinary humanity; and it seems to us that we get the best insight into the life which claims to be far higher than that, from the, for the most part, hard and stuttering prose of saintly writers. These seem to be serious arguments against expressly religious poetry generally—not against 'hymns,' which, as we all know, scarcely ever attempt to be poetry, but which have their necessary use in public devotion. But there is a very real sense in which poetry may, and ought to be 'religious': it should, and most of the best poetry in the world does, represent the fruits of religion in beautifully ordered life, and nature as seen by the eye which is interiorly illuminated by spirit.

'By grace divine,
Not otherwise, O Nature, are we thine,'

sings the special poet of nature, Wordsworth; but there are few serious poets who have been more careful than Wordsworth has been, when he has been most himself, to keep 'religion' at arm's length. The greatest religious poets have, in all ages, expressed themselves in purposely obscured and often playful myths and parables, of which the merely external sense has sufficient beauty to charm and satisfy the common reader, and to lure him away from their true significance, which is for other ears." (Champneys II, pp. 100–101.)

2. Spoken by *the foe,* this line is, of course, ironical.

4. The King James Version of Isaias XXXIII, 19, is: "Thou shalt not see a fierce people, a people of a deeper speech than thou canst perceive; of a stammering tongue, that thou canst not understand." In his essay, 'A People of a Stammering Tongue,' Patmore develops the theme of this ode at length.

5–11. Nature-poets were many in Patmore's time—Wordsworth, Shelley, Keats, Coleridge, *etc.*

8. *Seers:* in Nine Odes, "seers."

6–11. Speaking of the rhythmical excellence of the odes, Champneys, in his introduction to the complete edition of Patmore's *Poems* (p. xliii) calls attention to "the felicitous adaptation of sound to sense in such passages as this, in which the calm and pensive cadence of the last contrasting with the rapidity of the preceding line accurately represents the softening influence of the appeal to Love."

14. "The highest and deepest thoughts do not 'voluntary move harmonious numbers,' but run rather to grotesque epigram and doggerel." (*Aurea Dicta* CXLVII.)

12. *Views of the unveil'd heavens:* The vision seen in the mystical experience of such saints as Teresa and John of the Cross, and of such poets as Dante.

13. These *Prophets cannot sing,* not because they have had no vision, but because their vision is inexpressible. As St. John of the Cross says: "The aspiration of the Holy Spirit in the soul, whereby God transforms her into Himself, is so sublime and delicate and profound a delight to her that it cannot be described by mortal tongue, nor can human understanding, as such, attain to any conception of it." (*The Spiritual Canticle,* Stanza XXXIX, §3.)

15. *David* in the Psalms is primarily imparting divinely inspired truths. Incidentally he is poetic. *Dante* in the *Divine Comedy* is primarily a poet. Incidentally he gives us a glimpse of the vision of those who are divinely inspired.

28–32. Apropos of these lines we find this sentence in the writings of Francis Thompson: "I felt my instrument yet too imperfect to profane by it the highest ranges of mysticism." And Everard

Meynell comments upon Thompson's remark: "In 'The Mistress of Vision,' 'Dread of Height,' and particularly in 'The Orient Ode,' something is withheld." (*Life of Francis Thompson,* 1st. ed. p. 222.)

THE CHILD'S PURCHASE

Publication: First included in the sequence of the *Unknown Eros,* in *Odes* I–XLVI, 1878.

Theme: It is a hymn of praise of the Blessed Mother in whom are reconciled in their perfection conjugal love, maternity, virginity, and love of God. In her it was literally accomplished that "the Word was made flesh," and, "the Highest found His ultimate and crowning felicity in a marriage of the flesh as well as the Spirit." (*Knowledge and Science* VIII.) And in attaining this dignity as Mother of God, Mary remained a Virgin! Elsewhere, as in "The Contract" and "Deliciae Sapientiae," Patmore presents this theme by inference and in parable. Here we have the explicit statement and the reality: "The birth of Our Lord was the natural result of the virgin marriage in its perfection." (Page, p. 133.) Moreover, Our Blessed Mother immaculately conceived is the perfect Spouse of God. Hence, this ode is the glorious climax of the poet's song, the conclusion and crown of it all. As he meditated upon it in prospect, he wrote: "Perfect humanity, verging upon, but never entering the breathless region of Divinity, is the real subject of *all* true love-poetry; but in all love-poetry hitherto an 'ideal' and not a reality has been the subject, more or less. Here there can be no exaggeration, and yet all is quite simple, without strain." (Champneys I, p. 255.)

Originally, this ode was intended as introductory to a sequence to be called *The Marriage of the Blessed Mother*. This, like all of Patmore's similar plans was never carried out. But fortunately the ode is complete in itself. Speaking of it in a letter, Patmore remarks: "Though taking the form of a Prologue or Invocation for modesty's sake, it will be self-contained and not really require anything further." (Champneys I, p. 255.) A detailed description of the proposed sequence, later abandoned, is given by Mr. Page, pp. 129–46.

Inspiration: It flowed immediately from Patmore's general ideas (cf. *supra, Theme*), and from his deep personal devotion to Our Lady. The perfecting of this devotion, as Patmore himself tells it in his Autobiography, is one of the most interesting incidents in his life: "Before and ever since my reception into this Church my feelings had been, as it seemed to me, hopelessly out of harmony with the feelings and practice of the best Catholics with regard to the Blessed Virgin. I was in the habit, indeed, of addressing her in prayer, and believed that I had often found such prayers to be successful beyond others; but I could not abide the Rosary, and was chilled and revolted at what seemed to me the excess of many forms of devotion to her. Good I hoped might come of some practical contradiction of this repugnance, some confession in act and will of what my feelings thus refused to accept. I therefore resolved to do the very last thing in the world which my natural inclination would have suggested. I resolved to make an external profession of my acceptance of the Church's mind by a pilgrimage to Lourdes. This I undertook without any sensible devotion, and merely in the temper of a business man who does not leave any stone unturned when a great issue is at stake, though the prospect of attaining thereby what he seeks may seem exceedingly small. Accordingly, on the 14th of October, 1877, I knelt at the shrine by the River Gave, and rose without any emotion or enthusiasm or unusual sense of devotion, but with a tranquil sense that the prayers of thirty-five years had been granted. I paid two visits of thanksgiving to Lourdes in the two succeeding Octobers, for the gift which was then received, and which has never since been for a single hour withdrawn." (Champneys II, p. 56.) Speaking of the importance and significance of this passage, Edmund Gosse remarks: "It offers us the key of his life, his attitude, his entire contribution to literature; it offers us the key but it leaves to us the task of turning it in the lock. He does not mention here what was a part of his plan, that he hoped to get fresh inspiration for his Odes from the atmosphere of Lourdes." (*Coventry Patmore,* p. 144.)

Time of Composition: Late in 1877 at Old Mansion House, Hastings, near his daughter Emily, Sister Mary Christina who was then teaching at St. Leonard's-on-Sea. Patmore had meditated upon the theme for years and spent several laborious months of immediate preparation in the study of theology, especially of the *Summa* of St. Thomas. (Cf. Champneys I, pp. 249–262.)

Technique: Patmore's peculiar technique approaches perfection in this ode.

1–35. The poem opens with a parable. A child given a coin by its mother to spend upon a childish trifle, grows weary looking for something to buy and so returns the coin to its mother in exchange for a kiss. In like manner the poet to whom Mary has given the gift of poetry tires of spending it on themes of human love, and now returns that gift to her, asking only her love in return.

These lines sound like an adaptation of St. Ignatius' prayer, the *Suscipe:* "Take, O Lord, and receive all my liberty; my memory, my understanding, and my whole will. Thou hast given me all that I have and all that I possess; I restore it all to Thee and surrender it, that Thou mayest dispose of it according to Thy will. Give me only Thy love and Thy grace, and I am rich enough and desire nothing more."

14–19. There is an analogy between the poet's state of soul as described in these lines and the state of soul consequent upon the *touch of God* as described by St. John of the Cross: "The delicacy of the delight which is felt in this touch is impossible of description; nor would I willingly speak thereof, lest it should be supposed that it is no more than that which I say; for there are no words to expound and enumerate such sublime things of God as come to pass in these souls; whereof the proper way to speak is for one that knows them to understand them inwardly and feel them and enjoy them and be silent concerning them." (*Living Flame of Love,* Stanza II, §22.)

20. *God's Mother:* St. Thomas' explanation of how Mary may be said to be Mother of God is this: "In man on the part of his parents there is a twofold relation, the one of paternity, the other of motherhood, which are specifically diverse, inasmuch as the father is the principle of generation in one way, and the mother in another (whereas if many be the principle of one action and in the same way —for instance, if many together draw a ship along—there would be one and the same relation in all of them); but on the part of the child there is but one filiation in reality, though there be two in aspect, corresponding to the two relations in the parents, as considered by the intellect. And thus in one way there is only one real filiation in Christ, which is in respect of the Eternal Father: yet there is another temporal relation in regard to His temporal mother." (*Summa* III, q. 35, art. 5.) Again: "The Blessed Virgin is said to have merited to bear the Lord of all; not that she merited His Incarnation, but because by the grace bestowed upon her she merited that grade of purity and holiness which fitted her to be the Mother of God." (*Ibid.* q. 2, art. 11.)

My Mother: The title of Mother of all the Faithful was bestowed upon Mary as early as the time of Origen according to whom Christ lives in the faithful and thus Mary, Mother of Christ, is also Mother of the Faithful in whom Christ lives. (Cf. *Praef. in Jo.* 6, P. G. XIV, 32.)

"The doctrine of Mary's spiritual motherhood of men is contained in the fact that she is the antitype of Eve: Eve is our natural mother because she is the origin of our natural life; so Mary is our spiritual mother because she is the origin of our spiritual life." (*Catholic Encyclopedia.*)

In the Encyclical of Pius X written on the Jubilee of the Immaculate Conception, Feb. 2, 1904, we read: "Is not Mary the Mother of Christ? Then she is our Mother also. And we must in truth hold that Christ, the Word made Flesh, is also the Savior of mankind. He had a physical body like that of any other man: and again, as Savior of the human family, he had a spiritual and mystical body, the society, namely, of those who believe in Christ. 'We being many, are one body in Christ.' (Romans XII, 5.) Now the Blessed Virgin did not conceive the Eternal Son of God merely in order that He might be made man taking His human nature from her, but also in order that by means of the nature assumed from her He might be the Redeemer of men. For which reason the Angel said to the Shepherds: 'This day is born to you a Savior Who is Christ the Lord.' (St. Luke II, 11.) Wherefore in the same holy bosom of His most chaste Mother Christ took to Himself flesh, and united to Himself the spiritual body formed by those who were to believe in Him. Hence Mary, carrying the Savior within her, may be said also to have carried all those whose life was contained in the life of the Savior. Therefore all who are united to Christ and, as the Apostle says, are members of His body, of His flesh, and of His bones (Ephesians V, 30), have issued from the womb of Mary like a body united to its head. Hence, though in a spiritual and mystical fashion, we are all children of Mary and she is Mother of us all. Mother, spiritual indeed, but truly Mother of the members of Christ who are we." (S. Aug. L. de S. Virginitate, c. 6.)

24–35. This acknowledgment of Mary's inspiration in the past and the prayer for her continued inspiration in the future reminds us of Thompson's lines:

"Last and first, O Queen Mary,
Of thy white Immaculacy,
If my work may profit aught,
Fill with lilies every thought!
I surmise
What is white will then be wise."

("Motto and Invocation," ll. 14–19.)

(Cf. *infra,* ll. 155–57.)

31. *Sirius,* the brightest and whitest star in the heavens—the dog-star.

32–35. *thou only Fair:* In St. Bernard's Sermon on the Feast of the Nativity of the Blessed Virgin we read: "Let us see with what sentiments of tender devotion the Lord would have us honor Mary in whom He has placed the plenitude of all good; so that if there is anything of hope in us, if anything of grace, if anything of salvation, we may feel assured it has overflowed unto us from her who 'went up from the desert flowing with delights.'" (*Canticle of Canticles* VIII, 5.) (Cf. *infra,* l. 106.)

36–37. "The Word was made flesh and dwelt among us." (St. John I, 14.) This was the final consequence of Mary's answer to the angelic salutation: "Behold the handmaid of the Lord; be it done to me according to thy word." (St. Luke I, 38.)

In St. Bernard's Fourth Sermon on the Glories of Mary he thus addresses Our Lady: "Make haste, therefore, to answer the Angel, or rather to answer the Lord through the Angel. Say the word and receive the Word. Utter your human word and conceive the Divine Word. Pronounce the transitory word and embrace the Word everlasting."

39–40. The Magnificat (St. Luke I, 46–55) contains the first recorded words of Mary spoken after the Body of Christ had been conceived within her through the power of the Holy Ghost. (*Ibid.* 35.)

41–46. The *wonders* of grace that transpired in the solitude of Mary's soul during these months of silence are here suggested by Patmore, but wisely, he does not attempt to describe them. The *voiceless blue* is a perfect symbol of Mary's silence both before and after the *Magnificat,* as St. Bernard describes it: "How often Mary heard her Son not only speaking to the multitude in parables, but revealing to His disciples apart the mysteries of the Kingdom of God! She saw Him working miracles. She saw Him hanging on the cross. She saw Him breathing His last. She saw Him rising from the tomb. She saw Him ascending to Heaven. But how often in the midst of all these events do we find it mentioned that the voice of this most modest Virgin, of this most chaste Dove was heard?" (Sermon for the Sunday within the Octave of the Assumption, §11.)

42. Chief among the *wonders* heard by Moses on Mount Sinai were the ten commandments. (Cf. Exodus XX.)

43. The *wonders* imparted to St. John in the Apocalypse *when the seven thunders had uttered their voices,* like the wonders revealed to Mary, have not been transmitted to us. "As I was about to write," the Evangelist tells us, "I heard a voice from heaven saying to me: Seal up the things which the seven thunders have spoken and write them not." (Apocalypse X, 4.)

54. When the Second Person of the Blessed Trinity became Man, He *doff'd* His *rays* of divinity in the sense that His divinity was concealed beneath human nature. But, as St. Thomas says: "To be man

is newly predicated of God without any change in Him, by a change in the human nature which is assumed to a Divine Person. And hence, when it is said, *God was made man,* we understand no change on the part of God, but only on the part of the human nature." (*Summa* III, q. 16, art. 6.)

58–59. In Patmore's prose we find this very complete commentary on these lines: " 'Merit,' as the word is used in Scripture and by the Church, means rather *capacity* than *right.* Faith 'merits' because, without faith, there can be obviously no capacity. Christ took upon Himself the flesh and human nature of the Blessed Virgin, 'through whom we have *deserved*' (or been made able) 'to receive the Author of Life.' Emptiness of self is the supreme merit of the Soul, because it is the first condition of her *capacity* for God. 'My soul shall make her boast in the Lord: the humble shall hear thereof and be glad.' The Soul's boast and merit, as it were, her vanity, is the God-seducing charm of her conscious nothingness. She becomes through her

Mere emptiness of self, the female twin
Of Fullness, sucking all God's glory in.

The secret of obtaining and maintaining this humility, which is capacity, is not to deny the graces you have received, but to consider and be thankful for them all. If a sudden splendor shines about you in the night, and you see your Soul 'in the light of God's countenance,' as beautiful as a Goddess, never forget it, but remember that you are verily that Goddess for Him so long as you acknowledge yourself to be of yourself nothing but dust and ashes and a house of devils." (*Magna Moralia* IV.) (Cf. "De Natura Deorum," ll. 74–75; 137: "Psyche's Discontent," ll. 7–8, *etc.*)

Our Lady's words upon which these lines and the above commentary are founded, are: "And my spirit hath rejoiced in God my Savior. Because He hath regarded the humility of His handmaid; for behold from henceforth all generations shall call me blessed. Because He that is mighty hath done great things to me." (St. Luke I, 47–49.)

64. The paradox of this line finds its ultimate explanation in the last line of the opening stanza in the great hymn of Passion-tide, *Vexilla Regis:*

"Christ's royal banner flashes forth
The fulgent Cross' mystery:
Death crushes Life: yea, Life is slain
Yet death yields Life the victory."

65–73. " 'The Virgin's womb.' The narrowness of that dwelling, the darkness, the mode of nourishment: He could not hear, nor see, nor taste, nor move; He lay at all times fixed and bound:

And by that rapture of captivity
He made us free,
His blissful prisoners likewise to be."
(*Aphorisms and Extracts.*)

These lines may have been suggested by St. Bernard's prayer to Our Lady in the *Paradiso* Canto XXXIII, 1–7:

"Virgin and Mother, child of thine own Son,
More lowly and more high than all beside,
Of the eternal counsel chosen one,
So hast thou human nature magnified
That He who fashioned it did not disdain
Within His own creation to abide.
Within thy womb love's fire awoke again,
By whose effulgence, in the peace eterne,
This flower to its perfection did attain."
(Eleanor Vinton Murray, Translator.)

76–77. In *Vitis Mystica,* attributed to St. Bernard, Our Lady says of herself: "Mine is the lily of chastity because I first vowed to the Lord the preservation of virginity." (§ 56.)

78. By the grace of her divine Maternity, Mary was raised to a dignity above the Angels. (Cf. St. Bernard, Super *Missus Est,* Homilia I, § 5.)

79–81. White light containing the three primary colors is a particularly appropriate symbol of the Trinity. It is broken up, as it were, and made visible in Mary in whom we see reflected the power of the Father, the wisdom of the Son and the goodness of the Holy Ghost. (Cf. *Summa* I, q. xxxix, art. 7–8, and "Beata," *passim.*) In his essay, "The Bow Set in the Cloud," Patmore writes: "The individual Man, the *homo,* is the Image of God in so far as he is a substantial reflection of the Love, the Truth, and the Life, which last is the 'embrace' of Truth and Love, as the Holy Spirit is said by the Church to be the 'embrace' of the First Person and the Second."

79. *Prism:* "The spiritual body into which the bodies of those who love and obey God perfectly are from time to time transfigured, is a prism. The invisible ray of the Holy Spirit, entering its candid substance, becomes divided, and is reflected in a triple and most distinct glory from its own surfaces; and we behold Jesus, the Incarnate Second Person, and Moses (the Father) and Elias (the

Holy Ghost) talking with Him . . . This is the 'bow in the cloud' of man's flesh; the pledge that he shall no more be overwhelmed by the deluge of the senses, which are killed forever by this vision, as the flame of a tallow candle is killed by the electric light." (*Homo* XX.) (Cf. "Beata.")

82–83. The explanation of these lines is to be found in one of Patmore's favorite themes—human perfection is not to be found in its entirety in either sex (*vir* or *mulier*) but in the union of both (*homo*). (Cf. "Wedding Sermon," ll. 386–93.) This union, in effect, he attributes to Mary, conceived without sin. She, the fulfilment of all ancient types sacred and profane, is preeminently, "the *Bow set in the Cloud* of the renewed nature, for a promise that it shall never again be overwhelmed and destroyed by the deluge of the disordered senses." ("The Bow Set in the Cloud.")

86–87. "He who does the will of God is Christ's 'Mother, Sister, Brother,' and all other relations, Son, Daughter, Bride, and Bridegroom; for 'Christ,' says St. Augustine, 'is also the Bride, for He is the Body.' He could not be the 'satisfaction of all our desires,' as He has promised to be, were it otherwise." (*Magna Moralia* XXXV.)

90. *thy joyful Saint:* Saint Joseph.

93–97. Cf. "The Contract," *passim.*

104–115. These lines are redolent of the continuation of St. Bernard's prayer to Our Lady in the *Paradiso* to which allusion has already been made (*supra,* ll. 65–73):

"Lady, thou art so great, thy worth so high,
Who'er, grace seeking, has to thee not prayed,
Finds that his longing has no wings to fly.
And not alone thy goodness comes to aid
The one who prays, but often he will see
Thy bounty's there, before the prayer is made.
In thee is mercy, pity is in thee,
In thee munificence, in thee is won
All that of virtue in a soul can be."

(Eleanor Vinton Murray, Translator.)

104–108. "The Blessed Virgin, 'the holiest and humblest of creatures,' crowned with the glory and honor of bearing God in her womb, is the one woman in whom womanhood has been perfected, and in whom the whole of womanhood has been more or less reconstituted and glorified." ("Dieu et ma Dame.") Wordsworth's way of saying this was: "Our tainted nature's solitary boast." (Cf. *infra,* ll. 146–47, *etc.*)

108. Next to Our Savior, Mary was *Chief Stone of stumbling* to the Jews and Gentiles of whom St. Paul spoke and to those who have inherited their spiritual legacy. "We preach Christ crucified, unto the Jews indeed a stumbling block and unto the Gentiles foolishness." (1 Corinthians I, 23.)

108–116. The following passage illustrates the extremes to which critics may go when they do not share Patmore's views: "We despair of representing in words the impression which this sad medley of blessing and cursing has made upon us. We have said that we know no parallel to it. We beg pardon; the parallel is to be found in the last lines of Browning's 'Soliloquy of the Spanish Cloister':

'St, there's vespers! *Plena gratia*
Ave, Virgo! Gr-r-r, you swine!"
(Rev. D. C. Tovey, *Reviews and Essays,* p. 166.)

110. The hem of Christ's garment which the woman in the Gospel touched and was healed (St. Matthew IX, 20–22) is here made a symbol of Mary who bestows spiritual health upon *all* who ask her intercession. (Cf. *infra,* ll. 152–53.)

112–13. In his essay, "Distinction," Patmore quotes these lines to illustrate his affirmation of the doctrine of the Intercession of the Saints, according to which, "sinners, through them, approach Divinity."

The reasonableness of this doctrine when applied to Our Lady is thus explained by St. Bernard: "You were afraid, O man, to approach the Father; you were terrified at the sound of His voice and sought to conceal yourself (Genesis III, 8). Therefore He gave you Jesus as your Mediator. What shall not such a Son be able to obtain for you from such a Father? Doubtless He shall be 'heard for His reverence' (Hebrews V, 7): for 'the Father loveth the Son' (St. John III, 35). Surely you are not afraid of approaching Him also! 'He is thy Brother and thy flesh' (Genesis XXXVII, 27), 'tempted in all things like as thou art, but without sin' (Hebrews IV, 15), 'that He might become merciful' (*ibid.* II, 17). It is He that Mary has given you for your Brother. But perhaps you stand in awe of the Divine Majesty of Jesus. For although He has become man He has not ceased to be God. Perhaps you desire to have an advocate even with Him. If so, have recourse to Mary. In Mary human nature is found entirely pure, not alone pure from all defilement, but pure also from composition with another nature. Nor do I deem it doubtful that she likewise shall be heard for her reverence. Assuredly the Son will listen to the Mother and the Father will listen to the Son. My little children, behold the sinner's ladder. Behold the chief source of my confidence, the principal ground of my hope. What? Can the Son refuse anything to His own Mother or be refused anything by His Father? Can the Son deny a hearing to her or be denied a hearing by Him? Both suppositions are plainly impossible." (Sermon for the Feast of the Nativity of the Blessed Virgin Mary.) (Cf. *infra,* ll. 150–53.)

113–15. This is rather a bitter fling at those who spurn Mary's intercession and pray God directly. Pius X in his Encyclical on the Jubilee of the Immaculate Conception wrote: "Hapless are they who neglect Mary under pretext of the honor to be paid to Jesus Christ! As if the Child could be found elsewhere than with the Mother!"

120. *Suppliant Omnipotence:* As a creature, Mary was like every creature, a suppliant of God, her Creator. As Mother of Christ and Mediatrix of all Graces, she is, in a sense, omnipotent. (Cf. *supra* l. 20; *infra* ll. 152–53, *etc.*)

121. This is generally considered the finest apostrophe in the poem. Certainly it is one of the most Patmorean. It recalls "Legem Tuam Dilexi," and "The Body."

In a letter written about the same time as these lines, Patmore says: "We are quite of one mind in hating everything 'abstract'—abstract virtue, abstract truth, and all other abstractions which are the delight of philosophers, and, I believe, of devils." (Champneys I, p. 253.)

122–23. In Egypt, land of idolatry, the lives of the Israelites were made bitter "with hard works in clay and brick." (Exodus I, 14.)

124–29. These lines, an adaptation of the coming of the Magi, make the star that led them a symbol of Mary, the Star that leads the Magi of all time to the birthplace of God-made-Man.

131. The Prophet Aggeus alluding to the coming of the Savior, declared: "I will move all nations: AND THE DESIRED OF ALL NATIONS SHALL COME: and I will fill this house with glory: saith the Lord of hosts." (II, 8.)

132. An adaptation of Exodus III, 2: "And the Lord appeared to him (Moses) in a flame of fire out of the midst of a bush."

133–36. There is a reverent parity here drawn between the motive which, as it were, moved God to unite Himself with Mary, and the motive which impelled Him to create Eve. "And the Lord said: It is not good for man to be alone: let us make him a help like unto himself." (Genesis II, 18.)

138–39. "The Incarnation was an act done in eternity as well as time; the Lamb, the 'I am before Abraham was,' was 'slain from the beginning'; and, if we look from the point of view of eternity, we may see that effects of that act, apparently retrospective, were not really so; but that the Bread and Wine, without which 'there is no life in us,' may have been received from the hand of an invisible Melchisedech by many who, in time, have longed to see the Day of the Lord, and have done their best, by heroic purity and self-humiliation, to merit the Vision, and have thus attained to that love which, as St. Augustine says, 'supersedes all the sacraments.'" ("The Bow in the Cloud.")

139–40. Cf. "De Natura Deorum," ll. 123–24; "Child's Purchase," l. 106; "Legem Tuam Dilexi," ll. 31–36, *etc.*

143–45. This thought is the theme of the Church's hymn, *Stabat Mater,* read as the Sequence of the Mass on the Friday after Passion Sunday. Thompson made it the theme of his first published poem, "The Passion of Mary."

Pius X in his Encyclical on the Jubilee of the Immaculate Conception, February 1904, expressed it thus: "When the supreme hour of the Son came, beside the Cross of Jesus there stood Mary His Mother not merely occupied in contemplating the cruel spectacle, but rejoicing that her Only Son was offered for the salvation of mankind, and so entirely participating in His Passion, that if it had been possible she would have gladly borne all the torments that her son bore. And from this community of will and suffering between Christ and Mary she merited to become most worthily the Reparatrix of the lost world and Dispensatrix of all the gifts that Our Savior purchased for us by His Death and by His Blood."

146–47. Mary's reparation of the evil done by Eve is thus beautifully expressed by St. Bernard: "Eve was the thorn. Mary was resplendent as the rose. Eve, the thorn, by inflicting a wound; Mary, the rose, by healing it. Eve, the thorn, imparting death to all; Mary, the rose, restoring health to all. From the thorn is extracted a liquid from which is made the purple ink in which is written: 'From your carnal mind arises the flow of concupiscence which transmits actual sin to Eve herself and to Adam, and original sin to posterity.' Apropos of this the Apostle declares: *The letter killeth, but the spirit quickeneth* (2 Corinthians III, 6). As if he would say: *For by a man came death and by a man the resurrection of the dead. And as in Adam all die, so also in Christ all shall be made alive.*" (1 Corinthians XV, 21–22.) ("Sermo de Beata Maria," Mabillon text, Vol. II, Part I, 1369.)

The clear dogma of the Church on this and similar questions will be found in the Apostolic Letter of Pius IX Concerning the Dogmatic Definition of the Immaculate Conception, 1854. Here is the opening paragraph: "When the ineffable God had foreseen from all eternity that the lamentable ruin of the entire human race was to follow from Adam's trangression, and when in a mystery hidden from the ages (God) had decreed by a more hidden mystery the completion of the first work of His goodness through the Incarnation of the Word, in order that man who contrary to His merciful design, had been led into sin by the crafty deceit of diabolical wickedness, should not perish, and that what would fall in the first Adam should more happily be raised up in the second [Adam], He chose and decreed for His Only-begotten Son from the beginning of time and before all the ages, a mother from whom made flesh, He should be born in the happy fulness of time; and He [God] honored her before all creatures and showed her so great a love in preference to all creatures that in her alone He found the greatest delight with the most perfect complacency. Therefore far above all angelic spirits and saints He so wonderfully filled her with an abundance of all heavenly gifts taken from the treasure of His Divinity, that she might always be *entirely free* from every stain of sin and wholly beautiful and perfect, and should show forth that fulness of innocence and holiness, than which under God, no greater can be conceived, and which besides God no one can reach even in thought."

Read the hymn *Ave Maris Stella* by Venantius Fortunatus, sung at Vespers in the Little Office of Our Lady.

148–49. This is a beautiful suggestion of the chief facts commemorated on the feast of The Assumption of the Blessed Virgin—her departure from this life and the assumption of her body into heaven. (Cf. "To The Body," l. 46, and *Assumpta Maria,* by Thompson.)

150–53. The inspiration of these lines is found in the title which the Church has conferred upon Mary—Mediatrix of all Graces—a title honored by Benedict XV with a special Mass and Office for May 31st. One of the clearest expressions of the doctrine of the Church on this subject, is the following passage from the Encyclical of Pius X commemorating the Jubilee of the Immaculate Conception, February 2, 1904: "It cannot, of course, be denied that the dispensation of these treasures [of grace] is the particular and peculiar right of Jesus Christ, for they are the exclusive fruit of His death, who by His nature is the Mediator between God and man. Nevertheless, by this companionship in sorrow and suffering already mentioned between the Mother and the Son [cf. *supra,* notes on ll. 143–45], it has been allowed to the august Virgin to be the most powerful mediatrix and advocate of the whole world with her Divine Son."

"We are, then, it will be seen, very far from attributing to the Mother of God a productive power of grace—a power which belongs to God alone. Yet, since Mary surpasses all in holiness and union with Jesus Christ, and has been associated by Jesus Christ in the work of redemption, she merits for us *de congruo,* in the language of theologians, what Jesus Christ merits for us *de condigno,* and she is the supreme Minister of the distribution of graces. Jesus 'sitteth on the right hand of the majesty on high' (Hebrews I, 3). Mary sitteth at the right hand of her son—a refuge so secure and a help so trusty against all dangers that we have nothing to fear or to despair of under her guidance, her patronage, her protection." (Pius IX in Bull *Ineffabilis.*) (Cf. *supra,* ll. 112–13.)

155–62. Mr. Osmond in *The Mystical Poets of the English Church* (p. 339) speaks of these as the most significant lines in the ode, "lines in which the poet gives us what is both a bird's-eye-view of his own mystical trend and a partial indication of his earlier Anglican verse."

155–56. The sentiment of these lines and of many other lines in this ode bears a close resemblance to St. Bernard's Hymn to Our Lady in the *Paradiso,* Canto XXXIII:

1 Virgin and Mother, child of thine own Son,
More lowly and more high than all beside,
Of the eternal counsel chosen one,
4 So hast thou human nature magnified
That He who fashioned it did not disdain
Within His own creation to abide.
7 Within thy womb love's fire awoke again,
By whose effulgence, in the peace eterne,
This flower to its perfection did attain.
10 To us above, thy noontide ardors burn,
Of charity, while earth bound, ere men die,
A living spring of hope, to thee they turn.
13 Lady, thou art so great, thy worth so high
Whoe'er, grace seeking, has to thee not prayed,
Finds that his longing has no wings to fly.
16 And not alone thy goodness comes to aid
The one who prays, but often he will see
Thy bounty's there, before the prayer is made.
19 In thee is mercy, pity is in thee,
In thee munificence, in thee is won
All that of virtue in a soul can be.
22 Now, this man, who his course hereto has run,
From where the deeps of evil do extend,
And seen the lives of spirits, one by one,
25 Implores thee, of thy grace, such strength to send
That, through his eyes, uplifted he may be
More near to Him who is salvation's end.

28 And I, who for myself more ardently
Ne'er sought the vision, than for him, my best
Of prayers—may they not lack—I proffer thee,
31 That thou wilt rid him of each cloudy rest
Of his mortality, thy praying gain
For him the sum of joy made manifest.
34 Yet more I pray thee, Queen, who canst obtain
Whate'er thou willest, see that he withstands
After such vision, his affection's wane,
37 Protect him from the fret of human bands.

(Eleanor Vinton Murray, translator.)

Students of Chaucer will recall his translation of this prayer in the *Prologe of the Second Nonnes Tale.*

155–56. These lines are almost a literal translation of the same thought as expressed in Dante's lines quoted above.

157–60. In expression as well as in sentiment these lines remind us of Thompson's quoted *supra,* ll. 24–35.

161–62. It was literally true of Patmore that in the *Angel in the House* and in *Victories of Love* when he sang the beauty of the love of mortal woman, and the *graces* of Honoria and Jane, he was really singing the beauty of a love found in its perfection in Mary alone. (Cf. "Sponsa Dei," ll. 30–34.)

In one of Patmore's notes on his proposed poem, 'The Marriage of the Blessed Virgin,' we read: "Mary. She alone is what all lovers mean when they love; and thus the likeness of all Christian women to her love is no longer extravagant.

"All who approach womanhood in holy awe and belief in her perfection and with the mystic passion of refusal which is the first motion of love, believe in, love, and worship thee.

"Every noble Lover, though he may never have heard of Her, sees and loves Her and no one else, when he first beholds with awe and honor, with a passion of refusal, her whom he calls Emily or Laura." (*Patmore, A Study in Poetry,* Page, p. 142.)

Again: "Every pure soul is pure woman to God . . . Hence the ready honor and love of all mankind for the Blessed Virgin who alone represents the true attitude of the human soul." (*Ibid.* p. 144.)

An example of his early *Song of Lady's graces* is this passage from the *Angel in the House,* Bk. I, Canto ii, Prelude 1, ll. 33–40:

"Nay, might I utter my conceit,
'Twere after all a vulgar song,
For she's so simply, subtly sweet,
My deepest rapture does her wrong.

Yet is it now my chosen task
  To sing her worth as Maid and Wife;
Nor happier post than this I ask,
  To live her laureate all my life."

168–69. There is no better commentary on these lines than the following excerpts from Patmore's *Aphorisms and Extracts:* "O Holy Mother, who wast not afraid to undertake to utter the Word, but simply answered to Gabriel's invitation, 'Behold the Handmaid of the Lord'; so I, invited by God to speak such a word as has not been uttered since thou inspiredst the Florentine, will not refuse the vocation of Him Who has in this regarded the humility of my soul, His handmaid, who trusts to Him the whole execution of that which He has put upon her."

And this: "Dear Lord, for forty years I tried to raise in the wilderness a house for Thy abode. I painfully gathered bricks, and worked a cornice here, and there a capital; but as I put it together all would suddenly fall, and still I gathered up material, though the more I gathered the greater seemed the chaos; but one day, why none could tell, except perhaps that I felt more despair than ever I had done before, I heard a winnowing of unseen wings, and lo, the bricks and stones all took their place,

And a gay palace fine
Beyond my deepest dreamt design.
May He who built it all
Take care it does not fall."

(Champneys II, p. 71.)

DEAD LANGUAGE

Publication: One of the original Nine Odes, 1868.

Theme: It is the soul-cry of a rejected prophet who realizes that his message has fallen on deaf ears. In his introduction to the Nine Odes Patmore attributes his abandonment of poetry to the feelings here expressed. "I meant to have extended and developed this series of Odes," he wrote, "until they formed an integral work, expressing an idea which I have long had at heart; but feelings which are partly conveyed by the concluding Piece have discouraged me from fulfilling my intention."

This, the darkest period in Patmore's life, endured until he went to live at Hastings. There he was happy once more and poetic inspiration returned so completely that in 1877 he wrote: "I have written as much in the last three weeks as the whole of the Nine Odes." And before the end of this year the completed sequence of the *Unknown Eros* made its appearance. Subsequently the sympathetic criticism of those whose judgment Patmore respected, greatly increased the joy of his life and work.

Then followed another period of dejection marked by the destruction of his greatest prose work, *Sponsa Dei,* and the loss of the friendship of Mrs. Meynell. It was terminated only with death. But his last words to his wife, quoted at the conclusion of the Biographical Notes, show how completely his reconcilement of divine and human love pervaded his life as well as his art, to the very end. All this, reflected in Sargent's famous portrait, finds verbal expression in the following excerpt from Thompson's poem inspired by Sargent's work—a poem from which other lines are quoted apropos of the frontispiece of this volume.

"Love, worship if ye can
The very man.
Ye may not. He has trod the ways afar,
The fatal ways of parting and farewell,
Where all the paths of painèd greatness are;
. . . .
You the stern pities of the gods debar
To drink where he has drunk—
The moonless mere of sighs,
And pace the places infamous to tell
Where God wipes not the tears from any eyes,
Where-through the ways of dreadful greatness are."
("A Captain of Song.")

2–8. The full significance of these lines in which dogmatic truth and poetic truth are contrasted, is best learned from the following excerpt from Patmore's prose: "The Poet is, *par excellence,* the *perceiver,* nothing having any interest for him unless he can, as it were, see and touch it with the spiritual senses with which he is preeminently endowed. The Saints, indeed, seem for the most part to have had these senses greatly developed by their holiness and their habitual suppression of the corporeal senses. But, as a rule, they do not speak, perhaps from the fear of being too implicitly believed; or, if they do, they are careful

To make Truth look as near a lie
As can comport with her divinity,

in order to adapt it to the public capacity. But the Poet has this advantage, that none save the few whose ears are opened to the teaching which would be ridiculed or profaned to their own destruction by the many, will think that he is in earnest or that his flights into regions of perception, in which they can perceive nothing, are other than flights of fancy. He occupies a quite peculiar position—somewhere between that of a Saint and that of Balaam's ass." ("Religio Poetae.")

And again: "I once asked a famous theologian why he did not preach the love and knowledge of God from his pulpit as he had been discoursing of them for a couple of hours with me, instead of setting forth

Doctrine hard
In which Truth shows herself as near a lie
As can comport with her divinity.

He answered that, if he were to do so, his whole congregation would be living in mortal sin before the end of the week. It is true. The work of the Church in the world is, not to teach the mysteries of life, so much as to persuade the soul to that arduous degree of purity at which God Himself becomes her teacher." (*Knowledge and Science* XXII.) (Cf. "Tristitia," ll. 60–63.)

Patmore himself spoke with *double voice of Truth.* In the Political Odes he smites *the brutish ear with doctrine hard,* but in the Psyche Odes his words are

tender-soft as seem
The embraces of a dead Love in a dream.

3. Not all scorn is pride, as Patmore shows in the following passage from his essay, "Distinction": "There can be no 'distinction,' in life, art, or manners, worth speaking of, which is not the outcome of singular courage, integrity, and generosity, and, I need scarcely add, of intellectual vigor, which is usually the companion of those qualities habitually exercised. An accomplished distinction, as the sight of it gives the greatest delight to those who have it or are on the way to the attainment of it, so it is the greatest of terrors to the vulgar, whether of the gutter or in gilded chambers. Their asserion of their sordid selves it rebukes with a silence or a look of benevolent wonder, which they can never forgive, and which they always take for indications of intolerable pride, though it is nothing other than the fitting and inevitable demeanour, under the circumstances, of the 'good man in whose eyes,' King David says, 'a vile person is despised'; or that recommended by St. Augustine who tells us that, if a man does not love the living truth of things, you should 'let him be as dirt' to you; or by a still higher Authority who directs you to treat such an one as a 'sinner and a publican,' or, in modern phrase, a 'cad.' "

12. *the Imperial tongue:* Latin, the *dead language* in which the truths of the Church are *decently cloak'd.* In his essay, "The Language of Religion." Patmore writes: "Her whole system of language and rites proves either that the Church, who can speak her mind plainly enough when there is occasion for plainness, wantonly and habitually indulges in the folly of delivering a large part of her message in a language that few can understand, or that there is a body of knowledge which ought not to be and cannot be effectually communicated to all; and that, in her reticence, she is but obeying the command: 'Tell not the vision to any man till Christ be risen' in him."

13–16. In Our Lord's excoriation of the Scribes and Pharisees He prophesied how they and their successors would receive those who would dare to affront their *liberty* with *Heaven's:* "You serpents, generation of vipers, how will you flee from the judgment of hell? Therefore behold I send to you prophets and wise men and scribes; and some of them you will put to death and crucify, and some you will scourge in your synagogues, and persecute from city to city." (St. Matthew XXIII, 33–34.)

16. *Heaven's liberty:* Attained by subjection to God's law—the liberty that is an affront to *acorn-munchers* of truth is the theme of "Legem Tuam Dilexi."

18. This line reflects the complete dejection of Patmore's spirit at this time when he had assumed the attitude of a rejected prophet. (Cf. *supra, Theme.*) Gosse explains the rejection of Patmore's poetry by saying: "All England had its ears open to brilliant melodies such as Mr. Swinburne's; no other music could be heard." And Thompson goes to the root of the matter in the lines quoted apropos of the frontispiece in this volume.

Aristotle's answer to Alexander's complaint that in a certain book the philosopher had published *secrets,* might have been given by Patmore to his *monitor:* "They are published and not published, for none will learn from any book anything but that which he already knows." After citing this reply in his essay, "The Language of Religion," Patmore continues: "And I will add that neither in ancient nor in modern times has there been a poet worthy of that sacred name, who would not have been horrified had he fancied that the full meaning of some of his sayings could be discerned by more than ten in ten thousand of his readers." (Cf. "Eros and Psyche," ll. 206–207.)

1877

Publication: In *Odes* I–XXXI, 1877. In 1878, however, when *Odes* I–XLVI appeared, this ode was omitted and it has not been included in subsequent arrangements.

Theme: It is substantially the same as the theme of the other Political Odes, especially "1880–85." Mr. Shane Leslie suggests: "The *Bald-pate* is presumably the Tory seer, the *dyke* is the limited Franchise, the *garrulous clans* are the voters, and the rest reads like modern history." (*Studies in Subline Failure,* p. 142.)

1. *'Go up thou Bald-pate':* "And he (Eliseus) went up from thence to Bethel: and as he was going up by the way, little boys came out of the city and mocked him, saying: Go up, thou bald head; go up, thou bald head. And looking back, he saw them and cursed them in the name of the Lord: and there came forth two bears out of the forest, and tore of them two and forty boys." (4 Kings II, 23–24.)

8. *The check:* The dyke, symbol of limited Franchise.

L'ALLEGRO

Publication: One of the poems in *Amelia,* first published in 1878.

Composition: Written after his second marriage and after taking up his residence at Heron's Ghyll where he was released from previous worry and labor regarding finances. Champneys says of it: "The *strenua inertia* of his new occupation, and the tranquility of his days, forcibly portrayed in the ode 'L'Allegro,' gave such change and rest as were needed to prepare the mental soil for the new harvest of poetry. Of this a portion was at once reaped, though the whole was not fully gathered till after many succeeding years." (*Poems,* Introduction, p. xxix.)

Theme: Contemplating Autumn the poet sees in it a symbol of *The Spouse of Honour, fair Repose* (l. 24)—that spiritual rest attained, "In the soft arms of happy Certitude." Together with "Saint Valentine's Day," "Wind and Wave," and "Winter," it completes the seasonal sequence. Compared with the other three odes of the sequence, there is in this one less of nature and more of man. (Cf. "Saint Valentine's Day," and "Winter," *Theme.*)

1. *Felicity:* This, the keynote of the poem, suggests Traherne's *Poems of Felicity.* But even a casual reader cannot fail to see how much more austere is Patmore's ideal.

2–3. In these lines is contained one of the paradoxes of Christianity. On one hand Christ bids us in the Sermon on the Mount: "Seek and you shall find: knock, and it shall be opened to you." (St. Matthew VII, 7.) And here the poet stresses the gratuity of grace, as did St. Paul when he wrote: "Therefore He hath mercy on whom He will." (Romans IX, 18.) Clearly the poet's meaning is that *Felicity ope'st to none that knocks,* seeking first his own good and his own will, inverting the order established by Our Savior when, in the Sermon on the Mount He bade us: "Seek ye therefore first the kingdom of God and His justice." (St. Matthew VI, 33.) The arbitrariness of human love is expressed in the *Angel in the House* (Bk. I, Canto viii):

"The moods of love are like the wind,
And none knows whence or why they rise."

4–5. The freedom of God's bonds willingly accepted is the freedom which alone will retain and sustain *Felicity* in our souls. (Cf. "Legem Tuam Dilexi.") In the *Angel in the House,* (Bk. I, Canto x, Predude 1) Patmore says of human lovers:

"They live by law, not like the fool,
But like the bard, who freely sings
In strictest bonds of rhyme and rule,
And finds in them, not bonds, but wings."

8. "Friendship and love differ mainly in this: that, whereas the felicity of friendship consists in a mutual interchange of benefits, intellectual and otherwise, that of love is in giving on one part and receiving on the other, with a reciprocal perception of how sweet it is to the endower to endow and the receiver to receive." ("The Weaker Vessel.")

10–13. During his days at Heron's Ghyll, the solitude of the place fostered Patmore's solitude of soul and increased its joy. (Cf. *infra,* ll. 42–49.)

15–20. The poet followed his own teaching as regards his own first-love and the love that followed. (Cf. "The Wedding Sermon," ll. 442–85.)

24. The soul's *Repose* as Patmore conceives it in this line is far removed from Quietism.

25. Cf. *infra,* ll. 42–49.

25–26. The dependence of the joyousness of love upon truth is one of Patmore's favorite themes. (Cf. "The Wedding Sermon," ll. 155–68.)

28. This line is the best explanation for the inclusion of the Political Odes in the sequence of the *Unknown Eros.* Their subject is *God's remoter service, public zeal.* (Cf. "1867," " 1880–85," "Peace.")

35. Patmore never tires of insisting upon the necessity of *Certitude* in life and in religion. "A very small minority of mankind,

but a minority which includes almost all who have attained the highest peaks of heroic virtue and many who have been no less eminent for power of intellect and practical wisdom, have declared that, to them at least, God is knowable, communicable with, and personally discernible with a certainty which exceeds all other certainties." ("Thoughts on Knowledge, Opinion and Inequality.")

42–49. The poet here describes that spiritual solitude so necessary to judge the world and worldliness as they are judged in the lines that follow. "Solitude of heart may be had without being present in a holy place, or in the sacred sanctuary . . . True solitude consists in withdrawing from all that is on earth, from the world and from men, and drawing nigh to Heaven and God. You cannot of yourself acquire solitude of heart. It is a gift of God." (Marie Lataste, III, p. 24.)

St. Bernard thus expresses the same thought: "A Spirit before your face is Christ the Lord, and He requires solitude of soul, not of body. Yet, to retire sometimes from the company of others, as the opportunity presents itself, is not unprofitable especially in the time of prayer.

"The only solitude that is enjoined you, then, is solitude of mind and spirit. You are alone if you do not think of common things, if you are not affected by things present, if you despise what many admire, if you loathe what all desire, if you avoid strife, if you do not feel temporal losses, if you do not dwell upon past injuries. Otherwise you are not really alone even if there is no one with you. Do you not see that you can be alone in the midst of a multitude, and that you can be in the midst of a multitude when you are alone?" ("Sermons on the *Canticle of Canticles,* Sermon XL, § 5; Translation, pp. 159–60.) (Cf. "Magna est Veritas," ll. 5–6.)

56–72. Champneys suggests that these lines are based upon the following passage in a letter from Patmore to his wife in which he describes a day of activity at Heron's Ghyll: "Yesterday I had my last harvest thrashed out. We thrashed 170 sacks in about twelve hours. I think that when we have got used to the steam-engine we shall not think it unpoetical. I am sure Goethe would have made a splendid passage out of the *rapidity* with which the hopes of the long year are 'realized': the grain pouring from the many mouths of the machine all at once, the numbers of men feeding the furnace, oiling the engine, tying up the sacks as they fill, building up the mountainous stacks of straw, the sacks accumulating in the barn, *etc.* It is a very invigorating sight and I wish that you were there to see it." (Vol. I, pp. 235–36.)

73–74. The severity of the judgment here expressed is directed against such external activities and worldly wisdom as destroy all sense of spiritual values and the power of contemplation. It is the world's ever-recurring alternative where there is question of the invitation of Christ—a farm, or a yoke of oxen. (Cf. St. Luke XIV, 18–19.)

75. *Golden-Tongue:* probably Gladstone. (Cf. "1880–85," ll. 23–24.)

77. *the great Clever Party:* The Liberal Party. (Cf. "1880–85," and "1867.")

78–80. "He (Patmore) had no belief whatever in the collective wisdom of the multitude—failed to see:

How many grains of sifted sand,
Heap'd, make a likely house to stand,
How many fools one Solomon."

(Champneys II, p. 14.)

These lines appear to be a brief summary in verse of a prose passage from Sir Thomas Browne quoted by Patmore in his review of Greenhill's edition of *Religio Medici, Letter to a Friend,* and *Christian Morals:* "If there be any among those common objects of hatred I do contemn and laugh at, it is that great enemy of Reason, Virtue, and Religion, the Multitude; that numerous piece of monstrosity which, taken asunder, mean men, and the reasonable creatures of God; but confused together, make but one great beast, and a monstrosity more prodigious than Hydra. It is no breach of charity to call these Fools; it is the style all holy writers have afforded them, set down by Solomon in Canonical Scripture." (*Courage in Politics and Other Essays,* p. 57.) (Cf. "1880–85," ll. 29–46.)

81–83. The *Science* here spoken of is clearly pseudo-science as is evident from *Knowledge and Science* XXX, too long to quote. In a briefer passage Patmore clearly describes such science as he condemns: "Science without the idea of God, as the beginning and end of knowledge, is as the empty and withered slough of the snake, and the man, however 'wise and learned' and 'well conducted,' who has freed himself in thought from the happy bondage of that idea, is among the most sordid of slaves, and viler and more miserable than the most abandoned profligate who is still vexed by a conscience, or even a superstition. The latter, though miserable, is still alive; but the former is dead and feels 'no bonds in his death.'" (*Ibid.* XXXII.) (Cf. "The Two Deserts," "Sing Us One of the Songs of Sion," and "The Cry at Midnight.")

These lines are reflected in Thompson's "An Anthem of Earth," l. 202:

"Science, old noser in its prideful straw."

86. *Certitude:* The term, *kind twin-sister* of *Felicity,* is par-

ticularly Patmorean. Insistence upon the necessity of certitude is the chief theme of the essay, "Thoughts on Knowledge, Opinion and Inequality," from which the following passage is taken: "A great and increasing proportion of persons would, if you asked them, maintain that all convictions are merely opinions. But it is not so. A fool may opine absolutely that a wise man is a fool, but the wise man knows that the fool is one . . . Those who opine hate those who know, and who speak as those who know. They think it an assumption of superiority, whereas it is only its reality, and cannot but appear more or less in its manner of expression. Those who know are contemptuous or indifferent only towards such as impudently or ignorantly opine."

And again: "There can be no absolute certitude about the impressions of the senses or the inferences drawn from them. There can be about moral and spiritual things. The knave may sincerely opine that it is best for his interests to lie and cheat; but the honest man knows that he is a being whose interests are above all external contingencies, and that under certain circumstances it would be madness to behave otherwise than in a way which would be directly opposed to every argument and persuasion of the senses."

87–88. This is a peculiarly happy description of the Agnostics and Sceptics of the Nineteenth Century, to whom nothing was philosophically certain.

89–92. These lines always recurred to Champneys as particularly representative of Patmore's life at Heron's Ghyll. (Cf. *Composition, supra.*)

93. The *charming Wonders three* here alluded to are not easily identified. They may have been Patmore's second wife and his two daughters, Bertha and Gertrude—Emily was at this time in the convent. (Cf. Champneys I, p. 239.) The allusion is suggestive of "Beata," l. 7.

KING COPHETUA THE FIRST

Publication: One of the poems in *Amelia,* first published in 1878.

Theme: The legend here adapted to the poet's theme is cited in the notes to "Eros and Psyche," ll. 88–89. The development of the theme in this poem is too obvious to need any explanation in view of the notes on its less obvious development in the Psyche Odes.

BIBLIOGRAPHY

SOME EDITIONS OF PATMORE'S WORK STILL IN PRINT

[A bibliography of principal editions will be found in Champneys' *Memoirs and Correspondence of Coventry Patmore,* vol. I, p. xxv.]

Poems, edited with an introduction by Basil Champneys (1928, G. Bell & Sons, London).

Selected Poems of Coventry Patmore, edited with an introduction by Derek Patmore (1931, Chatto & Windus, London).

Principle in Art, and Other Essays (1912, G. Bell & Sons).

Principle in Art: Religio Poetae and Other Essays (1913, Duckworth, London).

The Rod, The Root, and the Flower (1923, G. Bell & Sons).

Courage in Politics and Other Essays (1921, Oxford University Press).

SOME BOOKS ON PATMORE

Memoirs and Correspondence of Coventry Patmore, by Basil Champneys (1901, G. Bell & Sons, London).

Coventry Patmore, by Edmund Gosse (1904, Hodder & Stoughton, London).

Portrait of My Family, by Derek Patmore (1935, Harper & Brothers, New York: Cassell & Co., London).

The Idea of Coventry Patmore, by Osbert Burdett (1921, Oxford University Press).

Patmore: A Study in Poetry, by Frederick Page (1933, Oxford University Press).

Further Letters of Gerard Manley Hopkins Including his Correspondence with Coventry Patmore, edited by C. C. Abott (1938, Oxford University Press).

SOME SOURCES OF PATMORE'S INSPIRATION

The Writings of St. Thomas Aquinas, St. John of the Cross, and St. Teresa.

The Picture of Love Unveil'd, by John Norris—A Translation of Robert Waring's *Amoris Effigies.* (A Modernized edition of this work has been edited by the present writer and privately printed at the Graduate School of Boston College.)

Saint Bernard on the Love of God, translated by Marianne Caroline and Coventry Patmore (1884, Burns & Oates, London). (The present writer has recently made an original translation of the selections found in the translation by Patmore and his wife. It is published by the Spiritual Book Associates, New York, and by Burns & Oates, London.)

Letters and Writings of Marie Lataste, translated from the French by Edward Healy Thompson (1893, Burns & Oates, London).

INDEXES

INDEX OF FIRST LINES

TITLE-INDEX OF POEMS AND NOTES